IN THE WAKE OF
9/11

IN THE WAKE OF 9/11

The Psychology of Terror

Tom Pyszczynski, Sheldon Solomon, and Jeff Greenberg

American Psychological Association

Washington, DC

First Printing July 2002
Second Printing September 2002
Third Printing February 2003
Fourth Printing July 2003
Fifth Printing January 2005
Sixth Printing October 2006
Seventh Printing February 2008
Eighth Printing September 2010

Published by
American Psychological Association
750 First Street, NE
Washington, DC 20002
www.apa.org

To order
APA Order Department
P.O. Box 92984
Washington, DC 20090-2984

Tel: (800) 374-2721, Direct: (202) 336-5510
Fax: (202) 336-5502, TDD/TTY: (202) 336 6123
On-line: www.apa.org/books/
E-mail: order@apa.org

In the U.K., Europe, Africa, and the Middle East, copies may be ordered from
American Psychological Association
3 Henrietta Street
Covent Garden, London
WC2E 8LU England

Typeset in Goudy by NOVA Graphic Services, Inc., Ft. Washington, PA
Printer: United Book Press, Inc., Baltimore, MD
Cover Designer: NiDesign, Baltimore, MD
Project Manager: NOVA Graphic Services, Inc., Ft. Washington, PA

The opinions and statements published are the responsibility of the authors, and such opinions and statements do not necessarily represent the policies of the American Psychological Association.

Library of Congress Cataloging-in-Publication Data
Pyszczynski, Thomas A.
   In the wake of 9/11 : the psychology of terror / Tom Pyszczynski, Jeff Greenberg, Sheldon Solomon.—1st ed.
      p. cm.
   Includes bibliographical references (p.) and index.
   ISBN 1-55798-954-0 (alk. paper)
      1. September 11 Terrorist Attacks, 2001—Psychological aspects.   2. Terrorism—United States—Psychological aspects.   3. Terrorism—Psychological aspects.   4. Terror.
5. Fear of death.   I. Greenberg, Jeff, 1954–   II. Solomon, Sheldon.   III. Title.

HV6432 .P97 2003
155.9'35—dc21

2002067561

British Library Cataloguing-in-Publication Data
A CIP record is available from the British Library.

Printed in the United States of America

To my mother, Mary Anne Cavadias, for all she's done for me,
and to my wife, Wendy Matuszewski, and my daughter,
Marya Myszczynski, for making life mean so much.

Tom Pyszczynski

To Maureen, Ruby, and Sam.

Sheldon Solomon

To my favorite New Yorkers: my mother, Edith Greenberg, and
the Krauses—my sister Debbi; her husband, retired NYPD officer David;
and my nephews David and Michael.

Jeff Greenberg

CONTENTS

PREFACE

In late October of 2001, we were asked by the publisher at the American Psychological Association to write a book using terror management theory and research to shed light on the 9/11 terrorist attacks on the World Trade Center and Pentagon. We were immediately excited about the opportunity, but we had some ambivalence as well. Personally, like many Americans, we were still reeling from the aftershock of the events of 9/11. Professionally, we wondered whether, given the continually growing mountains of information and analyses that had already been presented about these events, we had anything unique, important, or useful to add. But we were struck by the amazing parallels between the way thousands of research participants in our laboratory and field studies have responded to reminders of their own mortality and the way many Americans seemed to be reacting to the events of 9/11. And for years, we have believed that our analysis provides useful insights into the genesis of the prejudice, hatred, and hostility that lies at the root of the major wars and minor skirmishes that have marked our species' history on this planet. Ultimately, we hoped that we could add something to the discussion of the events of 9/11, and global terrorism in general, that would be useful to others struggling to cope with these tragic events and seeking solutions to the problems that we are now facing.

Since the beginning of our professional careers, we have been firmly committed to the belief that a central task for social psychology is to develop broad theories of human behavior capable of explaining human activities as they unfold in a cultural and historical context. We are also committed to presenting such ideas in an accessible fashion to academics, public officials, the business community, and the interested lay public—with the ultimate goal of promoting constructive social and individual change. What follows is our effort to follow through on this commitment by using the ideas that have sprung from our theoretical and empirical work over the past two decades in the hope of providing insight into the issues surrounding the terrorist attacks on 9/11 and their aftermath.

We are experimental social psychologists who have been investigating the core motives that affect human social behavior. Inspired by the seminal work of Ernest Becker, we developed *terror management theory*, which posits that the uniquely human awareness of death and our efforts to cope with this awareness provide the psychological impetus for a wide variety of superficially disparate human activities. This book begins with a presentation of terror management theory and more than 15 years of research testing hypotheses derived from the theory. We then apply the theory to understanding the causes and consequences of the events that transpired on 9/11 and to suggesting positive steps for coping with the aftermath. Our hope is that this book will be of value to those directly or indirectly affected by the attacks; to those trying to help; and to those in government, academia, industry, and elsewhere attempting to reduce the likelihood and impact of similar terrorist actions in the future.

Because our intention in writing *In the Wake of 9/11: The Psychology of Terror* was to apply a specific theoretical perspective—terror management theory—to this problem, we did not attempt to comprehensively present other social psychological, clinical, political science, or sociological viewpoints pertaining to these matters. There has been a plethora of analyses from these perspectives, and we certainly acknowledge that many such analyses will be necessary to fully address the issues surrounding 9/11. However, we believe that our work, while not itself sufficient to completely understand 9/11 and its consequences, is a very necessary component of any adequate account of those events and that any serious effort to make sense of 9/11 without recourse to terror management processes will not fare well.

In writing this book, we have made certain assumptions and perhaps exhibited certain biases that one might expect from a book written by American psychologists. One is that, although our goal is to understand the motives and psychological forces that led to the events of 9/11, these and other terrorist attacks, like all violence directed intentionally at civilians, are horrible acts that cannot be morally justified by *any* political agenda. A second assumption is that, although it is a difficult and daunting task, there is hope that the prevalence and effects of such terrorist actions can be reduced in the future. A third assumption is that this book will be read primarily by Americans, although we hope that it will also be read by others interested in a psychological analysis of the attacks and their aftermath. Based on this assumption, the discourse is directed toward this audience. Of course, we welcome readers from all cultures and are hopeful that our analysis will make sense to anyone who reads the book with an open mind.

Our final and perhaps most important assumption is that, at the heart of things, all human beings are fundamentally the same, with the same biological and psychological needs. We are all members of the same species; our behavior and motivation can, therefore, be best understood through the use of the same general biological and psychological principles. At the same time, we recognize that people live out their lives within frameworks provided by the particular culture in which they live. Thus, the precise manner in which universal psychological needs and processes are played out in individual lives depends on a host of cultural and historical factors, which vary from person to person. We are certainly not exceptions to this general rule. Although we have attempted to keep our own biases in check, we know that this cannot be fully accomplished.

ACKNOWLEDGMENTS

Responsibility for the writing and content of this book is shared equally by the three authors. Many people and organizations have made this book possible. Thanks to Bruce Sales, who first provided us with the opportunity to prepare a book for the American Psychological Association (APA) and graciously allowed us to shift our focus to this project, and to Gary Vanden Bos, for inviting us to prepare this book and for motivating us to complete it in a timely fashion. Thanks, too, to Ed Meidenbauer, Robin C. Bonner, and the staffs at the APA and NOVA Graphic Services for the excellent editorial and production help they have provided. We are also grateful to Fathali M. Moghaddam, professor of psychology at Georgetown University, and Julie Clancy-Smith, associate professor of history at the University of Arizona, who are experts in Near and Middle Eastern Politics and Affairs, for the helpful feedback they provided on various parts of this volume. We also appreciate the generous financial support we have received for terror management theory and research in the form of numerous grants from the National Science Foundation, the Ernest Becker Foundation, and the Alexander von Humboldt Foundation, and for the resources provided by our home institutions, the University of Colorado–Colorado Springs, Skidmore College, and the University of Arizona.

Sincere thanks also to a wide array of current and former students and colleagues, each of whom in their own unique way supported or made substantial contributions to the theoretical and empirical work that constitutes the foundation of this book: Teresa Abend, John Allen, Jamie Arndt, Steve Breckler, Jack Brehm, John Burling, Mark Dechesne, Neil Elgee, Victor Florian, Jamie Goldenberg, Eva Jonas, Eddie Harmon-Jones, Sander Koole, Jean Intermaggio, Joel Lieberman, Deborah Lyon, Shannon McCoy, Holly McGregor, Mario Mikulincer, Dave Myers, Randolph Ochsmann, Jonathan

Porteus, Abram Rosenblatt, Jeff Schimel, Linda Simon, and Bob Wicklund. Special thanks are due to our current students Cathy Cox, Ben Kluck, Mark Landau, and Andy Martens for the helpful discussions and feedback they provided while we were writing this book and for their invaluable help in preparing the final version of the manuscript.

Writing this book required us to shift our efforts away from other aspects of our professional and personal lives. In the professional sphere, thanks to our graduate students for keeping our research programs going strong during this time. Finally, we would like to thank our families—Wendy Matuszewski and Marya Myszczynski; Maureen Monaghan and Ruby and Sam Solomon; and Liz, Jonathan, and Camila Greenberg—whose unwavering love and confidence have been our greatest support.

IN THE WAKE OF
9/11

1

TERROR IN AMERICA:
THE DAY OUR WORLD CHANGED

History . . . is a nightmare from which I am trying to awaken.
—James Joyce, *Ulysses* (1922/1960, p. 40)

9/11

On September 11, 2001, Americans awoke to the nightmare of a well-coordinated, devastatingly effective, multipronged suicidal terrorist attack conducted by adherents of the radical Islamic group al Qaeda, orchestrated by their leader Osama bin Laden. At 8:46 a.m., 92 people on hijacked American Airlines Flight 11 were flown into the North Tower of the World Trade Center. At 9:03 a.m., 65 people on hijacked United Airlines Flight 175 were flown into the South Tower. As firefighters and police rushed to help those inside the burning buildings, both towers imploded on themselves and collapsed in rapid succession, killing between 2,000 and 3,000 people who were unable to get out in time (the body count is still not completely certain), in addition to those who already had been instantly vaporized from the impact of the planes or had jumped off the building to avoid incineration. The death toll also included hundreds of their courageous would-be rescuers. At 9:40 a.m., hijacked American Airlines Flight 77 and its 64 passengers crashed into the northwest wall of the Pentagon, in Washington, DC, killing 125 people in the building. A fourth hijacked jetliner, United Airlines Flight 93, carrying 45 passengers, then crashed in rural Pennsylvania at 10:10 a.m.; this jetliner had been headed to Washington,

DC, with the White House as its probable intended target. Fortunately, a heroic passenger rebellion thwarted that mission.

Word and images of these tragic events spread quickly. Most government buildings and many businesses and schools were closed. For the first time in the history of commercial aviation, all flights over American territory were grounded in an attempt to avert further attacks. The military was put on its highest level of battle preparedness. The president was shuttled between various secure locations while other essential government personnel were taken to other safe locations under heavy security.

In a matter of moments, the United States had become a gravely disoriented country tottering on the brink of chaos. Although terrorist attacks of various sorts had occurred throughout the world for most of the 20th century, nothing like this had ever happened here before, on our home soil, in the United States. When 168 people died in the bombing of the Alfred P. Murrah Federal Building in Oklahoma City in 1995 (Pressley, 1995), many Americans felt strangely comforted by the fact that this horrible atrocity was committed by disaffected American right-wing radicals rather than a plot hatched by enemies from abroad. And despite a previous attempt to destroy the World Trade Center by a related group of Middle Eastern terrorists in 1993 and several foiled plots to bomb airports in celebration of the millennium, Americans still felt safe at home and believed that no one could penetrate our defenses and perpetrate the type of large-scale terrorism that we all experienced on 9/11. Obviously, we were wrong.

The American people—and many others around the world—were stunned, terrified, saddened, and angered by the attacks. The nightmare of 9/11 affected every American, and we were certainly not exempt, as the following testimonies show:

> J.G.: Though I've been living in Tucson for many years now, I'm a New Yorker, born in the South Bronx and raised by working-class parents there and in Queens. In fact, I flew out of LaGuardia Airport on Monday morning, September 10, after visiting my mom in Queens, still basking in the afterglow of having seen my favorite band, Yes, at Radio City Music Hall two nights earlier. I arrived safely that night back in Tucson to reunite with my wife, Liz, and kids, Jonathan and Camila. The next morning I arose to get ready to hit the salt mines when Liz called me into the family room, saying, "You have to see this." What I saw on the television, along with millions of other Americans, was the World Trade Center, with a burning hole in the tower on the right, as if it were bleeding. Before I could even formulate a thought, a plane came around the burning tower from the right, and made a sharp left turn into the second tower, like a stab wound into the heart of New York. As I gaped at the scene, I thought it must be fake, a movie promo. Then after about 30 seconds, it sank into me that it was real, and my first postrealization thought was, Ok, now it's on. You attack my home; you're gonna pay.

S.S.: "What a Difference a Day Makes." On Monday, September 10, 2001, I was on the first floor of the World Trade Center at 9 a.m. after taking the train from Newark, New Jersey, heading to work at Brooklyn College. I always enjoyed my brief foray through the World Trade Center twice a week; the people at the excellent bakery I frequented knew how I liked my coffee and that I always got a corn muffin. Tuesday, September 11, was a different story. I drove to Brooklyn at 6 a.m., noting how the rising sun gave lower Manhattan, and especially the twin towers of the World Trade Center, a splendid glow. I arrived at my classroom at 8:30, and by 8:50 agitated pale-faced students began dribbling into the classroom with cell phones pasted to their heads. Apparently a plane had crashed into one of the towers of the World Trade Center. I went ahead teaching my class until the second plane hit. Clearly, something very terrible was taking place.

Hysterical students called their friends and families to beg them to leave the building immediately; I have no doubt that many people at the World Trade Center are alive today because of their cell phone–toting CNN-watching friends and loved ones who had a better sense of the disaster than those at what would soon become Ground Zero. I called my house in upstate New York and left an incoherent message to the effect that something very bad had happened. Classes were canceled; so I sat in my office for hours, my mind whirling at a breakneck pace, with the occasional intrusion of that annoying song "What a Difference a Day Makes." I thought about how I would get to work the next day and wondered if they would still have corn muffins at my favorite bakery at the World Trade Center (it had not yet occurred to me that the entire building falling might adversely affect the businesses on the first floor!). I was fuming at the thought of our country having been so savagely attacked and was eager to witness (on CNN, of course) the utter obliteration of those responsible. Then it hit me: I had been in the World Trade Center twice a week for the past 2 years. I was in the World Trade Center 24 hours ago. If today were yesterday, I could be part of the rubble instead of watching it from my office. "What a Difference a Day Makes."

T.P.: On September 11, I dropped off my 12-year-old daughter, Marya, at the bus stop for school and vaguely overheard a conversation about an airliner being hijacked by terrorists. When I got home, I had received an e-mail from Sheldon telling me that he wasn't going to be able to see Jeff, who was visiting New York City, because Jeff had to get to the airport too early for them to connect. That's when my wife called and told me what had happened. Wanting to know more, I turned on the television. The first thing I, like many people, saw was a small black cloud of smoke coming out of one of the walls of the World Trade Center. Then the second plane crashed into the other tower, and it became clear that this was not an accident. This was followed by the horrifying scene of the first tower collapsing. Where was Jeff? He told me he would be back from New York on Tuesday. Sheldon had written that Jeff had to catch an early flight. I wondered if Jeff might have possibly been on one of the doomed flights. For some reason, I just assumed that he was safe, imagined him sitting in the airport, perhaps not knowing what had happened, and cursing about the delayed flight. It wasn't till 2 hours later that I was able to get in touch with Jeff and find out that he had actually flown out the night before and had meant that he would be back at his office on Tuesday.

Then my thoughts turned to vengeance, but I worried about the possibilities of the even greater horrors that might lead to. I found some solace in the fact that Colorado Springs is far from the places that were targeted, but then I heard planes flying overhead. Looking out the window, I could see they were military planes, which reminded me that just beyond the other side of the mountain I live on is the North American Aerospace Defense Command (NORAD), the control center for the country's nuclear arsenal. Later in the day, I was surprised at how well my daughter Marya was dealing with all this. But when she heard planes flying overhead later that evening, she broke down into uncontrollable sobbing and wanted to know if they were coming to get us next.

Other Americans' reactions were wide ranging. Almost immediately after the attacks, many flocked to blood banks, hospitals, and Red Cross offices, hoping to give blood to help the survivors; sadly, very few required such assistance. Generous donations poured in to all types of relief organizations in the days and weeks after the attacks. General goodwill, heightened civility, excessive kindness, and heroic efforts to help everyone in need were in great abundance. But not all of our responses were so noble. In Mesa, Arizona, Balbir Singh Sodhi, a Sikh man from India who had dark skin and wore a turban, was shot and killed in his store by a patriotic American seeking revenge (Anchors, 2001). The Council on American-Islamic Relations reported hundreds of threats and incidents of violence and discrimination against Muslims. In the wake of the attacks, many Muslims throughout the country lived in fear of their fellow Americans who might be seeking vengeance and federal authorities who might believe them to be linked in some way to the people responsible for the attacks.

Meanwhile, the rest of the country dreaded the possibility of further acts of violence. Flying changed from a convenient means of rapid transportation to a risky and tedious proposition that, even to this day, many Americans have decided they can do without. After people in Florida, New Jersey, New York, and Washington, DC, died following contact with letters containing the deadly anthrax virus, even the U.S. mail became a source of fear. Threats of additional attacks led people to curtail many of their favorite activities, from eating out to shopping, traveling, and attending entertainment events. The economy has been reeling from these aftershocks, with profits decreased and unemployment increased. Simultaneously, sales of American flags, patriotic tattoos, and Osama bin Laden rifle range targets (and toilet paper) have been at an all-time high.

We have also witnessed more than our share of bizarre, almost surreal reactions to the tragedy. In the Midwest, nail clippers were confiscated from retired women traveling to Disney World, whereas Middle Eastern nationals in white sedans carrying box cutters and diagrams for nuclear power plants were released by police officers who did not even contact the FBI. In the weeks immediately after the attacks, more than a few flights were canceled when passengers noticed dark-skinned fellow travelers on board who might be of Middle Eastern heritage. On his nationally syndicated radio program, Rush Limbaugh suggested that all postal workers wear gas masks at work in response to the anthrax attacks. And at Ground Zero, New York City firefighters and police officers exchanged blows over the right to excavate the bodies of their dead colleagues.

THE SUDDEN RELEVANCE OF TERROR MANAGEMENT THEORY

As the smoke from the attacks has gradually cleared, so have our heads. For most Americans, paralysis, worry, anger, patriotism, and bloodlust have given way to a more sober perspective and sincere effort to understand what happened and why. The events of 9/11 have led to unprecedented attention in government, academic, and public arenas: Editorials, expert analyses, panel discussions, books, documentaries, songs, episodes of popular television dramas, and even stand-up comedy routines abound. By now you have probably heard from eyewitnesses; police and firefighters; military, political, and religious leaders; historians; political scientists; economists; psychotherapists; radio and television news and talk show hosts; comedians; engineers; and aviation, security, and terrorism experts. Who has not chimed in? George W. Bush, Colin Powell, Katie Couric, Rush Limbaugh, Madonna, George Carlin, and Pat Robertson all commented publicly; about the only major voice in America we have not heard from is that of Britney Spears—and perhaps that is just a matter of time. Is there anything possibly left to say, any constructive insight or recommendation yet to be offered?

We think there is. To our knowledge, no one has yet attempted to place these events in the context of a broad understanding of human motivation: why people behave the way they do. For the past 20 years we, as experimental social psychologists, have developed and tested an existential psychodynamic analysis of human behavior we call *terror management theory*. In the past, people sometimes mistook our theoretical analysis of the existential contradictions of the human condition for a practical guide as to how to manage terrorism. The occasional inquiries from the media regarding what we knew about managing terrorists used to amuse us. Even more amusing was the time one of us arrived to do a presentation on terror management theory for a symposium at a conference in Portugal and found that the rest of the panel consisted of military personnel from various NATO countries in full uniform, ready to discuss ways to (literally) combat the growing problem of terrorist violence. But as the shock from the events of 9/11 gradually subsided, we began to realize that our theoretical analysis fit what was going on in the world surprisingly well. Although working in relative obscurity except within our little academic circles, after 9/11 we were inundated with calls from radio and television stations and from magazine and newspaper reporters. Suddenly, our work seemed to have some immediate practical significance. It has been very strange for us, like gas mask manufacturers, security companies, and patriotic songsmith Lee Greenwood, to be garnering attention in the aftermath of these horrendous tragedies.

Why has our work so suddenly been recognized to be relevant to current circumstances? Terrorism, as the word implies, capitalizes on the human capacity to experience terror. Terror is, in turn, a uniquely human response to the threat of annihilation. Terror management theory is about how humans cope, not with the imminent threat of extermination but with the awareness that such threats are ubiquitous and will all eventually succeed: Death will be our ultimate fate. How then do we manage this potential for terror? And how does our answer to this question help us understand terrorist acts and the many short-term and long-term responses in their aftermath? The purpose of this book is to address these questions.

Terror management theory concerns the impact that awareness of the inevitability of death has on how we live our lives. Thus, it is essentially a theory about the effect of death on life. Perhaps the central insight to be gleaned from our work is that human beings attempt to fulfill culturally sanctioned dreams forged to escape the encompassing nightmare, not just of human history but also of human existence itself. Some Islamic terrorists dream of a heaven of dancing virgins overseen by Allah (one in Israel was found blown to bits but with extensive protection around his genital area; another had doused himself in cologne before his suicide attack), whereas Americans dream of amassing great fortunes, writing that great book, winning Nobel Prizes and Olympic gold medals, their kids' achievements, or entering one of a variety of theologically prescribed versions of heaven.

The horrific loss of life that resulted from the terrorist attacks of 9/11 is naturally a severe jolt to us all, although much more so, of course, to those who lost loved ones in the attacks. And beyond the shock of the events of 9/11, there is the continual threat of additional attacks. But if we step back for a moment and think about how we would be feeling so much more secure if there were no such thing as terrorism and terrorists, the question of why arises. Without terrorists, all we would have to worry about killing us is cancer, heart disease, diabetes, car accidents, Lou Gehrig's disease, AIDS, muscular dystrophy, multiple sclerosis, homicide, or if we are very lucky, a death in several decades due to the inevitable exhaustion of our bodies. Despite the new reality of homeland insecurity, terrorist hijacking of airplanes and anthrax are low on the list of things likely to terminate our existence. We are all far more likely to injure ourselves by climbing a stepladder in our own house or to get hit by a car than to be a victim of a terrorist attack. And yet, before 9/11, we all seemed much safer and infinitely more at ease. Why is it only now that we are in such psychological disarray?

According to terror management theory, what the terrorist attacks have done is to disrupt our normal means of managing our natural terror and, in so doing, threatened to undermine the psychological equanimity necessary for people to function effectively on a daily basis. In this book, we will present terror management theory, review the large and continually growing body of empirical research that supports it, apply this body of work to understanding the causes and consequences of the events of 9/11, and suggest possible remedial measures to help people cope with the threats we are now facing. Although it is not within our domain of expertise to argue for or against specific actions like the bombing of Afghanistan, we explore the implications of our work for constructive short-term responses to these anxiety-riddled times, as well as for long-term strategies to deal with the problem of Islamic fundamentalist terrorism. Just to whet your appetite a bit, one of the most consistent findings from our research has been that reminding Americans of their mortality increases the positivity of their reactions to anyone or anything that praises America and the negativity of their reactions to anyone or anything that criticizes America. We have seen this very same effect writ large across America in response to the terrorists' reminder to us all of our mortality.

PREVIEWING THE CHAPTERS TO COME

In our next chapter, we explain the basics of terror management theory, and in chapters 3 and 4, we provide an overview of the more than 150 studies that have provided support for the theory. A solid comprehension of the concepts that are the central focus of the terror management perspective is critical for understanding our analysis of the specific events and issues related to the 9/11 attack, and an appreciation of the many converging strands of empirical evidence that provide scientific support for these ideas is crucial for recognizing their validity and widespread applicability. Therefore, we have presented a rather thorough yet nontechnical discussion of central concepts and research findings in these chapters. From readers anxious to get to the core of our analysis of the causes and consequences of terrorist violence, we ask patience. Chapter 5 then shows how the theory can be used to understand the panoply of reactions that Americans have had to the attacks. Chapter 6 explores the various more extreme pathologic reactions that some people may have had to the attacks, such as acute anxiety disorders and posttraumatic stress disorder; this chapter also suggests some general strategies for helping people cope with the fears that the attacks have awakened. Chapter 7 uses terror management theory to shed light on the roots of the problem of ethnic and political terrorism and addresses the question, why would anyone want to do what the terrorists did? Chapter 8 discusses possible strategies for resolving the conflicts and social problems that gave rise to the hatred that led to such incredible devastation and loss of life; it also discusses the psychological conditions needed to foster peaceful coexistence in the very diverse multicultural world in which we live. Finally, in chapter 9, we briefly reflect on these ideas and place them within a broader perspective.

We certainly do not claim to have a monopoly on insights into the causes, consequences, or possible solutions to the problems of global terrorism and ethnopolitical conflict. Clearly, the causes of events such as these are exceedingly complex and will require input from virtually all the many disciplines concerning the human condition. And as our political leaders have repeatedly warned us, effective solutions will not come fast or be easy. Our species seems to have an inclination toward hatred, war, and the killing of innocent people. It has been happening since before the beginning of recorded history and continues to this day in all corners of the world. Some believe that a propensity for hatred and violence against our own kind is one of the characteristics that most clearly distinguish us humans from other species. Terror management theory offers important insights into this uniquely human propensity for destructiveness as well its specific manifestation in the form of international terrorism and its consequences. We turn now to a general overview of this explanatory framework.

2

TERROR MANAGEMENT THEORY: AN EVOLUTIONARY EXISTENTIAL ACCOUNT OF HUMAN BEHAVIOR

It is our knowledge that we have to die which makes us human.
—Alexander Smith, *Dreamthorp: A Book of Essays,
Written in the Country* (1857/1934, pp. 55–56)

To comprehend the tragic events of 9/11, we first need to acquire a general understanding of the core psychological motives that drive human behavior, an answer to the question, why do people behave the way they do? Only then can we make sense of the recent terrorist attacks and their far-reaching consequences. For almost 2 decades, we, as experimental social psychologists, have been developing and testing what we refer to as *terror management theory* (TMT; Greenberg, Pyszczynski, & Solomon, 1986; Solomon, Greenberg, & Pyszczynski, 1991a) in the service of acquiring such a broad account of human social behavior. TMT builds on the seminal work of cultural anthropologist Ernest Becker, especially *The Birth and Death of Meaning* (1962/1971), *The Denial of Death* (1973), and *Escape From Evil* (1975). Becker's thinking, in turn, was inspired by the earlier theorizing of some of the great minds of the past 2 centuries: Charles Darwin, Søren Kierkegaard, Sigmund Freud, Otto Rank, Erving Goffman, and Erich Fromm.

TWO FUNDAMENTAL QUESTIONS

Our theoretical analysis is intended to address two very basic questions about human behavior that seem to be superficially unrelated but are actually inextricably intertwined.

First, *why do people need self-esteem?* Psychologists have long recognized the importance of self-esteem; indeed, William James (1890) considered self-esteem an utterly indispensable psychological attribute in his classic *Principles of Psychology*. There is no more obvious psychological truth than that people want to feel that that they are worthy and valued and that their actions are righteous and justified. In fact, a massive array of empirical evidence has shown that low self-esteem is associated with poor physical and mental health and that threats to self-esteem engender anxiety and a host of psychological defenses (for a review, see Solomon, Greenberg, & Pyszczynski, 1991b). However, only recently have empirically oriented psychologists attempted to define what self-esteem is, how it is acquired and maintained, what psychological purposes it serves, and how it does so.

Second, *why do human beings have such a difficult time peacefully coexisting with other humans who are different from them?* Even a benevolent glance at human history reveals a continuous succession of violent ethnic cleansings and brutal subjugation of designated in-house inferiors. Assyrian bas-reliefs, circa 1200 BC, depict the residents of recently captured villages being skewered on stakes running from their groins to their shoulders. Jumping ahead several millenia, World War I ushered in the 20th century with new unprecedented horrors, such as machine guns, heavy artillery, submarines, poison gas, and trench warfare. World War II featured Hitler's clever juxtaposition of genocide and business; before "hitting the showers," concentration camp inmates served as slave laborers for major German corporations. More recently, 1 million of the Tutsi population of Rwanda were exterminated in fewer than 100 days by their Hutu neighbors, and Serbian soldiers in Yugoslavia gang-raped Muslim women while their colleagues played soccer with the recently decapitated heads of the women's children (Amnesty International Publications, 2001; Human Rights Watch, 1993).

As humankind staggers into the 3rd millennium AD, although the names change, it appears that the likes of Attila the Hun, Peter the Cruel, and Ivan the Terrible are still with us. Seemingly intractable ethnic strife, festering into brutal armed confrontations and staggering assaults on civilian populations, continues to proliferate from all corners of the planet where humans reside. The terrible, terrifying, terrorist attacks on the World Trade Center and Pentagon are only the most recent of our long history of sordid inhumane but nevertheless all-too-human atrocities: "Man's inhumanity to Man makes countless thousands mourn!" (Burns, 1786/1885).

EPISTEMOLOGICAL ASSUMPTIONS

Answering these two basic questions requires a theory that explains the motivational underpinnings of human behavior. In formulating such a theory, we were guided by four basic epistemological assumptions. First, it must be interdisciplinary in nature. Long before it became fashionable to give lip service to this concept, Becker cogently argued that each academic discipline focuses on only one aspect of the human organism and, therefore, cannot provide a complete view of human beings in their multidimensional complexity. Consequently, a comprehensive understanding of human affairs can be acquired only by considering central ideas from all areas of human studies—with an eye on recognizing commonalties between disciplines and efforts to integrate and synthesize insights from them. Accordingly, TMT combines ideas from biology, psychology, sociology, philosophy, anthropology, theology, literature, and popular culture.

Second, a useful theory must be scientific, in the sense of being amenable to empirical scrutiny. On the one hand, all ideas from all disciplines should be seriously considered; however, not all ideas are created equal (a currently fashionable belief in postmodern circles). Every idea has the right to be wrong. The best way to evaluate the merits of an explanatory proposition is to frame it in a way that renders it subject to disconfirmation and then to conduct the appropriate tests via historical analyses, anthropological studies, clinical observations, and our own specialty, laboratory experimentation.

Third, following the Enlightenment tradition and the pragmatism of 20th-century American philosophers (e.g., Charles Peirce and John Dewey), we believe strongly that theoretical accounts of human behavior should be framed so that they can be used to improve social conditions to maximize individual and collective well-being. Social science inquiry (or any inquiry for that matter) for the sake of acquiring knowledge, per se, without guidance by important questions and concerns, has led many academics to develop an ever-increasing array of highly specialized, insulated, and isolated branches of esoteric trivia masquerading as professional activity. The result is massive and chaotic piles of information that no one bothers to—or could possibly—make sense of or use for addressing important issues.

Finally, we believe that credible theories of human behavior should be grounded in evolutionary theory. Darwin's theory of evolution by natural selection has been incredibly successful in accounting for the fit between physical characteristics of living organisms and their environments and how the physical attributes (within and between species) of populations change over time. Explanations for human behavioral and psychological propensities are more likely to be correct if they are grounded in—or at least broadly consistent with—evolutionary principles.

GRAVE MATTERS: ON THE ROLE OF DEATH IN LIFE

Accordingly, our analysis of the human condition commences with the basic Darwinian assumption that all living things share a biological predisposition toward self-preservation, because such a tendency facilitates staying alive long enough to reproduce and pass one's genes on to future generations. We view this as a very basic adaptation that arose early in the history of life, long before humans, primates, or even mammals emerged as species. Different forms of life vary immensely, however, in terms of the structural, functional, behavioral, and (in some cases) psychological adaptations they have acquired in the context of millions (and in some cases billions) of years of evolution to render them fit for the specific environmental niches that they inhabit. Plants derive their sustenance by converting solar energy into carbon dioxide through photosynthesis; spiders construct elaborate silk webs in which they catch their food; turtles parry the thrusts of their predatory opposition by retreating into the bony or leathery shells erected on their backs; wolves travel in packs in coordinated search for prey and regurgitate half-digested food to feed their young. These are just a few examples of the seemingly infinite variety of effective adaptations to the demands of physical reality that various life forms have acquired to facilitate the arduous task of staying alive and perpetuating their genetic material over time.

What about human beings? Relative newcomers to the evolutionary scene, members of *Homo sapiens* do not at first glance appear to be a very formidable form of life or, for that matter, even a viable one. As individuals, we are not especially physically imposing (although upright bipedalism, opposable thumbs, and binocular vision are undoubtedly valuable attributes that have contributed to our survival): We are small and slow; our teeth and claws are impoverished, and so is our sense of smell. However, human beings are highly social and vastly intelligent creatures. Our gregarious nature fosters cooperation in the service of developing a host of elaborate behaviors (e.g., coordinated hunting and food sharing) and construction of social institutions (e.g., political, economic, and religious organizations) that facilitate our collective survival.

Large convoluted brains (especially forebrains) provide humans with an unprecedented degree of what Becker referred to as "freedom of reactivity"—behavioral flexibility in response to the demands of specific stimuli. Relatively simple-minded creatures respond reflexively and consistently in response to particular events; for example, hungry amoebas will always approach, envelope, and consume specks of glucose and flee from globs of acid; certain insects always fly toward light, even if it emanates from an open flame that subsequently incinerates them. Human beings, however, are able to inhibit reflexive responses, especially in novel and uncertain circumstances, to ponder behavioral alternatives; it is in this sense that they possess relative freedom of reactivity. Additionally, human beings are able to imagine things that do not presently exist, and then have the audacity and technical skills to transform their dreams into reality. Only human beings, in Otto Rank's words, "make the unreal real." In that sense, we are the only truly creative form of life. All other creatures must adapt themselves to the demands of physical reality as they encounter it; only human beings "just say no" to reality, conjure up an image of how they would prefer the world to be, and then transform it in accordance with their desires. The telephone, the helicopter, and the computer are just a few examples of what were originally figments of human imagination that have become quite physical and pervasive elements of human affairs. No wonder human beings, originally a small band among many other hominids (Tattersall, 2000) in a single neighborhood in Africa, have in a very short time proliferated and prospered in a wide variety of environmental niches.

One especially important aspect of human mentality, recognized by early Greek and Roman philosophers, and subsequently central to Kierkegaard's penetrating understanding of the human condition, is that human beings are both conscious and self-conscious. Other creatures are sensate and perceptive, but only human beings are aware of their awareness (consciousness) and of themselves as potential objects of their own subjective inquiry (self-consciousness may be expressed in this way: "I am and I know that I am; I know that I know that I am; I know that I know that I know that I am"). Consciousness and self-consciousness have important cognitive and affective consequences. Cognitively, we become time-binding animals (Becker, 1962/1971), able to reflect on the past and anticipate the future and, in so doing, enhance our prospects for survival in the present. Affectively, consciousness and self-awareness infuse us with awe and dread. To be alive and to know it is awesome: grand, breathtaking, tremendous, remarkable, amazing, astounding, and humbling. Every one of us, in our finer moments, is overwhelmed with the sheer joy of being alive. In Otto Rank's (1936/1978) lovely expression, we are "the temporal representative of the cosmic primal force" (p. 4): ultimately descended from, and consequently directly related to, the first living organism, as well as everything that has ever been alive, is currently living, and will ever live in the future.

However, consciousness and self-awareness also necessarily engender dread: fear, trepidation, anxiety, alarm, fright, horror, and, in due course, unmitigated terror. First, knowing that one is alive and being able to anticipate the future inevitably produces the unsettling awareness of one's inexorable death. As Faulkner (1936/1990) observed:

> It has always seemed to me that the only painless death must be that which takes the intelligence by violent surprise and from the rear so to speak since if death be anything at all beyond a brief and peculiar emotional state of the bereaved it must be a brief and likewise peculiar state of the subject as well and if aught can be more painful to any intelligence above that of a child or an idiot than a slow and gradual confronting with that which over a long period of bewilderment and dread it has been taught to regard as an irrevocable and unplumbable finality, I do not know it. (pp. 141–142)

Second, people also recognize that death not only is unavoidable but also can often occur quite tragically and prematurely (relative to an individual's normal life span) for reasons that can never be adequately anticipated or controlled. Californians know that the next earthquake might shake them off the face of the earth; Indians know that the next tidal wave might wash them into the sea; skiers know that their next downhill run might end by turning their heads into Jackson Pollock paintings on the sides of trees; we all know that our next stomachache may be a softball-sized malignant tumor, a harbinger of our impending demise. We have for a long time known but are now especially aware that our next plane trip, whether for business or pleasure, may not end happily; we also now know that the white dust that fell from the unexpected greeting card we just received in the mail may kill us; we know that life is precarious and that each of us is ultimately vulnerable and helpless in the wake of the virtually infinite number of mundane and arcane ways our existence might be terminated; we know.

Finally, we also know and are horrified by the realization that we are corporeal creatures—sentient pieces of bleeding, defecating, urinating, vomiting, exfoliating, perspiring, fornicating, menstruating, ejaculating, flatulence-producing, expectorating meat—that may ultimately be no more enduring or significant than cockroaches or cucumbers. The continuous awareness of these circumstances within which we live, faced with inevitable death, compounded by the recognition of tragedy magnified by our carnal knowledge makes us humans vulnerable to potentially overwhelming terror at virtually any given moment. Yet people rarely experience this existential terror directly.

What saves us is culture. Cultures provide ways to view the world—worldviews—that "solve" the existential crisis engendered by the awareness of death. Cultural worldviews consist of humanly constructed beliefs about the nature of reality that are shared by individuals in a group that function to mitigate the horror and blunt the dread caused by knowledge of the reality of the human condition, that we all die: "Death is the obverse of the self-preserving, appetitive drive or 'desire' of all living organisms: It can therefore be seen as the hidden mainspring of the created world." (Maclagan, 1977/1999, p. 27)

Terror Management Theory

At the most fundamental level, cultures allow people to control the ever-present potential terror of death by convincing them that they are beings of enduring significance living in a meaningful reality. This is the core proposition of TMT. And the core implication of TMT is that to maintain psychological equanimity throughout their lives, people must sustain

1. faith in a culturally derived worldview that imbues reality with order, stability, meaning, and permanence; and

2. belief that one is a significant contributor to this meaningful reality.

By providing a view of reality as stable, orderly, meaningful, and permanent, cultural worldviews allow us to deny that we are merely transient material organisms clinging to a clump of dirt in a purposeless universe fated only to die and decay. Instead, we live out our time on earth believing we are eternally significant contributors to a meaningful reality.

Of course, people are rarely, if ever, aware of how deeply their views of their existence are molded into this form by their cultures. Consider this very moment. What time is it? What day is it? What year? Where are you? Who are you? What are you doing? All these questions are easily answered. Right now for me, it's 9:48 a.m., Friday, December 7, 2001—Pearl Harbor Day; I am in Tucson, Arizona; my name is Jeff Greenberg; and, of course, I am writing an extremely important book. And this means there will be another 9:48 and another Friday and another December and more years, and centuries and millennia, and I am a significant, permanent contributor to this orderly, meaningful reality. But if we strip away my cultural worldview, then what's left? A nameless (scared!) creature pecking away with its digits on a piece of plastic, experiencing an ongoing stream of thoughts and sensations, each moment never to be experienced again. This stream started with my birth—or a bit before—and will end with my death—lights out.

All of my perceptions of time, place, name, meaning, and significance at this precise moment (and every other moment) are based entirely on my immersion in a culturally constructed and ultimately fictional framework for organizing my thoughts and sensations. Different cultures mold their members' transient experiences quite differently, but fortunately for them, all cultures provide order, stability, meaning, and personal enduring significance, just as America does for me. And precisely because cultures do this, the vast majority of people can function securely, safely tucked within their death-transcending worldviews. In this way, we live as valued participants in a culturally based symbolic vision, rather than as vulnerable animals fated only for death and decay. One of our favorite passages from Irvin Yalom's book *Existential Psychotherapy* (1980) makes this point most poignantly:

> Not too long ago I was taking a brief vacation alone at a Caribbean beach resort. One evening I was reading, and from time to time I glanced to watch the bar boy who was doing nothing save staring languidly out to sea—much like a lizard sunning itself on a warm rock, I thought. The comparison I made between him and me made me feel very snug, very cozy. He was simply doing nothing—wasting time. I, on the other hand was doing something useful, reading, learning. I was, in short, getting ahead. All was well, until some internal imp asked the terrible question: Getting ahead of what? How? And (even worse) why? What was brought home to me with unusual force was how I lull myself into a death-defeating

delusion by continually projecting myself into the future. John Maynard Keynes puts it this way: What the "purposeful" man is always trying to secure is a spurious and illusive immortality, immortality for his acts by pushing his interests in them forward in time. (p. 124)

Meaning, purpose, and significance functioned to elevate Dr. Yalom above lizard status to someone of eternal value, until that irksome imp, who may visit many of us on fleeting occasions, momentarily provided a glimpse through the cultural illusion. He recovered nicely though, by using this episode purposefully in his extremely important book. And we suspect that the bar boy did not see himself as a lizard, but more likely was daydreaming within his worldview, perhaps envisioning working his way up the ranks at the resort, thinking warmly of a special loved one, or dreaming of becoming the island's next great reggae singer.

Cultural Worldviews

Of course, providing meaning and significance to large numbers of what Becker referred to as "gods with anuses" is no easy task. Rather it requires that cultures provide answers to universal cosmological questions (e.g., Where did I come from? What should I do on earth? What happens to me after I die?) that convey a sense that the world is orderly, stable, and meaningful. And, indeed, all cultures do that, albeit in very different ways. Consider creation stories, which tell us where we came from and set up the culture's explanation of what our purpose here is. For example, in the Judeo-Christian tradition that most of us are familiar with, a manly bearded God created heaven and earth and all of its inhabitants in 6 days before taking a well-deserved break on the 7th day. But this view is not widely shared by a significant proportion of the rest of our species. For the Thompson Indians, in the northwest frontier of India (Verrier Elwin, 1958, as quoted by Long, 1963), creation is viewed in the following way:

> At first Kajum-Chantu, the earth, was like a human being; she had a head, and arms and legs, and an enormous fat belly. The original human beings lived on the surface of her belly.
> One day it occurred to Kajum-Chantu that if she ever got up and walked about, everyone would fall off and be killed, so she herself died of her own accord. Her head became the snow-covered mountains; the bones of her back turned into smaller hills. Her chest was the valley where the Apa-Tanis live. From her neck came the north country of the Tagins. Her buttocks turned into the Assam plain. For just as the buttocks are full of fat, Assam has fat rich soil. Kajum-Chantu's eyes became the Sun and Moon. From her mouth was born Kujum-Popi, who sent the Sun and Moon to shine in the sky. (p. 35)

Long (1963) also reports a South Pacific creation myth in which the universe is conceived of as a giant hollow coconut shell divided into different levels that communicate with one another. Mortals live in the upper world, but everything originates from a thick stem at the bottom of the shell where a formless spirit, Te-aka-ia-Roe (*The-root-of-all-existence*), perpetually sustains "the entire fabric of the universe."

The Ainu, original inhabitants of Japan, believe that the earth was initially lifeless mud and water until a heavenly creator sent a bird to make the earth and that humans are descended from the polar bear. The Bushmen of the Kalahari Desert in southwest Africa believe that God created everything after assuming the form of a praying mantis. The Eskimos of Kukulik Island in the Bering Strait believe that a Creator-Raven made the world—then after a brief rest, turned pebbles into people, who were subsequently instructed to throw pebbles into water; these became whales. The earth was created by a dung beetle out of mud according to the Negritos, pygmy people of Malaysia; and the Papua in New Guinea are quite certain that the first humans came out of a palm tree (all of these examples are from Leeming & Leeming, 1994).

Despite the wide diversity of mutually exclusive accounts of the origin of the universe and humankind—mutually exclusive in the sense that the literal veracity of any given account would almost certainly disconfirm all others, Leeming and Leeming (1994) observe that:

> When creation myths are compared, certain universal or archetypal patterns are discovered in them. Behind the many individual creation myths is a shadow myth that is the world culture's collective dream of differentiation (cosmos) in the face of the original and continuously threatening disorder (chaos).
>
> The basic creation story then, is that of the process by which chaos becomes cosmos, no-thing becomes some-thing. In a real sense this is the only story we have to tell. . . . It lies behind our attempts to "make something" of our lives, that is, to make a difference in spite of the universal drive toward meaninglessness. (p. viii)

These creation stories thereby set the foundation for the meaning systems by which people live, and building upon them, other creation stories, like those of tribes and nations, contribute greatly to this meaning. For example, for patriotic Americans, the Revolutionary War, George Washington, the Declaration of Independence, and so on serve vital roles in their meaning systems. In this meaningful worldview, being a patriotic American makes one significant—no longer a purposeless, transient animal, one is now an eternally significant contributor to a great nation that represents eternal values of freedom and democracy. In this way, cultural worldviews set up the path to immortality, to transcendence of one's own death. By being valued contributors to such a meaningful world, we become permanent constituents of an eternal symbolic reality, instead of just corporeal beings in a wholly material reality.

Of course, as with the creation stories, cultures vary greatly in the paths to immortality they provide. Indeed, in *Psychology and the Soul*, Rank

(1931/1961) described the historical evolution of cultural modes of immortality striving, with the one constant theme being that some essence of the person continues beyond death either individually or merged within a death-transcending collective. Building on this work, in *The Broken Connection: On Death and the Continuity of Life*, Robert Jay Lifton (1979/1983) distinguished between literal immortality involving an afterlife and symbolic immortality through enduring social connections and cultural contributions. Symbolically, for example, humans can attain a sense of immortality by contributing to art, science, the building of magnificent pyramids or commanding skyscrapers, or, more modestly, by making some small but lasting contribution to ongoing life. Besides these many varieties of achievements, people can pass on their genes, inheritance, and values to their own children, assuring some lasting mark on future generations. And they can sustain some sense of immortality simply by being a valued part of a larger collective such as a tribe or the nation that will live on in perpetuity. Indeed, in *Revolutionary Immortality: Mao Tse-Tung and the Chinese Cultural Revolution*, Lifton (1968) argued that this was the fundamental psychological appeal of Mao's communist worldview. With symbolic immortality, although the person may not believe in an individual soul that survives forever, he or she can feel that some physical manifestation of individual existence will endure nonetheless.

However, human beings (present company included) have always preferred their immortality to be quite literal. Woody Allen put it this way: "I don't want to achieve immortality through my work: I want to achieve it by not dying" (http://www.quoteworld.org).

This is undoubtedly the primary appeal of virtually all religions. In *The Evolution of the Idea of God* (1897/2000), Grant Allen[1] concluded from his anthropological study of religion that

---

[1] Allen (1897/2000) went to great lengths to note that his analysis of the origin of religion has no bearing on the question of the existence of God per se:

> To analyze the origin of a concept is not to attack the validity of the belief it encloses. The idea of gravitation, for example, arose by slow degrees in human minds, and reached at last its final expression in Newton's law. But to trace the steps by which that idea was gradually reached is not in any way to disprove or to discredit it. The Christian believer may similarly hold that men arrived by natural stages at the knowledge of the one true God; he is not bound to reject the final conception as false merely because of the steps by which it was slowly evolved. A creative God, it is true, might prefer to a make a sudden revelation of himself to some chosen body of men; but an evolutionary God, we may well believe, might prefer in his inscrutable wisdom to reveal his own existence and qualities to his creatures by means of the same slow and tentative intellectual gropings as those by which he revealed to them the physical truths of nature. I wish my inquiry to be regarded, not as destructive, but as reconstructive. It attempts to recover and follow out the various planes in the evolution of the idea of God, rather than to cast doubt upon the truth of the evolved concept. (p. 9)

We agree and have advanced a similar argument in one of our original formulations of TMT (Solomon et al., 1991a):

> Although our reasoning seems to imply that an absurdist, atheistic depiction of the world is an accurate perspective, our argument is not based on the notion that such a conception is absolutely true but rather on the notion that as we develop cognitively we necessarily entertain this horrific possibility and can never unequivocally disconfirm it. (p. 94)

the concept of a god is nothing more than that of a Dead Man, regarded as a still surviving ghost or spirit, and endowed with increased or supernatural powers and qualities. [There is a] universal god-making tendency in human nature . . . this universal tendency to worship the dead has ever since persisted as fully as ever, and is in fact the central element in the entire religious instinct of humanity . . . the universal feeling in favour of the deification or beatification of the dead, with the desire for immortality on the part of the individual believer himself in person. (p. 141)

The notion that literal immortality is a central feature of all organized religions was echoed a century later by Charles Panati (1996) in *Sacred Origins of Profound Things: The Stories Behind the Rites and Rituals of the World's Religions*. As an example of the many ways in which religions provide literal immortality, Panati provides a 7th-century description of Islamic Heaven:

The celestial Paradise is a place of consummate joy and bliss, consisting of seven grades of pleasure . . . and where admission is granted only by the will of Allah, God.

The bodies of the dead remain in their graves until the end of the world, when everyone will be resurrected to stand before Allah at the Final Judgment. Allah will require each person to walk the Path, which is the Zoroastrian-like bridge that stretches over Hell and ultimately ascends to the heights of Heaven. The righteous will walk the full length of the bridge, but the damned will fall off along the way, plunging into fiery pits of Hell, where they'll be roasted, boiled and afflicted with pus.

As in early Judaism, the Islamic Heaven physically resembles the Garden of Eden, though it is no longer populated with only one man and one woman. There are many available young maidens in this male-oriented Paradise, which brims with an abundance of fresh figs, dates, and sweet libations. (pp. 446–447)

This account of the afterlife is still quite seriously entertained by many Islamic fundamentalists, as evidenced by Islamic Jihad's Sheik Abdulla Shamni's 1995 (reported by Abu-Nasr, 1995, p. 1A) description of heaven as "a world of castles, flowing rivers, and lush fields" where the blessed "can eat the most delicious food, the most luscious fruits and the tenderest cuts of meat."

Many Eastern religions, such as Hinduism, believe in reincarnation. Individuals may be originally born as insects or potatoes, and then gradually work their way up to personhood; each is then successively reincarnated as a different person for many lifetimes, until reaching Nirvana, at which time one perpetually exists in an ethereal mist. And a firm belief in heaven is also central to the cultural worldview of the average American. Panati (1996) reported (based on a 1994 poll) that 77% of the American public believe that heaven exists and that 76% feel that they have an excellent chance of residing there some day. Heaven is a peaceful place, free of stress, and with ample leisure time—according to 91% of those who believe in its existence—and more than 70% believe that in heaven they will be in God's eternal presence, meet up with family and friends, and be surrounded by humor and frequent laughter.

In sum, all cultural worldviews serve an important anxiety-reducing function by providing a sense of meaning and a recipe for attaining either symbolic or literal immortality. Cultures vary a great deal (historically and at present) in terms of the specific manner in which they serve these purposes. Although the average enculturated individual believes in the absolute veracity of his or her personal but culturally derived conception of reality, no culture's account of the origin of the universe and plan for salvation is likely to be literally true. Consequently, cultural constructions are maintained over time primarily by social consensus and by altering physical surroundings, whenever possible, to render them in accordance with the vision of reality prescribed by the culture. Psychologically, then, the function of culture is not to illuminate the truth but rather to obscure the horrifying possibility that death entails the permanent annihilation of the self.

Self-Esteem

Psychological equanimity thus requires us to believe that we live in a meaningful universe in which some form of ourselves continues to exist forever. But it is important to note that simply believing in cultural worldviews does not, in and of itself, guarantee immortality; we must first meet the standards of value prescribed by our worldviews. In other words, individuals must perceive themselves as valuable and significant participants in the cultural drama to which they subscribe in order to qualify for the security-providing sense of death transcendence. Accordingly, all cultures have social roles with prescriptions of appropriate conduct; those who meet or exceed those standards obtain *self-esteem*: the belief that one is a person of value in a world of meaning. The primary function of self-esteem, then, is to buffer anxiety, especially anxiety associated with vulnerability and death.

We view the need for self-esteem as universal (anthropologist Walter Goldschmidt, 1990, called this ubiquitous human desire "affect hunger"), although the specific ways in which self-esteem is acquired and maintained vary across cultures and historical eras. So, for example, in contemporary American culture, ruggedly individualistic people who advance their fiscal well-being by being viciously competitive and actively strive to eliminate others who engage in similar pursuits are highly regarded and perceived as the paragons of civic virtue. But in a more collectivist culture, such as that of the Hopi Indians, where it would unthinkable to advance one's interests at the expense of another member of the community, the same person would be despised and ostracized for his or her arrogant antisocial proclivities. For the Sambians in New Guinea (reported by Herdt, 1982) adolescent boys perform oral sex on the male elders of the tribe as a normal rite of passage into adulthood; not to do so would be considered an abomination. In America, such behavior is generally frowned upon; and indeed, according to Jerry Falwell (with Pat Robertson's concurrence on *The 700 Club* on 9/13/2001), behavior of this kind was directly responsible for the events of 9/11.

A heroic accomplishment for a Crow Indian warrior was to gallop into an enemy camp and touch one of their warriors without injuring him; Tlingit Indians are regarded in proportion to how many blankets and other objects they have accumulated and then either given away or destroyed; Yurok Indians value ceremonial goods such as skins of albino deer and obsidian blades but would be loathe to give them away and horrified at the prospect of destroying them; Dinka men are measured by the number of cattle they possess; a Trobiand Island man is assessed by the size of the pyramid of yams he builds in front of his sister's house and leaves to rot (examples from Goldschmidt, 1990). For the Igbo of Western Africa, adolescent girls are fed high-calorie foods in a period of ritual seclusion to develop a plumpness that is considered an essential aspect of beauty (Dissanayake, 1992). American girls spend their adolescence starving themselves (or binge eating and purging) to make themselves thinner than linguini.

The main point here is that although everyone needs self-esteem, no one procures self-esteem directly for the self through the self because self-esteem is ultimately a cultural contrivance in that the standards by which we judge ourselves to be persons of value are invariably derived from the cultural milieu each of us inhabits. Just as no one cultural worldview has an absolute lock on the truth, no specific culturally inculcated standards of self-esteem are inherently more valid than others. As Nietzsche noted in *Beyond Good and Evil* (1886/2001) and *On the Genealogy of Morals* (1887/1989), there are no absolute barometers of goodness or wickedness. This is not to suggest that all value systems are equally admirable. Becker (1973) argued that one useful way of evaluating cultures is in terms of their ability to provide meaning, value, and physical sustenance to the largest proportion of their members with the least cost to themselves and their neighbors. Such an evaluation, of course, starts with the assumptions that human life is, in and of itself, valuable and that all humans have the right to survival and happiness. But even these very basic values are not universally held by all humans.

Culture, Self-Esteem, and Security

Our analysis so far has been at the level of culture and the psychological functions culture and self-esteem serve for the individual. An important question that arises at this point is how self-esteem acquires its anxiety-buffering qualities. How do the twitching blobs of acultural biological protoplasm we call human infants become members of a humanly constructed symbolic universe (culture) from which they derive a sense of meaning and value (self-esteem)? An individual, developmental focus is needed to answer this question, and our answer must dovetail with the cultural level aspects of the theory; fortunately, it does.

We start by noting the profound helplessness and immaturity of the human neonate. As many evolutionary theorists from Darwin on have noted, there is a direct relationship between cognitive complexity and degree of immaturity at birth and consequent prolonged period of dependence. Simple-minded creatures are born as relatively complete, albeit often miniaturized versions of, adult forms. Baby guppies are up and running (or rather swimming) the moment they descend from their mother's interior; a mare's foal is upright and walking moments after birth; kittens and puppies can be completely weaned from their mothers in 6 weeks.

The human infant is, by comparison, a pathetic and helplessly immature specimen, unable to perform even the most rudimentary acts and completely dependent on the care and goodwill of their primary caretakers for many years. For Darwin, profound immaturity and prolonged dependence are the evolutionary price that we pay for our vast intelligence and adaptability. We humans are incredibly flexible creatures, able to adapt to widely varying circumstances and to take active control over our environments, because our nervous systems develop a great deal after birth in response to experience, as opposed to being nearly fully formed at birth, as is the case for simpler creatures whose behavior is more directly bound to instinctual responses (although surely not impervious to experience). Although human behavior is far less rigidly determined by instinctual action patterns than that of other animals, humans are by no means devoid of instincts; quite the contrary, we all enter the world predisposed to grasping things in our hands, sucking things that our lips encounter (especially useful for getting fed), and orienting our visual attention toward human faces, especially those who provide us with something nutritious to suck. Infants also enter the world with a heightened capacity for experiencing anxiety when their basic needs are unsatisfied or when they feel threatened in any way. As Freud often noted, although anxiety is immensely unpleasant and we generally try to avoid it at all costs, it is nevertheless quite adaptive, especially for creatures unable to care for themselves. Hungry or wet infants cannot cook themselves a crepe or hop into fresh diapers, but they can certainly accomplish the same ends by emitting excruciating screams that attract the attention and consequent need-fulfilling responses from their parents.

According to the seminal work of John Bowlby (1969, 1973, 1980), infants' raw undifferentiated terror instigates the formation of attachments, at first to their mothers and eventually to others in their interpersonal universe. Bowlby argued that it made evolutionary sense for profoundly immature creatures to strive to maintain close proximity (at first physical and subsequently psychological) to those in a position to best provide for and protect them. Babies thus derive an utterly essential inchoate sense of security from being in direct contact with, or physical proximity to, seemingly omnipotent, omnipresent parental figures who magically intervene every time hunger, thermodynamic conditions, loud noises, or wet diapers render them frightened or uncomfortable. Accordingly, Bowlby observed that infants who are agitated and distressed are immediately comforted by physical contact with, and even the mere presence of, their primary caretaker and eventually use the mother as a secure base from which to explore their surroundings.

At first, very few social or cultural demands are imposed on infants, although they are already being psychologically and physically inculcated into the vagaries of their humanly constructed cultural surroundings, for example, by the names ascribed to them by their parents as a function of their gender and culture (an American boy is very unlikely to be named Mary, and we would be surprised to find indigenous residents of Iraq with the surname Smith); by the manner in which they are clothed (blue or pink in American households) and housed (in a crib in their own room in America; in bed with their mothers in most other cultures on the planet); by the removal of baby boys' foreskins or piercing of baby girls' ears. However, at a year or so of age, children begin to be more actively incorporated into their cultural order. This socialization requires parental efforts to get children to refrain from doing things they very much want to do and to begin to do things that they are ordinarily quite disinclined to do—both to adhere to cultural dictates and to keep them alive.

For example, there is nothing biologically problematic about hurling mud on the recently painted white living room walls to create dazzling and interesting visual spectacles, but many parents in Western cultures frown on this activity. There is nothing biologically problematic about loud burping after a meal or blowing one's nose into the open air on the street, but these are also contraindicated behaviors in many American households (although thoroughly acceptable and expected conduct in other cultures; Segall, Campbell, & Herskovits, 1966). It is, however, biologically problematic for a toddler to wander around naked in a blizzard or to touch the fascinating flickering flames of the blaze in the fireplace—even if doing so does not violate cultural dictates in any way. Thus, either because of culturally constructed standards of decorum or the sheer demands of physical necessity, parents must get their young charges to alter their behavior long before the infants are cognitively or emotionally mature enough to understand the rational or cultural basis for their parents' expectations.

Parents accomplish this arduous task by the conditional dispensation of affection. When children "do the right thing"—for example, put their muddy shoes on the door mat rather than on the kitchen table placemat; blow their noses in a tissue rather than on the silk curtains in the living room; wait for the swimming pool to be filled with water before jumping off the diving board—they are rewarded with the effusive, enthusiastic praise of their glowing parents. The same seemingly omnipotent, omnipresent people who in the past ministered to their every need and desire unconditionally now require certain behaviors to sustain their security-providing love and approval. In this way, being "good" by adhering to parental demands becomes associated with being safe and secure (good = safe and secure = alive). When, however, children do something at odds with cultural mandates or put themselves at risk for physical termination, parents react in a variety of ways—for example, physical punishment, verbal rebukes, or just appearing manifestly unhappy or disappointed—all of which share in common the very obvious lack of the enthusiasm and overt affection that are proffered when their behavior is more "appropriate." The absence of parental affection threatens the very basic inchoate sense of security previously engendered by proximity to the parents; consequently, being "bad" comes to be associated with feelings of anxiety and insecurity and the possibility of parental abandonment (bad = anxious and insecure = dead).

In this fashion, self-esteem acquires its anxiety-buffering qualities By adherence to parental demands that are, in turn, determined by, and are a reflection of, prevailing cultural standards, children sustain the parental love on which psychological equanimity, and effective instrumental behavior, ultimately depend. At the same time, children become increasingly familiar with their culture's socially constructed account of the universe and the standards of value associated with it, through constant exposure to cultural traditions and folklore. From Superman, Batman, Spiderwoman, and Mighty Mouse; to Hercules, Xena, Harry Potter, Jimmy Neutron, and Shrek; to Christopher Columbus, Paul Bunyan, and Johnny Appleseed; to Santa Claus, Freedom Fighters, Operation Desert Storm, and Operation Enduring Freedom, children are perpetually peppered with accounts of a world in which heroes routinely encounter and defy death, and where, generally speaking, good things happen to good people and bad things happen to bad people. And the cultural worldview is concurrently reinforced by a humanly altered physical reality that conforms to, and in so doing, substantiates the conception of reality provided by that cultural worldview. Churches look the way Biblical descriptions suggest they ought; flags and monuments (religious and secular) are physical testaments to the tangible reality of the culture's history and current vitality; Mickey Mouse really is at Disneyland, and Santa Claus really is at the mall.

Then between the ages of 3 and 10 years, or so, children become increasingly aware of their parents' mortality and their own (see Yalom, 1980, for a compelling discussion of children's concerns about death). This makes children simultaneously recognize (to varying degrees of consciousness) their extreme vulnerability—they could have been the ones who died of cancer at age 8 or were shot in the schoolyard or hit by a car or riding in an airplane that crashed into the side of that building in New York City—and their parents' ultimate inability to protect them from numerous potential dangers and eventual death. At this point, their security base must broaden to something bigger than their parents: something large enough to provide protection from these larger threats. Luckily, security-minded parents have been paving the way for this shift all along by teaching the deistic and secular beliefs and values of the culture, the very ones that also form their own security base. The child consequently shifts the basis of his or her psychological security from maintaining a sense of value in the eyes of the parents to maintaining a sense of value in the eyes of the culture at large and its deistic and secular representatives. As Geza Roheim points out in the book *The Origin and Function of Culture* (1943), now self-esteem is largely contingent on meeting or exceeding the standards of value shared by others in the culture: "The caressing and praise received from . . . parents is transformed into praise from . . . countrymen . . . fame and praise are socialized equivalents of love" (p. 31).

In this way, twitching blobs of biological protoplasm are transformed into culturally constructed symbol mongers who derive psychological equanimity through the belief that they are persons of value in a world of meaning and thus protected from harm in this life and assured a permanent place in the next one. The individual's self-worth is based on the roles and attributes valued within the cultural worldview to which the person subscribes, and cultures typically provide their constituents with a wide variety of valued attributes and roles that they can try to fulfill (e.g., smart, funny, athletic, doctor, scientist, entrepreneur). The ways in which people acquire and sustain their sense of self-worth change systematically across the life span; when we are little, we just need to be cute, clever, and obedient; later we may have to meet those sales quotas, cure those clients, or publish that book.

Summary of Terror Management Theory

In sum, TMT posits that the juxtaposition of a biological predisposition toward self-preservation that human beings share with all forms of life with the uniquely human awareness of the inevitability of death gives rise to potentially overwhelming terror. This potential for terror is managed by the construction and maintenance of cultural worldviews: humanly constructed beliefs about the nature of reality that infuse individuals with a sense that they are persons of value in a world of meaning, different from and superior to corporeal and mortal nature, and thus capable of transcending the natural boundaries of time and space and, in so doing, eluding death. For this reason, a substantial proportion of human activity is devoted to maintaining faith in one's cultural worldview and the belief that one is meeting or exceeding the standards of value derived from that worldview.

TWO FUNDAMENTAL QUESTIONS: REDUX

How, then, does TMT help us address the two fundamental questions posed at the outset of this chapter?

Why Do People Need Self-Esteem?

TMT explains what self-esteem is, how people acquire and sustain it, and what function it serves. Self-esteem is the culturally based belief that one is a valued participant in a meaningful reality. This belief is acquired and sustained by living up to a set of standards of value prescribed by the individualized cultural worldview that one has internalized over the course of socialization. We feel good and, therefore, protected when we fulfill the attributes and roles we have learned to value. This feeling of self-worth allows us to function with psychological equanimity despite our knowledge of our vulnerability and ultimate mortality. Self-esteem comes to serve this function over the course of childhood as meeting standards of goodness becomes the prerequisite for sustaining the parental love and protection that form the initial basis of the child's security. The larger culture, in its both secular and religious aspects, extends this equation of goodness and protection up through death transcendence, thereby facilitating the necessary shift of the bases of self-worth and security onto the grander stage of the cultural worldview. As long as we feel like valuable contributors within the cultural worldview to which we subscribe, we can pursue our daily activities feeling confident and secure.

Without these cultural trappings, however, we are all just nameless animals doomed only to die and decay. Only through our cultural beliefs and values and the powerful social validation of them by others (especially family, friends, lovers, and colleagues) can we sustain the sense that we are more than just such animals. To borrow The Who's phrase, self-esteem is an "eminence front," and although each of us can pick our own particular front, we can sustain that front only by a substantial measure of social validation of the attributes and roles by which we judge ourselves as valuable.

Thus, we spend our lives trying to be good little girls and boys, as our personal but culturally derived views of reality tell us how. Because self-esteem is ultimately a culturally based construction, different cultures teach us very different ways to feel good about ourselves, even, as 9/11 made abundantly clear, to the point where one cultural worldview's highest basis of self-esteem is to destroy members of another culture. This clearly illustrates the wide diversity of bases of self-worth across cultural worldviews but is obviously an extreme example. It is also a very rarely chosen route to self-worth, even within radical fundamentalist Islamic circles, which is something we will address more fully in subsequent chapters.

Less dramatically and destructively, people within American culture often sustain self-esteem in small ways, for example, by leaving tips for hotel maids and holding doors open for elderly people. And we do so in bigger ways by trying to be good Christians, Muslims, Hindus, Jews, or secular humanists; by striving to be good parents, friends, and lovers; and by fulfilling expectations of our occupations as the effective therapist, top-notch lawyer, dedicated doctor, dexterous short-order cook, invaluable housekeeper, and so on. Large cultures like that of the United States offer many ways to feel like valued contributors, although some attributes and roles are certainly more valued than others. Presumably doctors can generally derive more self-worth from their occupation than janitors both because of societal perceptions of the occupations and because of the amount of money society offers for those services. But the social consensus about occupational value can change. An interesting example in the United States is that in the wake of 9/11, there has been a surge in appreciation of police officers and firefighters; formerly taken largely for granted, they have at least temporarily attained a higher sense of value. These roles, which had diminished in popularity as routes to heroism, have made a real comeback, with one indication being the sudden increased popularity of firefighter and police officer action figures among American children.

Why Is Peaceful Coexistence So Difficult?

> Man's destructiveness and cruelty cannot be explained in terms of animal heredity or in terms of a destructive instinct, but must be understood on the basis of those factors by which man *differs* from his animal ancestors. The problem is to examine *in what manner and to what degree the specific conditions of human existence are responsible for the quality and intensity of man's lust for killing and torturing.* (Fromm, 1973, p. 186)

How does TMT help us understand "man's inhumanity to man" in general and the ghastly events of 9/11 in particular? From the perspective of TMT, a proper understanding of human cruelty follows from two problems associated with the death-denying aspects of cultural worldviews. First, if culturally constructed beliefs about reality serve a fundamentally death-denying function, the mere existence of people with alternative conceptions of reality is psychologically problematic. Encountering people with different beliefs and accepting the possible validity of their conceptions of reality necessarily undermines (implicitly or explicitly) the confidence with which people subscribe to their own death-denying conceptions and, in so doing, threatens to unleash the overwhelming terror normally mitigated by the secure possession of one's existing beliefs. If I believe that God created the earth in 6 days and someone else believes that God created the earth out of a giant drop of milk, one of us is clearly very wrong. To the extent that both of these beliefs function to protect us from anxiety, realizing that there are alternatives to our own beliefs undermines our faith in the absolute validity of our beliefs and thus makes us vulnerable to experiencing the anxiety that our beliefs function to protect us from.

Second, because culture is a symbolic solution to the very physical problem of death, in his final book, *Escape From Evil*, Becker argued that no culture (regardless of how powerful and convincing) can ever completely eradicate the terror engendered by the awareness of death. Clutching their rabbit's feet or fondling their rosary beads may have comforted people at the top of the World Trade Center on 9/11, but this did not alter their fate. Consequently, there is always residual anxiety that is repressed and subsequently projected onto something, typically a group of individuals inside or outside the culture who serve as scapegoats: socially designated all-encompassing repositories of evil. Participating in a heroic triumph over evil is one of the most effective ways of restoring our feelings of safety and security.

How, then, do we respond to people who are different from ourselves?

Conversion

On occasion, people react to encounters with alternative conceptions of reality by conversion to these alternative worldviews. An orthodox Jew convinced of the merits of Christianity becomes a Catholic; a fervent Communist Party member in the former Soviet Union becomes a committed free market capitalist. Conversion occurs primarily when, for one reason or another, the person is not attaining self-esteem and meaning from his or her own worldview, and consequently, he or she becomes alienated from it and searches for other avenues for emotional security. The infamous American Taliban member John Phillip Walker Lindh provides a quite rare but clear example of someone shifting worldviews. As an alienated 16-year-old boy, he gravitated toward Islamic fundamentalism, culminating in his joining the Taliban and accepting a worldview quite antithetical to the one within which he was raised (Tyrangiel, 2001). Consistent with a terror management account of such behavior, research (Paloutzian, 1981; Ullman, 1982) has found that just before a religious or political conversion, fear of death is high and self-esteem is low, but that fear of death decreases and self-esteem increases immediately following such conversions.

Derogation

Conversion in response to alternative conceptions of reality is extremely rare; why would people risk letting go of their security-providing worldview if it was providing them at least some modicum of security? It is much simpler and more common to defend against such alternative worldviews. To do so, people respond to others having different worldviews with a series of psychological and behavioral reactions that serve to bolster confidence in their own worldviews. The first line of psychological defense is to belittle people who are different. Sure the folks in the South Pacific believe the universe originated from a giant coconut shell; but these are "ignorant illiterate savages who live in mud huts without e-mail or CNN, so how could they possibly realize that God created us in his image along with all the other creatures in 6 days"? By disparaging those with different beliefs, the threat posed by those beliefs is diffused and no longer challenges the received wisdom of one's own cultural worldview.

Assimilation

However, if because of physical proximity to one's own group or resources treasured by one's group these people continue to be salient reminders of an alternative worldview, then additional measures must be taken. Because all cultural worldviews are symbolic illusions, in the sense that there are a multitude of ways to apprehend the universe, we are forced to rely on social consensus as our primary evidence of the validity of our own beliefs and values. When a disheveled guy at the Port Authority bus station in New York City shouts out that we should repent because the end of the world is near, it is tempting to shake one's head in pity and reach for the bottle of antipsychotic medication; but if a significant proportion of the human race were united in the very same belief it becomes quite a different, utterly "normal," and obvious "truth."

Psychologically speaking, then, the more the merrier. When large clumps of humanity become convinced of the merits of a cultural worldview, they legitimize it by virtue of their agreement. This is true not only for religious beliefs but also for virtually all aspects of self and life that people view as significant. Consider, as an example, spectator sports like professional basketball in the United States. The sight of 10 guys in shorts running around bouncing a rubber ball takes on great emotion-producing significance if you are a Lakers fan among 20,000 kindred spirits in the Staples Center and it is the NBA Finals. However, even a lifelong Lakers fan who goes back to the Elgin Baylor days would have a hard time seeing all this running around in gaily colored outfits as significant if he or she were the only one in the stands. In most other parts of the world, the similarly silly activity of soccer takes on the same magical meaning because of such social consensus.

Imagine the boost to your worldview if someone who initially sees little value in your views comes around to accept them—what better validation of the rightness of your worldview? This is the beauty of the second historically common strategy: to try to convince people who are different to dispose of their outlandish beliefs about reality and to adopt one's own instead. Missionary activity is one obvious example of this effort at assimilation: active efforts to get others to dispose of their religious beliefs and to adopt the "true" religion. So is political proselytizing; the Cold War was in some ways a battle between competing political ideologies, with the United States and Soviet Union vying with each other to convince the rest of the world that their political ideology was the "true" and only direction to adopt. Besides the obvious material and political advantages to converting others to one's belief system, there is a substantial psychological payoff when large groups of people adopt one's own culturally constructed vision of reality.

Accommodation

Sometimes certain aspects of an alternative way of living have an inherent appeal and thereby pose a threat that one's own worldview may lose followers. One common strategy, often employed when subcultures arise within a larger culture, is accommodation: incorporating appealing aspects of an alternative lifestyle into the mainstream worldview while divesting these aspects of that worldview of any potentially threatening meanings—meanings that challenge the central values of the mainstream worldview. For example, the hippie counter culture that arose in the United States in the 1960s advocated a simpler back-to-nature lifestyle of peaceful coexistence with others and de-emphasis of status and appearance. Aspects of this alternative value system included the wearing of "common-folk" clothes like blue jeans, eating health foods like granola bars, and listening to rock music. Over time, the mainstream culture co-opted these appealing features, separating them from the values from which they had sprung; now we have designer blue jeans, chocolate granola bars, and elevator music versions of (formerly iconoclastic) rock songs. Remember "We Won't Get Fooled Again"? Oh, yes we will.

Annihilation

Finally, if those others persist in holding on to their threatening alternative worldviews, something more drastic has to be done: If they refuse to join you, beat them—literally. Often, the most compelling way to eliminate the threat posed by people who are different, especially those who have become culturally designated repositories of evil, is to kill them and thus prove that your vision of reality must be right after all. "My God is better than your God, and we will kick your ass to prove it." From this perspective, then, ethnic strife and resultant armed conflict is ultimately the result of a psychological inability to tolerate those who do not share one's death-denying illusions. As Lifton points out in the book *The Broken Connection: On Death and the Continuity of Life* (1979/1983), "Wars and persecutions are, at bottom, expressions of rivalry between contending claims to immortality and ultimate spiritual power" (p. 315). In a related vein, Otto Rank noted the following in *Will Therapy* (1936/1945): "The death fear of the ego is lessened by the killing, the sacrifice, of the other; through the death of the other, one buys oneself free from the penalty of dying, of being killed" (p. 130).

The Middle East, Ireland, India and Pakistan, Turkey and Armenia, Rwanda, the Cold War, and the country formerly known as Yugoslavia are host to just a few of the many seemingly intractable conflicts, often going back thousands of years, in which each side denies the right of the other to exist. For example, the official policy of the Palestine Liberation Organization for many years was to push all Israelis into the ocean; Israelis countered with the quaint slogan "The only good Arab is a dead Arab." Former President Ronald Reagan fueled Cold War animosity by continual reference to the Soviet Union as the "Evil Empire," whereas the Soviet-supported Iranian fundamentalists countered by designating the United States as the "Great Satan."

Clearly, this is not the rhetoric of rational political and economic disagreement; it is the histrionic and terrified defense of death-denying ideologies unable to bear the psychological brunt of alternative conceptions of reality. And human history has been replete with a succession of unspeakable horrors, leaving oceans of blood and mountains of misery in their wake. And as Marcuse (1955) observed, there are few signs of such barbarism abating in modern times, when physical resources and technological development make the prospect of a peaceful planet a practical possibility. Instead, obscene amounts of energy and resources are currently devoted to development and deployment of increasingly lethal biological and nuclear weapons that make it quite possible that human beings will be the first form of life to become extinct through self-extermination. As Marcuse noted in the book *Eros and Civilization* (1955):

> Intensified progress seems to be bound up with intensified unfreedom. Throughout the world industrial civilization, the domination of man by man, is growing in scope and efficiency. Nor does this trend appear as an incidental, transitory regression on the road to progress. Concentration camps, mass exterminations, world wars, and atom bombs are no "relapse into barbarism," but the unrepressed implementation of the achievements of modern science, technology, and domination. And the most effective subjugation and destruction of man by man takes place at the height of civilization, when the material and intellectual attainments of mankind seem to allow the creation of a truly free world. (p. 4)

This is not to suggest that wars have no "rational" or "physical" basis. Of course they do: Wars are fought over strategic locations and valuable material resources. Landlocked countries often fight to gain access to the ocean to advance their trade interests, and Saudi Arabia would be of little interest to industrialized countries if it did not control the world's largest repository of oil. However, our point is that the psychological threat posed by competing worldviews and ideologies is necessary to generate sufficient amounts of rage and hatred to motivate ordinary citizens to put their lives on the line to do battle with an enemy. From this perspective, wars would occur even in the absence of political and material contentions because they are, in part, the result of conflicts between competing immortality ideologies. For example, Hitler viewed Germany's defeat in World War I as "deserved punishment by *eternal retribution*" because of the mixing of races that constituted "sin against the will of eternal *Providence.*" He argued that because of these sins Germany needed to purify itself by eliminating the filthy Jews and Gypsies and homosexuals (and anyone else who did not agree with him); this was a mission decreed by "the Creator of the universe" (all quotes from *Mein Kampf*, cf. Fromm, 1941/1969, p. 260). A little closer to home, when Iraq invaded Kuwait in 1990, President George Bush's original reaction (reported in the *New York Times* by Apple, 1990) was to frame public discourse about the conflict solely in economic terms: "Our jobs, our way of life. . . would all suffer if control of the world's great oil reserves fell into the hands of Saddam Hussein." But Americans were not about to risk their lives for a tank of gas or a job at Wal-Mart, so Bush's rhetoric changed substantially when it came time to actually fight (quoted in the *New York Times*, January 17, 1991):

> This is an historic moment. We have in the past year made great progress in ending conflict and cold war. We have before us an opportunity to forge a new world order, a world where the rule of law, not the law of the jungle, governs the conduct of nations. (p. A14)

Similarly, in a declaration of Jihad against Americans (Barr & Peterson, 2001), Osama bin Laden (and others) claimed that Americans are attempting to annihilate and humiliate all Muslims and that

> all these crimes and sins committed by the Americans are a clear declaration of war on God, his messenger, and Muslims. And ulema have throughout Islamic history unanimously agreed that the jihad is an individual duty if the enemy destroys the Muslim countries. . . . Nothing is more sacred than belief except repulsing an enemy who is attacking religion and life. . . . The ruling to kill the Americans and their allies—civilians and military—is an individual duty for every Muslim who can do it in any country in which it is possible. . . . We . . . call on every Muslim who believes in God and wishes to be rewarded to comply with God's order to kill the Americans and plunder their money wherever and whenever they find it.

All wars are thus ultimately holy wars; George W. Bush was just being honest when his initial reaction to the events of 9/11 was framed in terms of a "Crusade": "This crusade, this war on terrorism is going to take a while," Bush said in an unscripted remark on Sunday 9/15 after stepping off the presidential helicopter.

IS IT TRUE?

Hopefully by this point you will agree that TMT provides interesting and credible answers to the two fundamental questions posed at the outset of this chapter and a plausible account of human activity over the course of history. However, it is imperative to demonstrate that the theory does more than provide post hoc explanations for these phenomena; it should be able to generate novel empirical predictions that are supported by research specifically designed to test hypotheses derived from the theory. This endeavor has occupied us for almost 2 decades (with a growing number of students and colleagues also pitching in) and has not only yielded substantial support for the theory but also led to some important conceptual refinements. To this work we now turn.

3

TERROR MANAGEMENT RESEARCH: COPING WITH CONSCIOUS AND UNCONSCIOUS DEATH-RELATED THOUGHTS

It is not for us to confess that in our civilized attitude towards death we are once more living psychologically beyond our means, and must reform and give truth its due? Would it not be better to give death the place in actuality and in our thoughts which properly belongs to it, and to yield a little more prominence to that unconscious attitude towards death which we have hitherto so carefully suppressed? This hardly seems indeed a greater achievement, but rather a backward step . . . but it has the merit of taking somewhat more into account the true state of affairs.
—Sigmund Freud, *Thoughts for the Times on War and Death*
(1915/1959, p. 316–317)

After formulating terror management theory (TMT) in 1984, we found ourselves faced with a major challenge. How do we assess the validity of the theory so its relevance to many important forms of human behavior will be clear? More pertinent to present purposes, why should you the reader, or the public in general, take seriously what this theory has to tell us about the causes and consequences of the events of 9/11? This chapter and the next one provide our answers to these questions by presenting the growing body of research that has accumulated in support of the theory.

Not surprisingly, the theory seemed quite compelling to us from the start. And so we began presenting the theory at conferences and using it in our teaching. We found that students and colleagues from other disciplines tended to judge the ideas as either quite intriguing or obviously correct, whereas academic psychologists were often skeptical and viewed the ideas as obviously wrong. We expected some resistance from those in our own discipline because academic psychologists in the dark ages of the 1980s were prone to knee-jerk rejection of broad theories, especially if the theory is in any way connected to the psychoanalytic tradition. But we were surprised by the superficial nature of the opposition to the ideas. At talks, we often encountered responses such as "I don't think about death and am not afraid of it; therefore, this theory must be wrong." In response to our first paper on the theory, one review we received consisted of a single sentence: "I have no doubt that these ideas would be of no interest to any psychologists, alive or dead." You would think that, given the nature of the theory, at least some dead psychologists would be interested.

After considerable discussion regarding such reviews, a journal editor finally clarified things for us by pointing out that the ideas may have some merit but will not be taken seriously until they have been assessed empirically. This made sense to us. After all, patently obvious notions have a notoriously poor track record when they are ultimately subjected to empirical scrutiny. For example, the idea that the sun and the planets revolve around the stationary earth at the center of the universe makes a good deal of sense, squares with most peoples' experiences on the planet, and was upheld as absolute truth for thousands of years. Indeed, to believe otherwise was at one time considered heresy by the Catholic Church; Galileo was sentenced to life imprisonment in 1633 for his belief in the heretical Copernican notion that the earth revolved around the sun. Today we know better. Conversely, the idea that the same molecule, DNA, that directs the construction of a lizard or a grape also directs the construction of a human being seemed preposterously wrong-minded for centuries. Today we know better.

So in science, whether a theory intuitively seems to be obviously true or obviously false should not matter; the proof, as the quaint saying goes, is in the pudding. And the pudding in science consists of the results of research designed to test hypotheses derived from the theory. Accordingly, for the past 15 years, we, joined by some talented graduate students (now professors) and later by colleagues in independent labs around the world, have engaged in an extensive research program to test a host of hypotheses derived from TMT. The purpose of this chapter is to present an overview of the empirical support for the theory's most basic propositions and then discuss the research that led to an important distinction between ways in which people cope with conscious and unconscious death-related thoughts. This intricate line of research is described in some detail because the model that emerged from it is important for understanding both immediate and delayed reactions to 9/11. Chapter 4 then provides an overview of research on the role of terror management in two particularly central responses to the threat of death that are especially relevant to understanding the problem of terrorism: prejudice and striving for self-worth.

SELF-ESTEEM AS AN ANXIETY BUFFER

How could we assess the validity of such a broad theory, especially one that posits a pervasive influence of an unconscious and yet ever-present fear of death? We assess it the same way any theory is tested in science, by generating novel hypotheses that lead to empirical predictions and then designing studies and gathering data to test those predictions. After some pondering, we came up with two basic hypotheses. The first one concerned self-esteem. According to TMT, when people believe they are objects of value in a world of meaning, they should be able to function securely. In other words, self-esteem should serve an anxiety-buffering function.

Actually, by the time we had formulated TMT, there was already a host of evidence consistent with this idea. Literally hundreds of studies had found a *negative correlation* between self-esteem and anxiety; high self-esteem is associated with low anxiety and low self-esteem is associated with high anxiety. Indeed, low self-esteem has been found to be associated with a wide variety of mental and physical problems. Although this work is impressively consistent with the idea that self-esteem reduces anxiety, because this evidence is correlational in nature, it is also consistent with the quite plausible idea that anxiety-related physical and mental health problems reduce self-esteem. For a review of this evidence, see Greenberg, Pyszczynski, and Solomon (1986) and Solomon, Greenberg, and Pyszczynski (1991b).

Experiments help us gather more conclusive evidence of causation by manipulating a variable or set of variables of interest as possible causal factors (independent variables), holding other variables constant, and subsequently measuring the variables believed to be influenced by those independent variables (dependent variables). Existing laboratory experiments had already examined the effects of bolstering or threatening self-esteem, typically by rigging a test so that students would be randomly assigned to experience either success or failure. Consistent with the idea that self-esteem serves an anxiety-buffering function, students whose self-esteem was threatened by failure had been shown to experience increased anxiety and also to display a variety of psychological defenses against the threat, such as deciding that the test they had failed was invalid or making other excuses for their poor performance. In addition, research had shown that once the students defended against the threat of failure, their anxiety decreased. From the terror management perspective, this work seems to show that when the anxiety buffer is shaken, anxiety increases, defenses are marshaled, and anxiety then decreases as a consequence of these defenses.

A valid theory needs to be able to account for previously gathered evidence, and TMT was able to do so. But to be useful, a theory should also be able to generate novel hypotheses that are supported when tested. Therefore, based on the anxiety-buffering notion, we began proposing and testing such hypotheses. The first hypothesis was that raising people's self-esteem would lead them to experience less anxiety following a threat, even if that threat was unrelated to the domain in which self-esteem was increased. In our first experiment to test this hypothesis (Greenberg, Solomon, et al., 1992, Study 1), college students came to the laboratory and were told that they were participating in a study of the relationship between personality traits and reactions to emotionally arousing stimuli. More specifically, the students were told that they would be watching a short video and that we would ask them to give us some reactions to it, which we would then correlate with some of their personality traits that had been assessed by questionnaires that all of the students had completed earlier in the semester. The experimenter told the students that she was required to give them individual reports on the results of these personality assessments.

All of the students were then given what they thought were personalized psychological assessments based on their responses to the personality questionnaires, but which were actually one of two descriptions that were highly general in nature so that they could plausibly apply to all people. These descriptions were designed to convey either a positive or a neutral evaluation of the student's personality. For example, in the neutral feedback condition, the assessment stated, "Although you have some personality weaknesses, you are generally able to compensate for them" and "Some of your aspirations may be a bit unrealistic." In the positive feedback condition, the assessment stated, "Although you may feel that you have some personality weaknesses, your personality is fundamentally strong" and "Most of your aspirations tend to be pretty realistic." With the exception of such minor changes in wording to convey different meaning, the two forms of feedback were similar with respect to content and length, and our hope was that the self-esteem of the students who received the positive feedback would be temporarily elevated, whereas the self-esteem of the students who received the neutral feedback would remain unchanged. To check on the effectiveness of the self-esteem manipulation, the students completed the Rosenberg Self-Esteem Scale at the end of the study, and the positive feedback did indeed lead to higher self-esteem scores than did the neutral feedback.

After receiving the feedback, half of the students watched a 7-min video excerpted from the documentary *Faces of Death* that included actual footage of an autopsy and an electrocution, which was meant to serve as an anxiety-provoking situation. The other half of the students watched a 7-min video from the same documentary that was explicitly nonthreatening and had no graphic depictions or references about death. All of the students then completed the A-State form of the State Anxiety Inventory (STAI; Spielberger, Gorsuch, & Lushene, 1970), a standard self-report measure of anxiety, which was the primary measure of interest to us. Consistent with our hypothesis, students in the neutral self-esteem condition reported more anxiety in response to the death video than to the benign control video, indicating that the manipulation of anxiety through the use of the death video was successful; however, those students in the raised self-esteem condition did not report elevated levels of anxiety in response to witnessing graphic depictions of death.

The finding that people whose self-esteem had been temporarily elevated reported less anxiety than those whose self-esteem was not altered provided strong preliminary support for the notion that self-esteem causes a reduction of anxiety in response to threatening situations. However, one potential problem with that study was the use of a self-report measure of anxiety. Perhaps self-reports are not accurate indications of actual feelings, because participants were unaware of how they really felt, in which case they would be unable to provide an accurate assessment of anxiety, or because they were influenced by the desire to present themselves in a positive or socially desirable manner.

A second study (Greenberg, Solomon, et al., 1992) was consequently undertaken to conceptually replicate and extend the finding that raising self-esteem reduces anxiety in response to threatening circumstances by using a different manipulation of self-esteem and a different assessment of anxiety that was not subject to the problems associated with self-report measures. Students participating in this study were brought into a laboratory and told that we were interested in the relationship between cognitive and physical stimulation and physiological arousal. The students were then attached to a physiograph machine that measured skin conductance, an indication of autonomic arousal that is known to be highly correlated with anxiety (see, for example, Dawson, Schell, & Filion, 1990). After resting for 5 min in order to allow us to collect baseline measures of skin conductance, the students were told that the cognitive stimulation we were studying would be provided by a version of the "Thorndike Anagram Test," which was described as a highly accurate measure of verbal intelligence. The "Thorndike" was actually a bogus test consisting of 20 anagrams that were designed such that the average person would solve 16 to 18 problems correctly in 5 min while we ostensibly recorded their physiological responses.

The experimenter then told half of the students that because we were primarily interested in physiological responses to taking the test rather than performance, we would not score or look at the test (neutral self-esteem condition). The remaining students were told that we were especially interested in how well people performed on the anagram test and that, consequently, the test would be scored and they would receive feedback on their performance. The test was then scored by the experimenter, and the students were told that they had gotten N right (where N = the actual number of anagrams that each student had solved correctly), that no one in the experiment thus far had gotten more than $N - 2$ right, and that their score was in the 90th percentile. This feedback was designed to temporarily elevate self-esteem.

The students were then told that there would be a 90-s experimental period during which they would be exposed to physical stimulation while we measured their physiological responses. Half of the participants were placed in the threat condition and told that the physical stimulation would be provided by a series of mildly painful electrical shocks that would be administered through an electrode that was attached to their wrists at the outset of the study. The remaining participants served in the no-threat condition and were told that the physical stimulation during the experimental period would be provided by the light waves given off by a set of red and yellow lights in the lab. Presumably, the anticipation of electrical shocks during the experimental period would be more anxiety provoking than would peering at colored lights. The experimental period then occurred as described, except that no shocks were administered to any participants.

Our primary interest, of course, was to determine whether physiological arousal varied in anticipation of electrical shocks depending on whether or not self-esteem had been temporarily elevated. Skin conductance is a measure of the speed with which a small electric current travels between two fingers of the person's hand. All else being equal, the more anxious a person is, the more he or she will perspire, and because water is a good conductor, the more a person is perspiring, the faster the current will travel across the skin, that is, the higher will be the skin conductance. Not surprisingly, the results indicated that in the neutral self-esteem condition participants who expected to receive shocks exhibited higher skin conductance than those who gazed at colored lights. This showed that our manipulation of threat was most assuredly successful and allowed us to assess the effects of elevated self-esteem on skin conductance in an anxiety-provoking situation. In support of the self-esteem as anxiety buffer hypothesis and replicating the finding of the first study, students in the raised self-esteem condition who expected to receive electrical shocks exhibited no higher skin conductance than their counterparts in the nonthreatening control condition.

This finding is especially strong support for the notion that self-esteem causes a reduction of anxiety in stressful situations, for two reasons. First, the use of a physiological indicator of anxiety is not subject to the problem of unwilling ignorance or willful distortion that clouds interpretation of self-report measures. Second, if raised self-esteem made a person less anxious in response to someone else's calling him or her an idiot, this would be an important, but perhaps not surprising, indication of the anxiety-buffering properties of self-esteem because it would demonstrate that feelings of self-worth are effective for combating psychological assaults on one's self-worth. But to show that self-esteem buffers anxiety engendered by the expectation of electrical shocks, a physical assault on our very existence, is a much more potent demonstration of the pervasive effect of self-esteem on anxiety.

One could argue, however, that the results of both studies reported earlier have nothing directly to do with self-esteem. Rather, it could be that giving people very positive feedback about their personalities or telling them they have done very well on an intelligence test puts them in a good mood, and it is being in a good mood, rather than self-esteem per se, that is then responsible for the lower levels of anxiety that are subsequently observed in response to watching a death video or expecting to receive electrical shocks. A third study (Greenberg, Solomon, et al., 1992) was therefore conducted in which people were connected to a physiograph machine, and after baseline measures of skin conductance were obtained, they were given either positive or neutral personality feedback, the same manipulation of self-esteem used in the first study. Half of the participants then expected to receive electrical shocks, whereas the other half gazed at colored lights as we recorded their levels of skin conductance. Directly after this experimental period, everyone was asked to complete a standardized mood assessment questionnaire (the Positive and Negative Affect Schedule [PANAS]; Watson, Clark, & Tellegen, 1988).

The results were again consistent with the self-esteem as anxiety buffer hypothesis and with the findings of the previous studies. Specifically, people with temporarily elevated self-esteem exhibited lower skin conductance in anticipation of electrical shocks than those whose self-esteem was not altered. Additionally, subsequent analyses determined that these effects were due to how good the personality feedback made participants feel about themselves rather than the extent to which they reported being in a good mood following the experimental period. This finding thus supports the proposition that high self-esteem, and not simply being in a good mood, was responsible for the reduced anxiety in response to threat.

A subsequent set of studies (Greenberg et al., 1993) investigated the effects of self-esteem on defensive perceptions of vulnerability to illness and death. In previous work by Quattrone and Tversky (1984), half of the participants were told that people with a high tolerance for cold have longer life expectancies, whereas the remaining participants were told that people with a low tolerance for cold generally live longer. All of the participants were then asked to put one of their arms in ice water for as long as they could. Because people in this study were randomly assigned to experimental conditions, individual differences in actual cold tolerance should be evenly distributed across conditions, and consequently, there should have been no differences between the groups in how long they immersed their arms in cold water. However, the results indicated that people who thought that a high tolerance for cold was associated with long life kept their arms in the water much longer than those who were told that low cold tolerance was associated with longer life expectancies. Similarly, another study by Kunda (1987) demonstrated that frequent coffee drinkers were less convinced than infrequent coffee drinkers by research showing caffeine to be associated with health hazards. Presumably, distorting behavior or judgment in these cases serves to minimize anxiety about these threatening events (short life and bad health, respectively).

However, if self-esteem provides a buffer against anxiety, and the distortions we just described are attempts to minimize anxiety by denying one's vulnerability to early death, then enhancing self-esteem should reduce the tendency to distort perceptions in a vulnerability-denying manner. We tested this hypothesis in two studies. In Study 1, we gave participants positive or neutral feedback about their personalities to raise their self-esteem temporarily or leave it unaltered. We then told half of the participants that emotional people tend to die young and the other half that emotional people tend to have longer-than-average life expectancies. Afterward, we asked all of the people in the study to report on their own levels of emotionality. We found that people given neutral personality feedback engaged in vulnerability-denying distortion by reporting to be more emotional when emotionality was associated with longevity but less emotional when emotionality was related to shorter life expectancies. When self-esteem was raised by positive personality feedback, however, participants did not report differences in emotionality as a function of information that emotional people die young or live long. Raising self-esteem thus reduced the need to engage in vulnerability-denying defensive distortions.

Study 2 was then conducted to replicate the finding that high self-esteem reduces vulnerability-denying defensive distortions and to shed light on a theoretical concern that could be raised about all of our previous studies of self-esteem. Specifically, in all of the studies reported thus far, self-esteem was raised temporarily by giving people positive feedback about themselves or their performance. But some psychologists make a distinction between transient elevations of feelings of self-worth that result from these kinds of events, and enduring differences associated with chronic levels of self-esteem that exist above and beyond temporary situational fluctuations (e.g., Heatherton & Polivy, 1991; distinction between trait and state self-esteem). If self-esteem is a general anxiety buffer, then people with chronically high self-esteem should be less responsive to anxiety-provoking circumstances than those with chronically low self-esteem, even in the absence of momentary interventions that increase feelings of self-worth.

Accordingly, we had participants in Study 2 complete the Rosenberg (1965) Self-Esteem Scale before telling half of them that emotional people die young and the other half that emotional people live long, and we then asked them to report their own level of emotionality. Consistent with our prediction and the results of the first study, individuals with low self-esteem reported levels of emotionality that corresponded to those previously described as being associated with long life, but individuals with high self-esteem did not. Once again, high self-esteem eliminated vulnerability-denying defensive distortions. This finding thus demonstrates that self-esteem serves to buffer anxiety both when it is temporarily elevated and when it is chronically high.

Multiple studies have thus provided convergent support for a central proposition of TMT: Self-esteem functions to reduce anxiety in stressful situations.

MORTALITY SALIENCE AND UPHOLDING THE WORLDVIEW

The second basic hypothesis we derived from the theory has, up to this time, inspired more than 120 studies conducted in nine different countries. TMT proposes that cultural worldviews assuage the potentially paralyzing terror associated with the awareness of our mortality. To the extent that cultural worldviews serve this function, reminders of death should make people especially in need of the protection that their beliefs about the nature of reality provide for them. Thus, reminders of death should lead people to increase their defense and bolstering of their cultural worldviews. Our initial strategy to test this hypothesis was to ask people to think about their own death, which we will henceforth refer to as *mortality salience*, and then to make judgments about others who either violate or uphold important aspects of their cultural worldviews. After thinking about death, people should be especially likely to warmly welcome social validation of their worldviews but harshly reject anyone who calls the validity of their worldviews into question. People who violate important cultural values or subscribe to a different worldview threaten the individual's basis of psychological equanimity because they undermine the social consensus for those particular beliefs and values. Conversely, people who uphold important cultural values or merely share the same values that we do provide important evidence for the veracity of our socially constructed vision of reality. In response to mortality salience, therefore, people should be especially prone to derogate those who violate important cultural precepts and to venerate those who uphold them.

Mortality Salience and Moral Transgressions

Our first experiment (Rosenblatt, Greenberg, Solomon, Pyszczynski, & Lyon, 1989) was conducted with 22 municipal court judges in Tucson, Arizona, who volunteered to participate in the study. We assumed that the "laws of the land" were a central part of their worldviews and therefore designed a study to test the hypothesis that after mortality salience, the judges would be especially eager to uphold the law by making highly punitive judgments against a lawbreaker. The judges were told that we were interested in examining the relationship between personality traits, attitudes, and bond decisions (a bond is a sum of money that a defendant must pay before a trial in order to be released from jail). The judges then completed a set of questionnaires that consisted of some standard personality assessment instruments that were included to deflect attention from the actual purpose of the study. Embedded in the questionnaire packets for half of the judges (chosen by random assignment) was a Mortality Attitudes Personality Survey, described as a new form of projective personality assessment in which open-ended responses to questions about death were analyzed in the service of providing information about personality in general. Judges in the mortality salience condition were asked to write short responses to the following questions: "Please briefly describe the emotions that the thought of your own death arouses in you" and "Jot down, as specifically as you can, what you think will happen to you as you physically die and once you are physically dead." This has since become known as the classic mortality salience treatment. The other judges served as the control group and did not complete this questionnaire. All of the judges then completed a self-report checklist to assess emotional reactions to the mortality salience manipulation.

The judges were then presented with a hypothetical legal case brief that was virtually identical to those typically submitted to them before a trial. The case brief stated the arresting charge, prostitution, and the defendant's address, employment record, and length of residency. The brief also included a copy of the citation issued to the defendant, giving basic arrest information such as the location and date of the crime, the arresting officer, and the arresting charge. Notes from the prosecutor indicated that a lack of established community ties and the prosecution's inability to verify information provided by the defendant led them to oppose releasing the defendant on her own recognizance. The case brief was followed by a form that asked the judges to set bond for the defendant.

Our primary interest was in testing the hypothesis that the judges who were reminded of their mortality by the death-related questions would set an especially high bond for the alleged prostitute. We chose judges for the study because they are rigorously trained to make such decisions rationally and uniformly. Also, we had them pass judgment on an alleged prostitute because it is a crime that violates important moral convictions of most citizens in our culture.

The results of the study confirmed this prediction, with an average bond of $455 from the judges following mortality salience, versus an average bond of $50 from judges in the control group. This is a shockingly large difference given that all judges reviewed exactly the same materials, except for the presence or absence of the mortality salience manipulation. From a practical perspective, this result suggests that if one of these municipal court judges, in the course of his or her daily life, happened to have been reminded of his or her own death shortly before setting bond for a person accused of a crime, there is a good chance the unfortunate woman would have been required to come up with a substantial bond—or await trial in jail. This and related findings have led to a number of legal cases in which the excessive salience of death in the courtroom has been argued to be a factor introducing bias against defendants.

Of course, for ethical reasons, the court case in the study, although realistic, was hypothetical. However, none of the judges seemed to be aware of the true purpose of the study, so it is highly unlikely that they altered their behavior to "help" us with our research or to appear in a favorable light. An interesting finding was that none of the judges in the mortality salience group reported being upset by the questionnaire asking them to consider their own death. This was reflected by a lack of differences between the mortality salience and control groups on the self-report mood checklist and suggests that the mortality salience effect was not a result of simply putting the judges in a bad mood.

This result provided provocative initial support for the proposition that mortality salience engenders a greater need for cultural worldviews and consequently provokes more vigorous reactions to moral transgressors. However, no scientific finding can be taken seriously unless it can be replicated; recall that cold fusion was produced once in Utah but never taken very seriously because it could not be replicated elsewhere. Additionally, the findings of the study were based on the assumption that all the judges shared exactly the same worldview—in this case, the notion that prostitution is morally reprehensible. Finally, the findings could also be plausibly explained in several other ways. For example, perhaps thoughts of death simply irritate people in a way not detected by the mood measures and make them more negative about everything. Consequently, further studies reported in Rosenblatt et al. (1989) were undertaken to establish the robustness of the mortality salience effect, investigate a more refined prediction regarding the circumstances in which mortality salience would lead to harsher reactions to moral transgressions, and rule out alternative accounts of our original finding.

Having exhausted our supply of municipal court judges, our next studies employed the human version of the laboratory white rat: undergraduate college students in introductory psychology classes. In Study 2, we asked students to undergo the same procedure as the judges: to set bond for an alleged prostitute after completing some personality assessments in which the mortality salience manipulation was embedded for half of the participants; control participants in these studies completed a parallel questionnaire about innocuous topics like watching television. This was to rule out the unlikely possibility that the results of the first study were due to the judges in the mortality salience condition having completed more questionnaires than their control condition counterparts.

In this study, we assessed students' attitudes about prostitution in the packet of filler questionnaires before the mortality salience manipulation. We then looked at the responses of students who either strongly supported keeping prostitution illegal or felt that prostitution should be decriminalized. The results indicated that students asked to think about death set higher bonds for the alleged prostitute than those in the control group, but only if they had negative views of prostitution from the outset.

Two points are important here. First, this study replicated the basic finding of the study of the judges by demonstrating that moral transgressions are more severely punished after mortality salience. But second, the effect was obtained only if students found prostitution morally repugnant. This makes perfect sense given our theoretical perspective. Recall our claim that cultural worldviews serve to reduce anxiety surrounding death and that pondering one's mortality should engender a greater need for the protection afforded by one's worldview reflected by more vigorous responses to those who violate its most cherished prescriptions for appropriate behavior. But not everyone shares exactly the same beliefs, and consequently, we would expect mortality salience to provoke a response only if a belief that one seriously subscribes to has been violated or challenged.

To investigate further the possibility that mortality salience simply leads to indiscriminant negativity, after the students had completed the bond assessment in Study 2, they also rated how likeable, intelligent, moral, knowledgeable, and well adjusted they found the experimenter. If mortality salience put people in an indiscriminately negative frame of mind, then we would have expected to find the students who thought about their death derogating the experimenter, at least those students opposed to prostitution who had already prescribed higher bonds for the defendant in the hypothetical case. This did not occur; there were no differences between students in the various conditions in their ratings of the experimenter. This study thus demonstrated the highly specific nature of the increased bond assessment for the alleged prostitute following mortality salience, by showing that it happens only for people whose worldviews were violated and that such responses are confined to the violators themselves, and not indiscriminately to all others in the surrounding social environment.

Further studies continued to employ this basic paradigm to produce additional replications of the basic finding that mortality salience engenders more vigorous responses to moral transgressions, and to rule out other plausible explanations for this finding. One possibility is that thinking about death engenders physiological arousal. It is well known that such arousal leads to exaggerated responses to all kinds of social stimuli that may indeed be unrelated to the arousal itself; this is a phenomenon known as *excitation transfer* (Zillmann, 1971). If this were the case, then it would be arousal and not thoughts of death per se that could best explain our findings. This possibility was ruled out in Study 5, in which students set bond for an alleged prostitute following mortality salience or in a control condition while we monitored their physiological arousal. We once again replicated the by now very reliable and robust finding that mortality salience led to higher bonds but also demonstrated that students in the mortality salience condition were not more physiologically aroused than their control counterparts (in terms of skin conductance, pulse rate, and peripheral blood volume) and that levels of physiological arousal were uncorrelated with bond assessments.

It is also possible that the effects we found as a result of mortality salience would occur by asking people to think of any negative or anxiety-provoking event. This set of alternatives was ruled out in a series of studies (e.g., Greenberg, Simon, Harmon-Jones, et al., 1995; and for an extended discussion of this issue, see "What's death got to do with it?" on pp. 97–99 of Greenberg, Solomon, & Pyszczynski, 1997) comparing the effects of mortality salience with the effects of the salience of a host of other aversive circumstances, such as an upcoming exam, speaking in public, reacting to imagined or actual failures, dental pain, social exclusion, paralysis, and pondering the death of another person. In each study, basic mortality salience effects were reproduced, but contemplation of other negative events (even those that caused demonstrable anxiety) did not produce these effects, providing strong support for the claim that it is concern about one's own mortality that is responsible for exaggerated responses to moral transgressors.

Despite all of the studies and measures suggesting that the mortality salience effects did not result from negativity, there is still something unsurprising about the idea that thoughts of death lead to negative behavior. What really had us holding our breath, and what ultimately convinced us that we were really onto something, was the first study testing the hypothesis that mortality salience would lead to more *positive* behavior toward someone who *upheld* the values of the individual's worldview. Study 3 of Rosenblatt et al. (1989) had students prescribe a monetary reward to a person who behaved heroically by risking personal injury to report a suspected mugger to the police as well as setting bond for the now very familiar alleged prostitute. As in previous studies, mortality salience led to a higher bond for the alleged prostitute but, more important, also led to a higher reward for the hero ($3476 after mortality salience vs. $1112 in the control condition). This finding put the final nail in the coffin of any sort of automatic negativity idea and was the first of many studies to show that mortality thoughts lead to more positive reactions to those who uphold the worldview, as well as more negative reactions to those who violate it.

One possible problem with the research program as we have described it thus far is that it relies on the same manipulation of mortality salience (two questions asking people to jot down their feelings about death) and the same measure to assess the effects of this manipulation (setting bond for an alleged prostitute). Consequently, additional studies were conducted using different ways to manipulate mortality salience and different ways of assessing the effects of mortality salience.

Specifically, in Study 6 of Rosenblatt et al. (1989) participants completed a set of true-false questions that assessed their fear of death, instead of responding to the typical open-ended questions about death, as a manipulation of mortality salience. Control condition participants filled out a benign personality inventory of comparable length. Both groups then set bond for the alleged prostitute. The results were identical to those of previous studies: higher bonds following mortality salience.

Our basic finding that mortality salience produces exaggerated reactions to moral transgressors was subsequently independently replicated by

Florian and Mikulincer (1997); they made mortality momentarily salient by asking Israeli volunteers to complete the Fear of Personal Death Scale (Florian & Kravitz, 1983) that assessed both interpersonal (e.g., how one's death will affect significant others) and intrapersonal (e.g., how one's death will impact one's own sense of self) aspects of death. All participants then read vignettes describing some common moral transgressions in contemporary Israeli culture. Some of the transgressions were of an interpersonal nature and others were of an intrapersonal nature. All of the participants then rated the severity of the transgressions and were asked to rate the severity of the punishment that should be administered, similar to the bond assessment in our alleged prostitute paradigm that you are already quite familiar with by now.

The results indicated that, relative to a group of control participants, mortality salience engendered increased ratings of severity and magnitude of punishment for moral transgression, thus replicating our original finding. Additionally, mortality salience produced the largest increases in severity ratings and punishment when participants' specific concerns about death (intrapersonal vs. interpersonal) were congruent with the nature of the moral transgression. In other words, people were especially punitive toward interpersonal moral transgressions after being asked to ponder the interpersonal aspects of death, whereas they were especially punitive toward intrapersonal moral transgressions after being asked to ponder the intrapersonal aspects of death. This finding establishes (a) the multidimensional nature of concerns about death (i.e., death means different things to different people) and (b) the correspondence between specific mortality concerns and particular aspects of the cultural worldview that become differentially important to individuals as a function of this relationship.

Mortality Salience and Worldview Defense

Following the prostitute and hero studies, we began assessing the scope of these mortality salience effects. Among other things, the theory purports to explain hostilities among nations by utilizing the notion that national identity is a large component of most people's worldviews. Indeed, one of the key ways in which people think of themselves as more than just animals is by thinking of themselves as Americans, Italians, Germans, Iranians, and so on. Indeed, our names and values are most often derived from our nation's history and values. Therefore, we wanted to test the hypothesis that mortality salience would lead to especially positive reactions to those who praise one's country and especially negative reactions to those who criticize one's country. To do so, Greenberg et al. (1990, Study 3) had American college students read essays by authors that either strongly favored or opposed the U.S. political system following a mortality salience or control induction. We actually wrote the essays, but they were printed as an interview in *Political*

Science Quarterly (a bogus journal) with a Nobel Prize–winning political science professor at Harvard. The pro-U.S. essay recognized economic inequalities and foreign policy mistakes but was generally positive and concluded that "In this country, the people and not the government will be the final judges of the value of what I have to say. That is what makes this country a great place in which to be a free thinker." The anti-U.S. essay acknowledged the value of many parts of the American political system but then focused extensively on the influence of the power elite on the system and on the economically motivated and amoral behavior of the United States abroad. It concluded that "Morality has absolutely nothing to do with our foreign policy. That's why the idea that the U.S. is a promoter of world democracy and freedom is a total sham." This essay suggested that violent overthrow of the present government was in order. The students were then asked to rate how likeable and knowledgeable they found the author of the essay.

Results indicated that all participants liked the pro-American author and found him more knowledgeable than the anti-American author but that this effect was significantly exaggerated following mortality salience. Specifically, after thinking about their death, participants evaluated the pro-American author more positively and the anti-American author more negatively. Viewing the pro-American author positively bolsters the worldview, whereas viewing the anti-American author negatively defends it, by allowing one to dismiss the anti-American arguments. This finding established that mortality salience influences responses to those who support or oppose important aspects of cultural worldviews (in this case political values) in addition to the moral transgressions or heroic behaviors examined in the previous studies.

Since that study, this finding has become the most commonly replicated effect of thoughts of one's own demise, the prototypic demonstration of what we refer to as *worldview defense*: more positive evaluations of those who help validate one's worldview and more negative evaluations of those who challenge the validity of that worldview. We next wondered what would happen if, following mortality salience, we put people in a position of violating their own cherished beliefs. Greenberg, Simon, Porteus, Pyszczynski, and Solomon (1995) hypothesized that this would be an extremely uncomfortable experience. In this study, participants were asked to think about death or a neutral control topic under the guise of personality assessment and then were asked to complete two tasks designed to assess creative problem solving. In the first group, they were asked to sift sand out of black dye, and in the second group, they were asked to hang a hard plastic crucifix up on a wall; they were provided with a host of objects of potential use in accomplishing these tasks. For the control group, the only effective solutions to these problems involved hammering the nail into the wall with a block of wood, and sifting the sand by pouring the black dye through a piece of white cloth. For the experimental group, however, there was no block of wood, so the nail could be hammered into the wall effectively only with the crucifix itself, and the only cloth available to sift out the sand was a small American flag; thus for the experimental group, the only effective ways to solve the problems involved activities that are clearly sacrilegious if not downright blasphemous for the average American. We measured how long students took to accomplish these tasks and asked them to report afterward how difficult they found the tasks and how uncomfortable they were doing them.

Our prediction was that following mortality salience, personal transgressions involving cherished cultural icons would be especially upsetting, and this was borne out by the results of the study. Specifically, when students were asked to think about watching television before the creativity study, there was no difference in the time that it took them to complete the tasks as a function of the types of objects available, and there was no difference in their self-reports of task difficulty and discomfort. Similarly, mortality salient students who were asked to work with a piece of wood and a white cloth completed the tasks in the same amount of time and with the same affective consequences as their control counterparts. However, following mortality salience and needing to inappropriately use the crucifix and American flag to solve the problems, the students took twice as long to complete the problems and reported substantially more negative feelings about undertaking them. These findings establish that negative reactions to moral transgressions after thinking about death occur regardless of who commits them (oneself or others) and are engendered by inappropriate use of physical objects with symbolic value in the context of the individual's cultural worldview. As we asserted in that paper:

> Cultural icons function as concrete manifestations of the more abstract meanings and values of the cultural worldview, which constitute the individual's primary source of psychological equanimity. This reification of abstract concepts provides individuals with a tangible focus for their allegiance to the cultural precepts. . . . Indeed, Rank (1932) argued that these symbols are essential because such allegiance could not be sustained in the absence of physical artifacts that correspond to and thereby psychologically confirm the "truth" of the prevailing cultural ideology. (p. 1221)

Coffins and Consensus

The results of research conducted in laboratory settings provide important insights about human social behavior but involve a rather artificial reminder of mortality. How common are such reminders out in the real world? In actuality, they are quite common; in our daily lives, there are countless reminders of our mortality, ranging from fictional and news stories on television and in books and newspapers, to doctor visits and drives past cemeteries, to deaths of friends and relatives. Therefore, we thought it was important to establish that mortality salience effects could be obtained in such natural contexts. Accordingly, in Pyszczynski et al. (1996), we used proximity to a funeral home as a natural mortality salience induction and tested the idea that people would enhance their estimates of the number of people who shared their beliefs about important issues when they were in front of the home. Recall that TMT views cultural worldviews as fragile illusions that are sustained primarily by social consensus. If such worldviews serve a terror management function, then thinking about death should make us especially prone to inflate the extent to which we believe that others agree with us on important issues. In this study we interviewed German citizens, either directly in front of, or a short distance (100 m) away from, a funeral parlor. Participants were asked to report their attitudes about German immigration policies (for or against), an issue that was at that time being hotly debated in Germany, and then to estimate the percentage of the German public that agreed with them on this question. We considered being in front of the funeral parlor to be the mortality salience induction, while being 100 m to either side served as our control conditions. As predicted, people interviewed in front of the mortuary estimated a higher percentage of others agreeing with their views. This occurred primarily among people holding a minority position, presumably because they were most in need of greater consensus for their beliefs.

A similar study was then undertaken in the United States to replicate this finding, where people in Colorado Springs were interviewed in front of a funeral parlor or on either side of it, and asked about their beliefs about the teaching of Christian values in public schools, an issue of great debate in America in general and especially in Colorado Springs at the time. We again found that in front of the funeral home, people holding a minority position inflated their estimates of the percentage of others who agreed with them. These two studies suggest that mortality salience effects are not at all restricted to laboratory settings and may occur in a variety of natural contexts in which we are exposed, however subtly, to reminders of mortality.

Summary of the Mortality Salience Paradigm

The initial goal of this part of our research program was to empirically assess the hypothesis that cultural worldviews serve in part to assuage the anxiety associated with our awareness of death. We reasoned that to the extent that this is true, asking people to ponder their own demise (*mortality salience*) should engender an especially strong need for the protection that their worldviews provide and, consequently, provoke especially strong positive reactions to anything or anyone who upholds their personal—perfused through their culture, of course—vision of reality, and especially strong negative reactions to anything or anyone who violates or takes issue with this reality.

In support of the theory, a substantial body of research has shown that asking people to contemplate their own mortality does indeed engender such responses, even though people do not report being anxious or upset by thoughts of their own death and are not physiologically aroused by them. The basic findings of the mortality salience paradigm have been consistently replicated (in our labs and independent labs) and have been obtained using different manipulations of mortality salience, measuring different aspects of cultural worldviews, including personal transgressions with physical objects that are imbued with special significance in the context of a specific cultural ideology. Mortality salience effects have been produced in natural settings as well as in the laboratory. Additionally, plausible alternative accounts of these findings have been ruled out. The idea that beliefs about the nature of reality serve to alleviate concerns about mortality is thus supported by a wide range of converging evidence, and this body of evidence cannot be explained by other existing theoretical perspectives.

THE PSYCHODYNAMICS OF TERROR MANAGEMENT: THE DUAL DEFENSE MODEL

Besides the support they provide for the TMT proposition that concerns about death are uniquely responsible for mortality salience effects, the studies just reviewed raise some intriguing questions. Although we believe that people think about death far more often than they realize or are willing to admit, we certainly do not mean to imply that people are constantly obsessed with this basic existential problem. How, then, could the theory be correct? Could concerns about mortality be affecting people even though they rarely think about these issues? Such questions lead to some more concrete questions about the cognitive mechanisms through which the problem of death produces its effects. We turn now to this issue.

Obviously, mortality salience effects depend on bringing thoughts about death into consciousness. It is interesting, however, that doing so does not appear to engender negative affect. Participants do not report elevated levels of negative affect on scales designed to detect such responses (such as the STAI or PANAS), and they do not typically express very strong feelings in debriefings or in their responses to the questions about death that make up our mortality salience induction. In addition, our experimental procedures usually direct participants' attention away from mortality concerns and onto other matters before administration of the dependent measures. Just as we can write about the terror of death with relative equanimity, our participants can consider their mortality in a similarly calm fashion. Yet, our mortality salience treatments reliably produce systematic effects. If conscious thoughts of mortality are not sufficiently disturbing to cause rumination and create negative affect, and participants are likely to be distracted from such thoughts before our dependent measures are obtained, it is reasonable to ask why our mortality salience treatments produce worldview-bolstering responses at all

Our answer to this question is based on the original logic of the theory and the mortality salience hypothesis derived from it. Terror management is posited to be an unconscious and ongoing defense that serves to avert the potential for terror engendered by the knowledge of mortality. The theory posits that toward this end, people are constantly working to maintain faith in their worldview and personal value. Fear of death functions as a motivating force whether people are currently focused on this particular issue or not. The implicit knowledge of death, rather than current focal awareness, is the motivating factor. Just as a desire to get into graduate school is a motivating force for undergraduate students, whether or not they are currently thinking of this long-term goal, so, too, is the fear of death a motivating factor even when the issue is not in current focal awareness. Reminding participants of the fact that they will die someday signals a need for fortification of the cultural anxiety buffer, which then leads to bolstering of the cultural worldview and efforts to meet cultural standards of value. In a similar manner, reminding a student of his or her long-term goals is likely to signal the need to put greater effort into his or her academic pursuits (see Pyszczynski, Greenberg, Solomon, & Hamilton, 1990, for a more thorough discussion of the hierarchical relationship between terror management and other motives and goals).

According to this analysis, terror management processes are ultimately concerned with implicit knowledge of death rather than with thoughts of mortality that have recently entered consciousness. Death-related thoughts that enter consciousness are usually best confronted either by instrumental responses to avert the actual threat (e.g., hitting the brakes, avoiding the violent drunk, getting medical treatment) or by psychological defenses to remove the troubling material from current awareness. Defensive maneuvers in response to thoughts of death that have entered awareness include distracting oneself from the problem (avoidant thinking; e.g., Houston & Holmes, 1974), minimizing the apparent threat by altering perceptions of its severity (situation redefinition; e.g., Bennett & Holmes, 1975; Houston & Holmes; Lazarus, 1966), denying vulnerability to the threat (e.g., Greenberg et al., 1993; Jemmott, Ditto, & Croyle, 1986; Quattrone & Tversky, 1984), and emphasizing the temporal remoteness of the problem ("not me, not now"; Chaplin, 2000). Although all of these strategies can help remove thoughts of death from consciousness, none of them alter the problem of the ultimate inevitability of death. TMT posits that this problem—or, more precisely, the potential for the abject terror it engenders—is controlled by complete immersion in the cultural drama that provides meaning, value, and, consequently, a sense of security and immortality.

To summarize, we are proposing that adherence to a cultural worldview serves to keep potential terror from becoming manifest and that the reminders of one's mortality signal a need for securing that defensive structure. After all, people certainly seek self-esteem and faith in their worldviews in the absence of direct reminders of their mortality. The evidence reviewed earlier suggests, however, that these pursuits are substantially intensified after a reminder of the inevitability of death. When mortality is made salient, the direct rational *proximal* psychological defenses noted earlier are activated to reduce conscious awareness of death. Once the problem of death is out of focal attention but while it is still highly accessible, terror management concerns are addressed by *distal* defenses: bolstering faith in the worldview, as indicated by the mortality salience effects that we have uncovered in our studies (e.g., derogation of those who violate or challenge one's worldview and enhanced regard for those who validate the worldview).

The Role of Delay and Distraction

This analysis led us to consider the ironic possibility that the effects of thoughts of mortality on human judgment and behavior are greatest when they are accessible but no longer in focal consciousness or working memory. As noted earlier, in our original mortality salience studies, participants thought briefly about their own death and then moved on to other measures and tasks, which were often presented as part of a separate study. Thus, by the time our dependent measures are collected, it is highly probable that the participants are no longer consciously thinking about their mortality. If our reasoning is correct, this heretofore inadvertent delay and distraction from the thoughts of death between the mortality salience manipulation and the assessment of dependent measures may actually facilitate the occurrence of the effects because the more immediate concern of getting thoughts of mortality out of consciousness has already been addressed. Four studies provided support for that reasoning. In the first study (Greenberg, Pyszczynski, Solomon, Simon, & Breus, 1994), we tested the hypothesis that a more prolonged and extensive consideration of mortality than that employed in our previous studies would attenuate our usual mortality salience effect. In this study, mortality salient participants (exposed to our usual induction) exhibited an especially strong preference for a foreign student who wrote a pro-American essay over a foreign student who wrote an anti-American essay relative to control participants who were induced to think about watching television. However, in an additional condition in which, following the usual mortality salience treatment, participants were asked to consider their mortality further and express their deepest fears about it, pro-American preferences were significantly lower than those found for simple mortality salient participants. Thus, stronger mortality salience effects were found in response to a relatively subtle treatment than in response to a more extensive one.

Study 2 compared the effect of distracting participants from the problem of death after the mortality salience treatment with that of forcing participants to keep death-related concepts in mind. In addition to the usual conditions in which participants were induced to think about either death or television, we added three mortality salient conditions in which, after the mortality salience induction, we introduced a 3-min delay before participants were introduced to the pro- and anti-American essays. In the distraction condition, participants worked on a word search puzzle in which they were to find specific television-related words from rows and columns of letters; they would consequently have to keep mundane words like *drama* in their minds. In the continued death focus condition, the participants worked on the same word search puzzle, but the words they searched for, and thus were forced to keep in mind, were death related (e.g., *coffin*, *graveyard*). We also included a free thought delay condition in which participants were simply asked to write down whatever thoughts came to mind during the 3 min. As expected, distraction participants exhibited a strong mortality salience effect, whereas continued death focus participants did not. Free time delay participants' ratings were most similar to those of the distraction participants. Content analyses of these participants' thought listings indicated that all but three wrote exclusively of mundane matters unrelated to death; thus it is consistent with our analysis that, overall, these participants exhibited a strong mortality salience effect. In addition, ratings of the targets by the three participants who did list existential thoughts were more like those of the continued death focus and television control participants.

A third study was then conducted to rule out an alternative explanation for the effects obtained in Studies 1 and 2. In those studies, the critical manipulations were confounded with the amount of time that participants attended to death-related concerns. Specifically, in both the extensive mortality salience treatment used in Study 1 and the continued death focus treatment used in Study 2, participants focused on death-related thoughts longer than in the other conditions. Consequently, one could argue that this longer focus on the problem of death enabled participants to come to some sort of insight or resolution and thus eliminated their need to defend their worldviews. In other words, it could be argued that the critical variable underlying the effects found in Studies 1 and 2 was the amount of time that participants focused on mortality, rather than the extent to which death-related thoughts were in focal attention at the time that dependent measures were obtained.

Study 3 tested this alternative by comparing conditions in which the amount of death-related thought was held constant but the timing of a distraction was varied. The study included a mortality salient distraction condition, a television salient control, and a mortality salient continued death focus condition similar to those used in Study 2. Two additional mortality salient conditions were also included in which the amount of death focus was held constant but the timing of this focus was varied. In the first condition, the mortality salience induction was followed by a death puzzle that was then followed by a distraction (television) puzzle. In the second condition, the mortality salience induction was followed by a distraction puzzle that was then followed by a death puzzle. If longer consideration of death eliminates worldview defense (which would be reflected in this study by a smaller pro-American bias), then both latter conditions should be similar to the television control and the continued death focus conditions. If, however, the critical variable underlying mortality salience effects is the extent to which death-related thoughts are outside focal attention when the dependent measures are obtained, then worldview defense should be found in response to mortality salience when the distraction puzzle is the last task before the dependent measures but not when the death puzzle is the last task before the dependent measures. This is precisely what happened.

The findings of these studies thus suggest that worldview defense occurs after death has been made salient but only when concerns about mortality are no longer in active memory when dependent measures are assessed. If the problem of death must be activated but outside focal consciousness, exactly how does it produce increased defensive behavior? Research on the effect of time on the accessibility of recently activated thoughts provides two possible answers to this question. First, basic social cognitive research indicates that accessibility of primed concepts generally decreases over time (e.g., Fiske & Taylor, 1991; Srull & Wyer, 1980). If this were the case for the death-related concerns activated in our mortality salience studies, it would imply that the accessibility of those concerns must be relatively low before they produce increased defense of the cultural worldview. Second, Martin and Tesser (1993) found that experiencing a shortcoming in the pursuit of ego-relevant goals produces increases in the accessibility of goal-related thoughts, although this ruminative increase occurs only after a delay and distraction. They argue that participants initially defensively suppress goal-related thoughts to avoid the negative effect that such thoughts might entail. However, they also argue that over time such thoughts become more accessible because of a relaxation of this suppression, combined with a tendency toward perseveration regarding unresolved self-regulatory concerns (Pyszczynski & Greenberg, 1987, 1992) and the hyperaccessibility of previously suppressed thoughts (e.g., Wegner, 1994; Wegner & Erber, 1992). If this were the case, then in our mortality salience studies, the accessibility of death-related thoughts would actually be higher after a delay and distraction than it would be immediately after a mortality salience induction.

Our initial study of the accessibility of death-related themes (Greenberg et al., 1994) was conducted to evaluate these two alternative possibilities by measuring the accessibility of death-related thoughts in response to our mortality salience induction, either immediately after the induction or later, after a distracting task. Participants were exposed to the simple mortality salience or television salience inductions used in previous experiments, and the accessibility of death-related thoughts was then assessed with a word fragment completion task, similar to measures that have been used effectively in past research (e.g., Bassili & Smith, 1986). This measure asks participants to form words from 20 word fragments. Six of the fragments could be completed as either death-related or unrelated words. For example, coff__ could be completed as either coffin or coffee. The more someone has death-related thoughts close to consciousness, the more death-related completions they are likely to generate. Thus, for each participant, our measure of level of death thought accessibility consists of the number of death-related completions (out of a possible six).

The mortality salient distraction participants were distracted from the problem of death by reading a bland descriptive passage before the death thought accessibility measure; the mortality salience no distraction participants completed the accessibility measure before reading the passage. The television salient participants all read the passage before completing the accessibility measure, thereby controlling for any effects of the passage. If the increased worldview defense after mortality salience and distraction depends on a decrease in the accessibility of death-related thoughts, participants in the mortality salient immediate condition should exhibit the highest level of accessibility of such thoughts. If, however, the increased defense of the worldview results from an increase in the accessibility of death-related thoughts after distraction, participants in the mortality salient distraction condition should exhibit higher levels of death-related word completions than those in the other two conditions. The latter hypothesis was clearly supported. The fact that both increased defense of the worldview and increased accessibility of death-related thoughts emerge after a delay and distraction suggests that terror management effects emerge when the problem of death is high in accessibility but nonetheless outside current focal consciousness.

Proximal and Distal Defense

The foregoing analysis suggests that the initial response to mortality salience is to engage in simple, direct, threat-focused defenses that enable the individual to get death-related thoughts out of consciousness. These defenses involve distraction strategies or reassuring thoughts about one's health and the remoteness of the threat of death, that is, altering one's beliefs to deny vulnerability to early death, as in Greenberg et al. (1993). After the thoughts of death have been removed from consciousness, this process of active suppression is relaxed, and as a result, the individual experiences an increase in the accessibility of death-related thoughts. As the accessibility of such death-related themes increases, the individual engages in symbolic terror management defenses, bolstering self-esteem and the cultural worldview. Thus, the individual first deals with the problem of potentially unpleasant thoughts in consciousness by denying or getting rid of them (proximal defense) and then addresses the unconscious core concern with mortality (distal defense). If this sequence is correct, then in contrast to worldview defense, which occurs only after a delay, we should find that vulnerability-denying defensive distortions occur immediately after mortality salience but not after a delay.

To test this hypothesis, Greenberg, Arndt, Simon, Pyszczynski, and Solomon (2000) conducted a study in which, in addition to a television salience control condition, we included four mortality salience conditions in which we measured direct defense by assessing self-reported emotionality after informing participants that emotionality was associated with either a long or a short life expectancy, as in Greenberg et al. (1993), and worldview defense by having them evaluate pro- and anti-American essayists. Using four differently timed mortality salient conditions, whenever there was a delay between mortality salience and measurement of defense, worldview defense was high and direct defense was low. Whenever there was no delay, direct defense was high and worldview defense was low. Thus, it seems clear that proximal defenses that deal directly with the problem of death in a logical manner, such as biasing one's reports of emotionality so as to deny one's vulnerability to an early death, emerge only shortly after conscious thoughts about death, while such thoughts are presumably still in focal attention. On the other hand, distal terror management defenses, such as increased defense of the cultural worldview, occur only after individuals have been distracted from conscious thoughts of death (see Pyszczynski, Greenberg, & Solomon, 1999, for an extended presentation of this dual-process model of conscious and unconscious death-related thoughts).

The Role of Accessibility and Suppression

The studies reviewed earlier suggest that the finding of delayed worldview defense seems to coincide with a delayed increase in the accessibility of death-related thoughts. Therefore, we deemed it important to embark on further investigations of the role of accessibility of death-related thoughts in terror management processes. Recall that Greenberg et al. (1994) found that worldview defense in response to mortality salience occurs only when death-related thoughts are no longer in active memory and that the accessibility of death-related thoughts in response to a mortality salience induction is initially low but then increases over time. Our explanation for the difference in accessibility of death-related thoughts over time is based on the notion that people initially actively suppress thoughts of mortality to reduce negative affect, but that over time these thoughts become more accessible as suppression is relaxed or the previously suppressed thoughts become hyper-accessible (Wegner, 1994). The results of Study 4 of Greenberg et al. (1994) do not, however, allow us to differentiate between this account of increasing accessibility of death-related thoughts over time and the notion that such accessibility might be low initially because of the subtle nature of the mortality salience induction and that accessibility subsequently increases as people ruminate on the prospect of their demise—a qualitatively different psychological process that does not require recourse to the notion of active suppression.

Although the active suppression of death-related thoughts that we are positing transpires outside conscious awareness, it is unlikely that this could occur in the absence of sufficient processing resources (Wegner, 1994). Therefore, we reasoned that, if our previous results were due to such active suppression, denying people the resources to engage adequately in suppression should produce an immediate increase in accessibility of death-related thoughts following mortality salience. On the other hand, if no such suppression process is involved, no increase in accessibility would be expected to result from taxing participants' cognitive resources.

On the basis of this reasoning, Arndt, Greenberg, Solomon, Pyszczynski, and Simon (1997) designed a study to assess the effects of cognitive load on immediate and delayed death thought accessibility following mortality salience. Cognitive load was used as a way to "deprive participants of processing resources" (Gilbert & Hixon, 1991, p. 511) necessary for thought suppression. Accessibility of death-related thoughts was measured with a word fragment completion task similar to the one used in our prior studies. The results replicated our previous finding of low accessibility of death-related thoughts immediately after mortality salience that then increased over time, but only in the conditions in which participants were not under high cognitive load before death thought accessibility was assessed. In contrast, death thought accessibility was significantly elevated immediately after mortality salience in the conditions in which participants' cognitive load was high, presumably because participants were deprived of the cognitive resources necessary to suppress their thoughts about death. Thus these findings very clearly support the proposition that low levels of accessibility of death-related thoughts typically found immediately after mortality salience inductions are due to efforts to actively suppress thoughts of death from conscious awareness.

If high death thought accessibility triggers worldview defense, and such accessibility is high immediately after mortality salience because high load undermines suppression of such thoughts, then we should also find amplified worldview defense immediately after mortality salience under conditions of high cognitive load. To test this hypothesis, participants in a second study were burdened with the same cognitive load as in Study 1, which either was or was not released before the measure of worldview defense was obtained. We assessed worldview defense by having participants evaluate pro- and anti-American essays. The results in the low-load conditions replicated the findings of Study 3 of Greenberg et al. (1994): Specifically, a stronger bias in favor of the pro-American target was obtained after mortality salience when worldview defense was assessed after a delay but not when it was assessed immediately after the mortality salience induction. This presumably reflects participants in the delay condition having enough time and adequate cognitive resources to suppress thoughts of death, which then became more accessible over time as this suppression was relaxed. On the other hand, participants in the no-delay condition were still actively suppressing thoughts of death at the time they were evaluating the essays. However, under conditions of high cognitive load, a strong pro-American bias was obtained in response to mortality salience even in the no-delay condition, presumably because the cognitive load deprived participants of the resources necessary to suppress their death-related thoughts, which consequently were highly accessible immediately after the mortality salience induction. High accessibility of thoughts of death thus seems to be a necessary and sufficient precondition for the terror management effects engendered by mortality salience.

The Role of Consciousness in Terror Management Processes

This study, in turn, raised an interesting question regarding the role of consciousness in the production of terror management effects: Specifically, do mortality salience effects require an initial conscious consideration of one's own mortality, or do they occur whenever accessibility of death-related thoughts is high, even if people have not recently had explicit conscious thoughts about their inevitable demise? Arndt et al. (1997) addressed this question by investigating the effects of subliminal priming of the concept of death on both the accessibility of death-related thoughts and the amplification of cultural worldview defense. Previous research has demonstrated that subliminal exposure to a variety of stimuli increases the accessibility of the cognitive and emotional schemas associated with the primed concepts (e.g., mood, attitudes, interpersonal relationships) that, in turn, directly influence affect, attitudes, and behavior (e.g., Kihlstrom, 1987; Murphy, Monahan, & Zajonc, 1995). Accordingly, we hypothesized that subliminal exposure to the issue of death would *immediately* enhance the accessibility of death-related thoughts and produce mortality salience effects that have heretofore been obtained only following a conscious contemplation of mortality. Because people are not conscious of the heightened accessibility of death-related thoughts produced by subliminal priming, they would have no impetus to suppress this heightened accessibility.

In a preliminary study, participants were asked to view 10 pairs of words on a computer screen presented individually for 0.5 s each, and then to determine if the words were related and to indicate their responses by pushing specific keys on the computer keyboard. Actually, each pair of neutral words served as a forward and backward mask for a 42.8-ms exposure to either the word *death* or the word *field*, which was flashed in between the first and second words of the pair. Afterward, accessibility of death-related thought was assessed using the same word stem completion task employed by Greenberg et al. (1994). Participants were also asked if they saw more than two words flashed on the computer screen during each trial of the word relationship task and, if so, to list what other word they might have seen. Participants were then told to presume that an additional word was presented on each trial and to guess what that word was from a list of four words, including *death* and *field*. The results indicated that accessibility of death-related thoughts was significantly higher following subliminal exposure to *death* than to *field*, even though participants did not report seeing the subliminal stimulus and could not choose that stimulus from the four-word list at more than a chance level. This finding replicates prior research demonstrating the effectiveness of subliminal primes for activating schematic representations of relevant constructs. We were than able to subsequently determine if the heightened accessibility of death-related thoughts following subliminal death primes was sufficient to produce mortality salience effects in the absence of conscious contemplation of death by conducting a second experiment in which worldview defense was assessed after subliminal exposure to death.

In the next study, participants were led to believe that they would be participating in two different experiments, the first of which was described as an investigation of the relationship between personality characteristics and the ability to perceive relationships between words. Accordingly, participants completed some personality assessments, including our usual mortality salience induction (the two open-ended questions about death) for one third of the participants. Remaining participants received a parallel set of questions pertaining to their next important exam. All participants were then exposed to the subliminal priming procedure employed in Study 1: Participants in the subliminal death prime condition received the "death" prime, whereas those in the supraliminal mortality salient condition and control condition received the neutral "field" prime. Participants again did not report seeing more than two words on the computer screen during the subliminal exposure procedure, nor could they reliably select the specific word they had been exposed to when asked to pick it from a four-item list.

A measure of worldview defense was then obtained in a supposed second experiment by asking participants to evaluate pro- and anti-American essays supposedly written by foreign students. The results revealed that the standard mortality salience induction produced a greater pro-American bias than the control condition, as has been consistently found in our previous studies. More important for present purposes, exposure to subliminal death primes also resulted in elevated pro-American bias relative to the control condition, thus clearly establishing that worldview defense in response to thoughts of death does not require any conscious awareness of such thoughts.

We then conducted an additional pair of studies to replicate these findings and to compare a subliminal death prime (this time *dead*) with a prime consisting of another aversive word, *pain*, to determine whether non-death-related aversive words would also increase worldview defense (the change from *death* to *dead* was made to match the length of the aversive word control prime used in this study). We first demonstrated that the "pain" prime increased the accessibility of "pain"-related words without participants being aware of the prime. Then, in the next study, participants were subliminally exposed to either the "death" or the aversive word prime, after which affect and worldview defense were assessed. As in the previous study, the subliminally presented death-related word amplified worldview defense relative to the control word, and there was no evidence that this effect resulted from any affective reaction to the death word. Taken together, these studies indicate that increased worldview defense is a result of heightened accessibility of death-related thoughts outside of conscious awareness; this finding is highly consistent with the terror management contention that such worldview defense serves a deeply rooted unconscious concern.

Mortality Salience and the Cognitive Experiential Self

Freud (e.g., 1933/1965) repeatedly made a distinction between primary processes—psychological activities (including psychological defenses) that are not only unconscious but also fundamentally irrational—and secondary processes of a conscious and rational nature. More recently, cognitive experiential self theory (CEST; Epstein, 1983, 1994) made a similar distinction between rational and experiential thinking and posited that a substantial portion of human psychological activity is neither conscious nor logical. The rational system "is a deliberative, effortful, abstract system that operates primarily in the medium of language" (Epstein, 1994, p. 715), that is "experienced actively and consciously, and requires justification via logic and evidence" (p. 711). The experiential system, on the other hand, is "a crude system that automatically, rapidly, effortlessly, and efficiently processes information" (p. 715) and "is experienced passively and preconsciously and is self-evidently valid" (p. 711). Epstein argues that the experiential system is the default option or dominant system in most situations, because it is less effortful and more efficient, whereas the rational system is activated primarily in situations with cues, suggesting the need for rational analysis.

Consistent with the CEST distinction between rational and experiential thinking, research has shown that heuristic processing (e.g., Tversky &

Kahneman, 1974) occurs primarily when participants are in an experiential mode, whereas more logic-based inferences occur when participants are in a rational mode (e.g., Epstein, Lipson, Holstein, & Huh, 1992; Kirkpatrick & Epstein, 1992). Additionally, Sappington, Rice, Burleson, and Gordon (1981) and Sappington, Russell, Triplett, and Goodwin (1980) have found that emotionally based beliefs exert a stronger effect on social behavior than intellectually based beliefs (cf. Fazio, 1990), which is consistent with the notion that the emotion-based experiential system is most influential in the control of ongoing social behavior.

If, as we have argued, the fear of death is an unconscious, primal concern that stems from the individual's desire for survival, then mortality salience effects should occur primarily when an individual is in an experiential mode, and rational processing may undermine the use of terror management defenses in several ways. First, Freud suggested that people often actively seek to think about threatening material in an abstract, intellectual manner because this can be an effective way of detaching a stimulus from its threatening implications (e.g., Freud, 1933/1965). Epstein has similarly suggested that thinking in a rational mode may prevent the emotional impact of a threatening issue from registering or "sinking in." In support of this view of intellectualization as defense, Lazarus, Opton, Nomikos, and Rankin (1965) have demonstrated that an intellectual appraisal of potentially stressful events reduces negative reactions to such events. Second, given that there is no logical connection between the fact that one will die someday and faith in one's cultural worldview, thinking about death in a rational mode may instigate more direct and rational means of coping with mortality, such as promising oneself to quit smoking or get more exercise.

Simon, Greenberg, Harmon-Jones, Solomon, and Pyszczynski (1996) thus hypothesized and found in two studies that mortality salience is less likely to lead to increased worldview defense when participants are in a rational mode of thinking than when they are in an experiential mode of thinking. In Study 1, mode of thinking was manipulated by the appearance of the experimenter. In the formal condition, designed to put participants in a rational mode, a male experimenter wore a lab coat over long pants and black, horn-rimmed glasses and sat and talked stiffly behind a desk. In the informal condition, designed to put participants in an experiential mode, the experimenter wore shorts, a T-shirt, and Birkenstock sandals. He also sat on the desk and used his hands expressively as he talked. In Study 2, written instructions were used to manipulate rational and experiential modes of thought, patterned very closely after materials used by Epstein and colleagues (e.g., Epstein et al., 1992; Kirkpatrick & Epstein, 1992). Specifically, rational mode participants were instructed in this way: "On the following page are two open-ended questions; please carefully consider your answers to them before responding. We would like you to be as rational and analytic as possible in responding to these questions." Experiential mode participants were instructed in this way: "On the following page are two open-ended questions; please respond to them with your first, natural response. We are just looking for peoples' gut-level reactions to these questions." Participants in both studies then completed a mortality or television salience control questionnaire, followed by an evaluation of a pro- and anti-American target. The results of the studies revealed a strong pro-American bias in mortality salient conditions but only when participants were in experiential modes of thought.

A third study was then undertaken to determine if the absence of worldview defense in response to mortality salience by participants in a rational mode of thought was associated with a corresponding lack of heightened accessibility of death-related thoughts after a delay and distraction, as has been found in all prior studies in circumstances in which mortality salience does not produce worldview defense. As in Study 1, mode of thought was manipulated by the appearance of the experimenter, and participants were given a mortality salience or control induction. This was followed by an immediate assessment of the accessibility of death-related thoughts (the same word stem completion task employed in our prior studies), a brief excerpt from a short story to serve as a distraction during a delay period, and then a second measure of death thought accessibility. Experiential mode participants exhibited the usual pattern of death theme accessibility in response to mortality salience: Specifically, low initial accessibility of death thoughts were followed by an increase over time. However, mortality salient rational mode participants had low levels of accessibility of death thoughts both immediately and after a delay and distraction, suggesting that rational consideration of death facilitates suppression of subsequent death-related thoughts and, once again, that accessibility of thoughts of death is a necessary and sufficient condition to produce mortality salience effects.

Self-Esteem, Worldview Defense, and Death Thought Accessibility

Given the central role we have ascribed to the high accessibility of death-related thoughts in the production of mortality salience effects, it follows that such accessibility should be low in all circumstances when mortality salience effects are reduced or eliminated by moderating factors, and this has been shown to indeed be the case. For example, Harmon-Jones et al. (1997) demonstrated that enhancing self-esteem eliminates the delayed increase in the accessibility of death-related words after mortality salience. In this study, participants were given positive or neutral personality feedback and were induced to think about their mortality or a neutral topic. Participants then completed two word fragment completion tasks to assess the accessibility of death-related words—one immediately after the mortality salience manipulation and one after reading a distracting story. In the neutral self-esteem condition, there was a delayed increase in the accessibility of death-related thoughts similar to that found in Study 4 of Greenberg et al. (1994). However, for raised self-esteem participants, the accessibility of death-related words remained low both immediately and after a delay.

Finally, Study 3 of Arndt et al. (1997) and Greenberg, Arndt, Simon, Pyszczynski, and Solomon (2000) provided direct demonstrations that worldview defense following mortality salience produces a consequent decrease in the accessibility of thoughts of death. Participants in these studies were exposed to a mortality salience or exam salience control induction, read a short distraction passage, and were then asked to read the same pro- and anti-American essays employed in many of our other studies. Exam salient and half of the mortality salient participants then evaluated the merits of the essays and the integrity of the reputed author of them, while the remaining mortality salient participants were given parallel questions that allowed them to evaluate the essays in only a non-judgmental fashion (e.g., "What gender do you think the author is?"; "Approximately how many words do you think were in the essay?"). All participants then completed the word fragment task to measure accessibility of death thoughts. Results revealed elevated levels of death thought accessibility following mortality salience after a delay, as has been found in all previous studies, but only for those participants who did not have an opportunity to engage in worldview defense by evaluating the authors of the essays in judgmental ways. The mortality salient participants who were able to engage in worldview defense by derogating the anti-American essay and venerating the pro-American one took advantage of the opportunity to do so, as evidenced by a stronger pro-American bias relative to the exam salient control condition. More important for present purposes, however, these participants did not consequently show elevated levels of death-thought accessibility, suggesting that worldview defense serves its terror management function by reducing accessibility of thoughts of death.

The Effects of Separation Reminders on Death Thought Accessibility

Mikulincer, Florian, Birnbaum, and Malishkevich (2002) recently proposed that "separation from a close relationship partner is so distressing because it undermines the buffering of the terror of death. Specifically, close relationships help people buffer death concerns, and separation from a close relationship partner may leave them temporarily defenseless against death awareness and consequently result in distress" (p. 3). In support of this proposition, Mikulincer et al. report several studies in which asking participants to think about the dissolution of a close relationship produced heightened accessibility of death thoughts, especially in insecurely attached participants. These findings are especially important because they demonstrate that implicit concerns about mortality can be engendered by thoughts other than death per se.

Death Thought Accessibility and the Accessibility of Worldview-Relevant Constructs

A recent series of six studies by Arndt, Greenberg, and Cook (in press) have also found that the same conditions that produce high death thought accessibility increase the accessibility of nationalistic constructs in American men and relationship constructs in American women. This work suggests that for men, death thoughts are closely linked in memory to thoughts about America, whereas for women, death thoughts are most closely linked with romantic thoughts of such things as love and weddings. Arndt et al. suggested that this means that whereas both men and women will defend whatever aspects of their worldviews are threatened following mortality salience, high death thought accessibility generally activates the constructs most central to the individual's worldview, which generally seems to be national constructs for men and relationship constructs for women. Further research is needed to determine if this also means that when given a choice following mortality salience, men will bolster their patriotism, whereas women will bolster their relationships.

Summary of the Psychodynamics of Terror Management

All the research findings described in this section of the chapter converge on the proposition that mortality salience effects occur when thoughts of death are highly accessible but not explicitly conscious. Specifically, we have established that mortality salience effects occur when people are in an experiential "frame of mind" that is fundamentally nonrational and presumably involves processing of information without relying on closely monitored logical analysis. We also demonstrated that subtle reminders of mortality produce more vigorous worldview defense than more sustained (and therefore presumably more conscious or salient) mortality salience inductions. This was followed by the finding that worldview defense in response to mortality salience occurs only when people are distracted from thoughts of death before we obtain our dependent measures. We found that direct rational defenses occur immediately after mortality salience, whereas symbolic terror management defenses involving defense of the cultural worldview occur only after a delay. We established that death thought accessibility is low immediately following a mortality salience induction but increases over time during a distraction, presumably because the conscious awareness of death engendered by our usual mortality salience induction leads to active efforts to suppress such thoughts (hence the low accessibility of death thoughts immediately after mortality salience inductions). This hypothesis was subsequently verified by depriving people of the attentional resources necessary to engage in active suppression through the use of a cognitive load procedure and finding high levels of accessibility of death thoughts immediately following mortality salience. Additionally, subliminal death primes were shown to produce immediate increases in accessibility of death thoughts. Subliminal death primes also resulted in increased worldview defense, thus allowing us to conclude that heightened accessibility of death thoughts activated without conscious awareness is a sufficient condition for the instigation of terror management processes. We then demonstrated that factors moderating the vigorous worldview defense in response to mortality salience, such as high self-esteem and rational thinking, are also associated with lower accessibility of thoughts of death after a delay and distraction; this finding suggests that the dual-component cultural anxiety buffer (consisting of a cultural worldview and self-esteem) serves its terror management function by minimizing the accessibility of thoughts of death. Finally, we provided additional support for this possibility by establishing that accessibility of death thoughts after mortality salience is reduced after people are given an opportunity to engage in worldview defense.

Taken together, these studies point to the central role of accessibility of thoughts of death in mortality salience effects. We have presented the evidence for these central aspects of the theory in some detail to show that the theoretical analysis of human motivation on which our analysis of the causes and consequences of the 9/11 terrorist attacks rests is based on strong scientific ground. The flow chart presented in Figure 3.1 (next page) provides a summary of the processes activated by reminders of death. In our next chapter, we expand our coverage of mortality salience research to show its wide-ranging effects on people's evaluations of others who are different and on strivings for self-worth, two aspects of human behavior especially relevant for understanding the events surrounding 9/11.

Thoughts of death enter consciousness

V

Proximal defenses: Suppression & rationalization

V

Increase in accessibility of death-related
thought outside consciousness

V

Distal terror management defenses:
Worldview defense and self-esteem bolstering

V

Death thought accessibility is reduced and
potential terror is averted

Figure 3.1. Defensive processes activated by conscious and unconscious death-related thought. From "A Dual Process Model of Defense Against Conscious and Unconscious Death-Related Thoughts: An Extension of Terror Management Theory," by T. Pyszczynski, J. Greenberg, and S. Solomon, 1999, *Psychological Review, 106,* p. 840. Copyright 1999 by the American Psychological Association. Adapted with permission.

4

TERROR MANAGEMENT RESEARCH: PREJUDICE AND SELF-ESTEEM STRIVING

These creatures are for the most part malevolent and murderous by nature, able to tolerate others only insofar as they resemble themselves, capable of slaughtering each other because of a slight difference in skin colour or appearance. Also they cannot tolerate those who do not think as they do. Although they know perfectly well, theoretically, that the surface of the inhabited globe is divided into thousands of areas, each with its system of religious or scientific belief, and although they know that it is entirely by chance that any individual among them was born into this or that area, this or that area of belief, this theoretical knowledge does not prevent them from hating foreigners in their own particular small area and if not harming them, isolating them in every way possible.

—Doris Lessing, *Briefing for a Descent Into Hell*
(1971/1981, pp. 130–131)

Life . . . is arduous, difficult, a perpetual struggle. It calls for gigantic courage and strength. More than anything, perhaps, creatures of illusion as we are, it calls for confidence in oneself. Without self-confidence we are as babes in the cradle.

—Virginia Woolf, *A Room of One's Own* (1929/1981, pp. 34–35)

The research reviewed in the previous chapter established the basic effects of death-related thoughts on human judgment and behavior, and the processes through which these effects are produced. In this chapter, we review research on two consequences of concerns about mortality that we believe are most important for understanding the causes and consequences of global terrorism. The first line of work has documented the role of terror management processes in prejudice and aggression against people different from ourselves. The second set of studies is focused on various ways in which people strive for self-worth in response to death reminders. Both of these lines of research have clear implications for understanding the forces that motivate people to sacrifice their own lives in order to destroy others and the forces that influence how the targets of such terrorist actions are likely to respond.

THE ROLE OF TERROR MANAGEMENT IN
PREJUDICE AND INTERGROUP CONFLICT

As L. von Bertalanffy has noted in *Comments on Aggression* (1956; quoted in Fromm, 1973):

> There is no doubt about the presence of aggressive and destructive tendencies in the human psyche which are of the nature of biological drives. However, the most pernicious phenomena of aggression, transcending self-preservation and self-destruction, are based upon a characteristic feature of man above the biological level, namely his capability of creating symbolic universes in thought, language, and behavior. (pp. 186–187)

Is it really possible that fear of death engenders hostility toward others who are merely different from ourselves, as well as a heightened propensity to be physically aggressive toward them? Recall that we have already established that making mortality momentarily salient by asking people to ponder their own demise results in exaggerated punishment for moral transgressors and increased rewards for those who uphold cherished cultural values. We have also shown that when reminded of their mortality, Americans react especially negatively to people who criticize the United States and especially positively toward people who praise the United States. But in all of these studies, the target individuals actively bolstered or undermined participants' cherished beliefs, that is, by breaking the law or condemning the American way of life. Does the *mere existence* of those with worldviews different from our own pose a similar threat and lead to similar negative reactions?

Terror Management and Prejudice

To get a more direct indication of the effects of mortality salience on responses to people who have similar or different worldviews, we (Greenberg et al., 1990,) conducted a study in which Christian college students were led to believe that we were interested in the relationship between personality variables and how people form interpersonal judgments. To sustain this cover story, they completed a set of questionnaires in which they provided some personal information about themselves; participants were then randomly divided into mortality salient and control conditions. Following the mortality salience manipulation, participants received what they believed were questionnaires completed by two of the other students in the study and were asked to read them and then evaluate the people who wrote them. Actually, we generated two bogus descriptions of college students who differed slightly in terms of academic interests and political opinions (one was described as conservative, the other liberal) and then varied the religious affiliation of the students' parents (and by inference, the students themselves): Christian or Jewish. Consequently each of our Christian participants evaluated a Christian and a Jewish target, with the order of exposure of the targets counterbalanced.

Our primary interest was to determine if the Christian participants' evaluations of the target persons would vary as a consequence of thinking about death. The results indicated no difference between ratings of the Christian and Jewish targets by the Christian participants in the control condition, momentarily restoring our faith in humanity. However, as predicted, following mortality salience, participants increased their affection for the Christian target and had more negative reactions to the now significantly less desirable Jewish target. This work directly supports the idea that terror management concerns lead us to embrace those with similar worldviews but to derogate and reject those with different worldviews.

In an independent laboratory, cleverly using a very different mortality salience manipulation and very different measures, Nelson, Moore, Olivetti, and Scott (1997) also found that terror management concerns contribute to intergroup bias. After watching either gory depictions of automobile accidents to momentarily render mortality salient or benign highlights of traffic safety tips, college student participants read a scenario about a car accident in which the driver was suing either an American or a Japanese auto manufacturer and were asked to rate the degree of culpability and fiscal responsibility of the manufacturer. Nelson et al. (1997) hypothesized that watching fatal car wrecks would cause participants to increase their blame of the auto manufacturer, but only if the car was made in Japan. Results were entirely in accord with these predictions, lending convergent support to our basic claim that terror management concerns lead to positive reactions to aspects of one's own culture and negative reactions to aspects of other cultures.

In the first terror management studies conducted outside the United States, Ochsmann and Mathy (1994) provided additional support for this idea using a behavioral measure. German university students did not discriminate between German and Turkish targets in a control condition, but following mortality salience, the German target was rated more positively and the Turkish target more negatively. Then, in a clever second experiment, German university students participated in a study of personality attributes in exchange for modest remuneration. After completing a mortality salience or control questionnaire embedded in a packet of personality assessments, the students thought the experiment was over and were directed to a waiting room in order to receive their payment. In the waiting room there was a row of nine chairs with someone sitting in the middle chair. This person was actually a German confederate who, unbeknownst to the participants, was in collusion with the experimenter and who dressed either as she would normally appear or as a Turkish individual.

In this study, Ochsmann and Mathy were primarily interested in where participants would choose to sit as a function of whether they had been asked to ponder their mortality previously and whether the person with them in the waiting room appeared German or Turkish. They found that the apparent nationality of the confederate in the waiting room did not matter in the control condition: Participants sat the same distance from either the German or the Turkish target. But following a subtle reminder of death (remember that the mortality salience manipulation was embedded in a booklet of personality assessments completed some time ago in a different room and that people thought the experiment was over) the students sat closer to the German target and farther away from the Turkish target.

This was an especially important finding because it demonstrated behavioral responses to mortality salience in addition to the attitudinal differences obtained in prior studies. After thinking about their own death, people not only dislike those from another country or those who practice a different religion, but they also literally keep their distance from them. Next, we wanted to assess whether mortality salience would encourage direct physical aggression against people who pose a challenge to one's cultural worldview.

Terror Management and Aggression

Conceptually, such a demonstration would not be problematic: Just give people machine guns and have them think about death before exposing them to a confederate dressed like themselves or as a person from a different culture and see what happens! Two problems precluded this approach, however. We could not find anyone stupid enough to serve as a confederate, and there are ethics committees these days that frown on this kind of procedure. To approach this issue directly required some imaginative thinking, aided by a chance encounter with a newspaper report in the *Phoenix Gazette* (Phoenix, Arizona) on April 6, 1995:

> *Headline: Officer's Eggs Allegedly Spiked With Hot Sauce.* A breakfast cook at a Denny's was charged with assault for allegedly spiking two Vermont state troopers' eggs with Tabasco sauce. Michael Towne, 20, could get up to two years in jail and a $4,000 fine. Troopers Timothy Clouatre and Michael Manning, who had crossed into New Hampshire for breakfast on Feb. 7, said the eggs burned their mouths and upset one officer's stomach. . . . In court papers, police quoted an unidentified witness who claimed to have seen Towne put a large amount of Tabasco on the food. The witness "said that Towne did not like police officers and did it as a joke," police said. (p. A2)

As soon as we saw this, we knew we were onto something big! A quick review of newspapers and magazines revealed a surprising number of incidents in which hot sauce was administered with intent to assault or abuse. For example, on January 24, 1989, the *Los Angeles Times* reported an incident in which a mother and son who ran a foster-care home were accused of forcing children to drink hot sauce and eat hot peppers; on May 16, 2000, the *St. Petersburg Times* reported the beginning of jury selection for the first-degree murder trial of Walter Morris, who "is accused of shaking a 2-year-old boy, throwing him on the floor, pouring hot sauce down the boy's throat and punching him." In view of these real-life incidents, we decided to use hot sauce administration as a direct measure of physical aggression in an experiment on the role of mortality salience in human violence directed against people who possess dissimilar worldviews (McGregor et al., 1998).

In groups of four or five, college students were recruited to participate in an experiment, on the basis of having either fairly liberal or conservative political views, as determined by a battery of pretests administered earlier in the semester. Participants were unaware of the selection criteria when they were contacted to be in this experiment, and they believed they would be participating in two separate studies. The first study was described as an examination of the relationship between personality traits and impression formation. Everyone was escorted to private cubicles, was asked to write a short paragraph about his or her opinion of politics in the United States, and was expected to exchange essays with another member of the group later in the study. The paragraphs were then collected, and participants completed some standard personality assessments, followed by either a mortality salience or control induction.

At that point, the experimenter gave each participant an essay purportedly written by a student in one of the other cubicles; the essay was identified by a three-digit number, so although participants believed the writer of the essay was present in the group, they did not know who it was. In fact, we created two bogus essays: One was designed to conflict with a liberal but not conservative worldview (e.g., "Liberals are the cause of so many problems in this country, it's not funny. Not only that, but they get in the way of decent Americans who are trying to solve all those problems that they created in the first place. The bleeding heart stance they take of trying to help everyone is a joke and incredibly stupid."); the other was designed to conflict with the worldview of conservatives but not liberals ("Conservatives are the cause of so many problems in this country, it's not funny. Not only that, but they get in the way of decent Americans who are trying to solve all those problems that they created in the first place. The cold-hearted stance they take, of trying to help only themselves is a joke and incredibly stupid."). Consequently, regardless of the political orientation of each participant, half read an essay that threatened their worldview and half read an essay in accord with their political opinions. All participants were asked to make some nonjudgmental evaluations of the essays (e.g., to guess the author's gender and comment about the style of the prose) and were then informed that the "first study" was completed.

The "second study" was portrayed as an examination of the relationship between personality and food preferences. Participants believed they would taste and evaluate dry or spicy foods, and because the experimenter needed to remain ignorant of the type and quantity of food tasted, participants would administer the food samples to each other. Participants then completed a taste preference inventory in which they evaluated their affinity (or distaste) for sweet, salty, sour, spicy, creamy, and dry foods.

All of the participants were then actually placed into the same group—sampling the dry food and administering the hot sauce. They were all given an envelope that contained a saltine cracker (presumably prepared by another participant in the group) and were asked to eat the entire cracker and then rate how much they liked it. The experimenter then informed the participants that they would now prepare a sample of hot sauce, which the experimenter would then give to another person in the group. They were told that to minimize confusion, they would be allocating the hot sauce to the person whose essay they had read in the first study described earlier (recall that each participant knew the supposed political views of the person but not his or her identity). The participants were then asked to taste the hot sauce, which was prepared so as to be painfully hot. The experimenter mentioned that people are sometimes curious about the taste preferences of the participants they would be administering the hot sauce to; consequently, they were shown a bogus taste preference inventory indicating that they were about to administer hot sauce to someone who very much disliked spicy foods. After it was made very clear to them that the other person was the one who had written the essay they read in the first study and that person would have to eat all of the sauce (just as they had earlier been required to eat the entire cracker that was presumably given to them by another participant), each participant then spooned as much hot sauce as they felt was appropriate for the other subject to consume in a small covered Styrofoam cup.

Our primary measure in this experiment was the amount of hot sauce allocated to another person in the study who did not care for spicy foods, as a function of the person's political beliefs (worldview consistent or worldview threatening) and whether mortality or exams had been made salient to them in the first study. Results indicated no differences in hot sauce administration in the exam control condition: Participants doled out relatively modest and equivalent amounts of hot sauce regardless of the political views of the targets (15.20 g versus 17.56 g to worldview-threatening and worldview-consistent targets, respectively). However, following mortality salience, participants slightly reduced the amount of hot sauce allocated to targets who supported their political views (11.86 g, but this was not a statistically significant difference); more important, they gave a whopping (and very significant statistically) 26.31 g of hot sauce to those in opposition to their political beliefs. And when the study was completed and we talked to our participants, it was evident that they knew exactly what they were doing in terms of their heavy-handedness with the hot sauce; that is, they knew it was an act of aggression directed against those who threatened their cherished beliefs (although they were quite unaware that this behavior was the focal point of the study or that it was ultimately engendered by the mortality salience manipulation).

These studies, taken together, provide strong converging support for the disconcerting notion that mortality salience engenders negative attitudes, physical distancing, and physical aggression toward people who are different by virtue of subscribing to dissimilar cultural worldviews.

Terror Management in Minimal Groups

Having established that mortality salience engenders negative attitudes and physical hostility toward people who are different, Harmon-Jones, Greenberg, Solomon, and Simon (1995) empirically examined the notion that when people lack an obvious or existing outlet upon which to project their fear of death in the form of prejudice and violence, they will latch on to some fairly arbitrary and trivial basis on which to declare themselves superior to another, in order to preserve their psychological equanimity in the face of death. To determine if there is any merit to this claim, Harmon-Jones et al. used the minimal group paradigm (Tajfel, Billig, Bundy, & Flament, 1971) in which groups of previously unacquainted students came to the laboratory and were asked to look at, and evaluate, paintings by Paul Klee and Wassily Kandinski. After viewing slides of the paintings and expressing their opinions of them on a rating form, we randomly divided the participants into groups and had half think about death and half a benign topic; then we had all participants evaluate members of their own group, those purported to have the same artist preference they did, and of the other group, people purported to prefer the other artist. Consistent with previous findings, there was no difference in participants' ratings of those who liked Klee or Kandinski in the control condition; but when mortality was made salient before the evaluations, people reported a greater affection for others who shared their newly established artistic preference and more negative reactions to those with the alternative artistic preference. This finding suggests that mortality salience leads people to prefer similar others over dissimilar others, even when the basis of determining similarity is relatively trivial.[1]

---

[1]Jonathan Swift (1726/2001) fans will undoubtedly recall the hilarious description of this phenomenon in *Gulliver's Travels*, in which differences in opinions regarding on which side an egg should be cracked resulted in 36 months of violent enmity between the empires of Lilliput and Blefuscu:

When We "Like" Our Designated Inferiors

All of the studies we have reported thus far suggest that people dislike those who are different from themselves. But this is clearly not always the case, in that every culture generally consists of a dominant majority peppered with ethnic or racial minorities who typically serve specific and highly stereotypic (from the perspective of the dominant majority) roles in the culture. For example, there is still considerable evidence of prejudice, stereotyping, and discrimination against many groups, such as Blacks, Hispanics, Native Americans, Jews, Asian Americans, gay and lesbian Americans, and women. However, even those who harbor such prejudices typically acknowledge important, albeit stereotypic, roles such people serve in the context of mainstream American culture. African Americans are admired as dancers, athletes, and rappers; Jewish Americans as lawyers and doctors; Chinese Americans for their restaurants and martial arts; and gay men for their skills as interior decorators and hair stylists.

Given that cultural worldviews serve to assuage concerns about death, and minorities contribute to the scheme of things as long as they conform to our conception of them in the context of the dominant culture, when mortality is made salient, perhaps people will actually like the in-house designated inferiors to the extent that they are "in their place" and conform to the dominant cultures' stereotypic conception of them. And, if this is true, mortality salience might engender negative reactions to minorities who violate ethnic and racial stereotypes that would normally be welcome, in that they conform to the dictates of the dominant culture. In other words, a young Black rocket scientist or stock broker would ordinarily be much more appealing than a pimp or a rapper to a mainstream White American because the scientist and stockbroker appear to have embraced mainstream American values and succeeded in the context of them, whereas the pimp and rapper confirm all the traditional negative stereotypes that are typically associated with young Black men. But, following reminders of death, the need to validate their current vision of reality—including the sense, for example, that Black men are future felons; Jews are cheap; gay men are great hairdressers—may incline White Americans to prefer the Black pimp or rapper, who provide comforting confirmation of the existing worldview, and

---

Which two mighty Powers have, as I was going to tell you, been engaged in a most obstinate War for six and thirty Moons past . . . the Emperor . . . published an Edict, commanding all his Subjects, upon great Penaltys, to break the smaller End of their Eggs. The People so highly resented this Law, that . . . It is computed, that eleven thousand Persons have, at several times, suffered Death, rather than submit to break their Eggs at the smaller End. During the Course of these Troubles, the Emperors of Blefuscu did frequently expostulate by their Ambassadors, accusing us of making a Schism in Religion, by offending against a fundamental Doctrine of our great Prophet Lustrog. . . . Now the Big-Endian Exiles have found so much . . . encouragement from their Party here at home, that a bloody War has been carried on between the two Empires for six and thirty Moons with various Success . . . they have now equipped a numerous Fleet, and are just preparing to make a Descent upon us. (pp. 48–49)

deplore the Black professional, who now appears grotesquely at odds with accepted cultural stereotypes.

Schimel et al. (1999) tested this rather counterintuitive notion in an experiment at the University of Arizona in which groups of previously unacquainted White college students and a Black confederate working with us participated in what was described as an investigation of the relationship between personality traits and first impressions of people. To accomplish this, participants were ushered into private cubicles and asked to write a short essay about what they did the previous summer. They were also told that they would subsequently read essays written by two other students in other cubicles and evaluate the authors (anonymously in that the participants would not know who in the group had written the essays they would be reading and their evaluations of the authors would be private and anonymous). The essays were collected, and the subjects went on to complete some personality assessments, including a mortality salience or television salience control manipulation.

All participants then read two essays. The single Black participant appeared to have written one, and a White student appeared to have written the other (order or presentation was counterbalanced). Actually, we wrote bogus essays to ensure that everyone in the study was exposed to the same stimuli as a function of experimental conditions, which varied the physical appearance and content of the essay describing the summer activities of the Black confederate. The confederate was always easily identified as the author of one of the essays because it always began by referring, depending on conditions described below, to how few Black students, or "brothers," live in Tucson.

In the stereotype-consistent condition, the confederate wore high-top sneakers with untied laces, an Atlanta Braves shirt, black baggy shorts, dark sunglasses, and a backward baseball cap. He also carried a portable cassette player with headphones around his neck. The essay that was designed to be attributed to him described "brothers, splitting to L.A., serious hoop, slammin' nightlife, cruisin' for honeys, clubbing, getting stupid, a few run-ins, drinking forties" and concluded with "Man, coming back to classes was whack, but I don't want to trip on that." In the stereotype-inconsistent condition, the same confederate was conservatively attired: button-down dress shirt and tie with khaki dress pants, penny-loafers, and black framed glasses; and he was carrying a briefcase. The essay, after mentioning how few Black students live in Tucson, went on to indicate that the confederate's summer consisted of taking 9 hours of summer engineering classes at the University of Arizona while working 20 hours a week for a software company. The essay also stated that he spent his spare time reading and playing chess, and concluded with the following statement: "All in all, I had a very productive and exciting summer." Finally, in the neutral condition, the confederate dressed like a typical college student on this campus, in a casual T-shirt and shorts, low-top sneakers, and toting a backpack over one shoulder. His essay began by noting how few Black students live in Tucson, followed by one of two neutral essays. One neutral essay referred to taking a summer school class, going to parties with friends, watching videos, and playing board games: "By the way, I was the Monopoly champ of the summer." A second neutral essay referred to traveling in San Francisco, visiting family in Ohio, and going to a wedding in New Orleans: "We had a bachelor's party the night before on Bourbon Street. It was a blast." These essays were counterbalanced within the neutral condition, so that half of the time the traveling essay appeared to be written by the Black confederate and the other half by a White participant.

After reading each essay, we asked participants to rate how much they thought they would like this person and how interested they would be in getting to know the person, in order to determine if evaluations of the Black confederate would vary as a function of the extent to which he conformed to or violated cultural stereotypes and whether mortality had been made salient before the evaluation. The results indicated the following: Participants' evaluations of the Black confederate in the neutral condition did not differ from their evaluations of the White target or vary as a consequence of mortality salience. In other words, our control White participants seemed to view the neutral Black and White targets in this study without bias. All of the participants read the same essays (counterbalanced by race of target and order of presentation as described above) and did not respond in a biased fashion depending on whether they believed the author was Black or White. Also, mortality salience did not cause any changes in these evaluations. In the television salience control group, participants expressed a strong preference for the well-dressed, chess-playing, briefcase-toting Black confederate, as well as considerable disdain for the baggy-panted, baseball-capped, "brother" (in both cases, relative to the evaluation of the confederate in the neutral condition). However, in the mortality salience condition, this pattern of results was completely reversed: Now the participants were wildly enthusiastic about the same "brother" who inspired nothing but contempt in those in the control group and were incredibly hostile toward the scholarly Black confederate whom their control counterparts greatly preferred.

Four additional studies with American students found similar effects: that mortality salience led to a preference for women, Germans, and gay men who conformed to the cultural stereotype of that particular group. Thus, the same negative stereotypes that generally render minorities targets of constant derision become badges of honor when mortality salience inspires the need to bolster a cultural worldview that includes minorities serving specific roles that are not valued in any absolute sense except to verify our sense of things being the way we believe them to be. No wonder racial, ethnic, and gender prejudice is so insidiously difficult to overcome: We are fundamentally ambivalent about people labeled as designated inferiors.

On the one hand, we want them to dispose of the unseemly character flaws that make them who they are, embrace the values of the dominant culture, and become more like us. However, at the same time, we despise people who do this because in so doing they no longer conform to our cultural worldview, which requires that they "stay in their place" for the purpose of sustaining our psychological equanimity by keeping the prevailing cultural worldview intact.

MITIGATING FACTORS: DOES MORTALITY SALIENCE ALWAYS PRODUCE WORLDVIEW DEFENSE?

The tenor of the results of the studies presented so far suggests that making mortality salient inevitably produces worldview defense: increased affection and regard for those who share or uphold important aspects of cultural identity or values, and increased disaffection for and hostility toward those who are different or violate cherished cultural values. But is this always the case? And if not, are there theoretically predictable factors that moderate the effects of mortality salience on worldview defense?

High Self-Esteem

To the extent that self-esteem is an anxiety buffer, raising self-esteem should reduce or eliminate worldview defense following mortality salience. To test this idea directly, Harmon-Jones et al. (1997) gave participants either positive or neutral personality feedback to raise their self-esteem or leave it unaltered, and then had half of them ponder their mortality while the remaining participants thought about watching television. Everyone next read two essays that were supposedly written by foreign exchange students about their impressions of the United States and then completed evaluations of the essays and their authors. One of the essays was extremely positive about life in America, whereas the other essay portrayed America in very negative terms. The results indicated that mortality salience led to worldview defense in the neutral self-esteem condition but not in the raised self-esteem condition. Specifically, participants who received the neutral personality feedback and then thought about their deaths rated the pro-America essay more favorably and the anti-America essay less favorably than the students receiving the same personality feedback but who then thought about watching television. However, those who received the positive personality feedback did not have more extreme reactions to the essays following mortality salience relative to the evaluations of those who thought about watching television. Raising self-esteem thus eliminated the effects of mortality salience on worldview defense.

A second study then replicated this procedure but used students with dispositionally high and low self-esteem rather than personality feedback to create momentary elevations in feelings of self-worth. The results were identical to those obtained in the previous study. Low-self-esteem participants made more extreme evaluations of the pro- and anti-America essays following mortality salience relative to the television control group, but high-self-esteem individuals did not. Thus, after mortality salience, high self-esteem reduced the need for worldview defense, regardless of whether the high self-esteem was situationally induced or dispositionally high.

Liberal Worldview and the Value of Tolerance

Greenberg et al. (1990) found that high, but not low, authoritarians responded to mortality salience with increased derogation of attitudinally dissimilar others. According to Adorno, Frenkel-Brunswick, Levinson, and Sanford (1950), the authoritarian individual is characterized by a high regard for authority, rigidity, and conventionality. Thus, it was not surprising that those with the most rigid worldviews would defend them most vigorously in response to mortality salience. However, the absence of such an effect among low authoritarians suggests that some worldviews might actually militate against increased prejudice as a consequence of mortality salience, particularly those in which tolerance is an important value.

Greenberg, Simon, Pyszczynski, Solomon, and Chatel (1992) conducted two studies to assess this possibility. On the basis of the previous finding that low authoritarian individuals did not derogate attitudinally dissimilar others when mortality was made salient, the theoretical and empirically demonstrable relationship between authoritarianism and political conservativism (Stone, 1980), and the notion that American liberal political ideology espouses the value of tolerance of different others, we hypothesized that extremely liberal individuals would be less likely than their conservative counterparts to become increasingly intolerant following mortality salience. To test this hypothesis, we selected American subjects who were either extremely liberal or extremely conservative (as evidenced by their views on abortion, prayer in schools, flag burning, and the Reagan presidency) and then asked them to evaluate liberal and conservative targets under mortality salient or control conditions. We predicted that mortality salience would produce more favorable impressions of similar targets and more unfavorable impressions of dissimilar targets but that this would occur only among conservative subjects. Because liberal political ideology explicitly espouses tolerance for diversity (indeed, *liberal* literally means tolerant and open minded) and because mortality salience should intensify the individual's desire to fulfill the standards prescribed by their worldview, we expected to find that liberals would not show the usual derogation of dissimilar others when mortality was made salient and that they would in fact like the dissimilar target more than they would in the control condition. The predicted pattern of results was obtained.

In a follow-up study, we manipulated the salience of the value of tolerance instead of relying on individual differences in advocacy of tolerance. Although tolerance is a particularly potent value for liberals, it is likely to be advocated at least to a moderate extent by virtually all Americans. The Declaration of Independence referred to inalienable rights of all men, and the Constitution guarantees freedom of speech and religious practice. Thus, we thought that if asked on a questionnaire about the importance of tolerance, all of our American participants would advocate this value, and in doing so, the value would become salient to all participants asked about it. Furthermore, we hypothesized that if the value of tolerance was made salient in this way, reminders of one's mortality should motivate people to live up to that value as well as to defend their beliefs. Therefore, priming the value of tolerance should reduce or eliminate the tendency for mortality salience to engender derogation of those who are critical of one's worldview. In this study, mortality salience led to an especially large preference for a foreign student who praised the United States relative to a foreign student who was critical of the United States when the value of tolerance was not primed. However, priming the value of tolerance completely eliminated the effect of mortality salience on pro-American preferences. The converging findings of these two studies suggest the hopeful possibility that cultural worldviews can be constructed that do not inevitably lead to hostility toward those who are different, even when mortality concerns have been aroused. Worldviews that emphasize tolerance of those who are different may help insulate people against the interpersonal hostility that concerns about mortality and defending one's worldview might otherwise create.

Strong Belief in Symbolic Immortality

Lifton (1979/1983) proposed that culture provides opportunities for people to obtain symbolic as well as literal immortality. Although people may recognize that they will certainly die, they are comforted by a variety of vehicles that instill symbolic immortality and, in so doing, blunt the terror of death. According to Lifton, symbolic immortality can be obtained through five modes of experience: biological (one is the continuation of past generations and will continue to live in one's children); creative (a sense that one's work, teaching, and personal influence will provide a creative and enduring contribution to society that will persist after one's death); natural (a feeling that one is part of an eternal natural universe); spiritual and religious attainments (searching for a higher plane of existence); and experiential (intense peak experiences).

Accordingly, Florian and Mikulincer (1998) predicted that people who possess a strong sense of symbolic immortality will be less threatened by the prospect of their deaths and will respond less vigorously to a mortality salience manipulation. In Study 1, participants completed a Hebrew version of a symbolic immortality scale based on Lifton's modes of symbolic immortality developed by Mathews and Kling (1988), followed by Florian and Kravitz's (1983) Fear of Personal Death Scale to assess overt expressions of fear of death. Consistent with the hypothesis, results revealed a negative correlation between belief in symbolic immortality and fear of death (i.e., greater belief in symbolic immortality was associated with lower self-reported fear of death). In Study 2, individual differences in belief in symbolic immortality were assessed before the classic mortality salience manipulation. Participants then prescribed bond for an alleged prostitute (similar to the procedure used by Rosenblatt, Greenberg, Solomon, Pyszczynski, & Lyon, 1989). As predicted, mortality salience resulted in higher bond assessments, but only for participants with low belief in symbolic immortality; in other words, high belief in symbolic immortality eliminated the punitive reactions to moral transgression in response to mortality salience.

Secure Attachment

Recall that according to Bowlby (1969, 1973, 1980), raw undifferentiated terror instigates the formation of attachment to primary caretakers that serves as a basis for psychological equanimity in infancy and adulthood (for theory and research about how attachment in infancy persists through adulthood, see Shaver & Hazan, 1993). The anxiety-buffering properties of self-esteem based on adherence to the standards of value prescribed by one's cultural worldview are ultimately derived from this process. Bowlby's original formulation of attachment theory made a broad distinction between secure and insecure attachments. Although all normal human infants form attachments, securely attached individuals (by virtue of either their genetic predisposition or the positive manner in which they are treated by their caretakers) are generally comfortable with, and confident about, their relationships with others (and life in general). Insecurely attached individuals, in contrast, become either excessively anxious and ambivalent about their relationships with others or avoidant in the sense of maintaining great emotional distance in their relationships.

On the basis of prior findings that securely attached individuals report less fear of death than insecurely attached individuals (Mikulincer, Florian, & Tolmacz, 1990) and more confident beliefs in symbolic immortality (Florian & Mikulincer, 1998), Mikulincer and Florian (2000) predicted and found in their first study that greater ratings of severity and ascription of punishment for moral transgressions as a result of mortality salience would be obtained only among insecurely attached people. Subsequent experiments (Studies 4 and 5) demonstrated that securely attached individuals were not impervious to mortality salience; rather, they reacted in a different (and theoretically predictable) fashion. Specifically, following a mortality salience induction, securely attached participants showed increased confidence in their belief in their symbolic immortality and an increased desire for intimate relationships (as assessed by Brennan, Clark, and Shaver's Experience in Close Relationships Scale, 1998).

Summary of Mitigating Factors

These findings provide an important qualification to the general finding that momentary reminders of death foster negative attitudes and increased hostility to those who violate cherished cultural values or subscribe to a different worldview. Specifically, high self-esteem, a liberal political orientation or salient reminder of the value of tolerance, a confident belief in symbolic immortality, and secure attachment style all serve to reduce the otherwise pernicious effects of mortality salience.

CONCLUSION: "ISMS" MAKE SCHISMS

Following Ernest Becker in *Escape From Evil*, terror management theory (TMT) asserts that the uniquely human awareness of death results in the development and maintenance of cultural worldviews: humanly created beliefs about the nature of reality that provide meaning and associated standards of value that, in turn, allow for the acquisition of self-esteem as the basis of psychological equanimity. But to the extent that psychological equanimity requires the preservation of culture as a fragile symbolic construction perpetually sustained by social consensus, the mere existence of people with different beliefs (i.e., other cultures) undermines the absolute validity of any particular culture and engenders a host of negative reactions toward those who are different, as a means to restore confidence in the dominant culture: derogation, assimilation, accommodation, and annihilation.

Then, to make matters worse, in-house scapegoats are arbitrarily chosen whenever there are not enough foreigners about to hate, because residual anxiety (inevitable in that no cultural construction can completely eliminate the overwhelming horror of death) must be constantly projected onto tangible repositories of evil to sustain psychological equanimity. Finally, to make an already bad situation completely untenable, designated inferiors become an integral part of the dominant culture; and although we generally despise them, when they seem to conform to our negative stereotypes, after subtle reminders of death, we despise them when they appear too much like ourselves! Prejudice and ethnic strife thus seem to be a nearly inevitable result of the use of cultural worldviews to assuage the fear of death.

In support of these claims, research has demonstrated that mortality salience produces increased affection for those who share one's cultural worldview and greater negative reactions to those who are different. After thinking about death, people maintain greater physical distance from different others and are more likely to be physically aggressive toward those who threaten their cultural worldviews. Additionally, mortality salience produces hostility toward those who differ from us in even trivial dimensions, such as preference for a particular abstract artist, and renders people prone to disparage members of disadvantaged groups who deviate from negative cultural stereotypes of the group.

Can fear of death account for all human hatred and violence? Of course not! Life is complex, and surely a variety of factors contributes to these phenomena. Nonetheless, in light of the accumulated evidence presented in this chapter, we believe that TMT should be an essential component of any sincere effort to understand human hatred and violence. In short, terror management needs contribute to the formation and defense of isms, and *isms make schisms!*

Does this mean the human race is doomed to extinguish itself as destructive technologies improve? Is consciousness as a form of mental organization and the resultant need for cultural constructions a fleeting, florid outburst, a short-lived evolutionary dead-end? Does understanding the terror management function of prejudice and violence and the factors that mitigate such reactions provide any practical insight about how to minimize "man's inhumanity to man"? These are questions that we return to in upcoming chapters.

TERROR MANAGEMENT AND SELF-ESTEEM STRIVING

As the presentation of terror management research so far suggests, the majority of mortality salience research to date has focused on hypotheses concerning how death-related thoughts increase the bolstering and defense of the individual's cultural worldview. This work has emphasized the dark side of terror management—defending one's worldview by reacting negatively to those who explicitly or implicitly violate or challenge the validity of one's worldview.

However, TMT is not primarily about defending one's cultural beliefs. It is about how we sustain a sense of security, of death transcendence, despite the knowledge of our mortality. Faith in a meaning-providing worldview sets the foundation for that psychological equanimity. However, people have to establish and maintain a sense that they are significant contributors within that meaningful reality to feel truly protected and transcendent. Thus, a major component of our everyday efforts to manage terror consists of activities designed to establish and sustain our self-worth by living up to our personal, albeit culturally derived, standards of value. If these sorts of behaviors do indeed serve a terror management function, then we should find that reminders of mortality increase both self-esteem striving and self-esteem defense. A growing body of research has found support for these ideas.

BEHAVIORAL EVIDENCE OF ENHANCED SELF-ESTEEM STRIVING

In the first research to test directly whether self-esteem striving serves a terror management function, Taubman Ben-Ari, Florian, and Mikulincer (1999) brought Israeli soldiers into their laboratory and first assessed the extent to which they used their driving ability as a source of self-esteem. In a series of studies, they then manipulated mortality salience and assessed these soldiers' proneness to engage in boldly risky driving, sometimes using their responses to hypothetical driving scenarios and sometimes using their performance on a driving simulator. They consistently found that following mortality salience, the soldiers who used their driving ability as a source of self-esteem reported an especially great willingness to try risky driving maneuvers and actually drove especially fast in the driving simulator. Subsequent research by this group has found additional evidence that for men mortality salience often increases the willingness to take risks. In addition to providing evidence that mortality salience increases striving for self-esteem, this line of work indicates that reminders of one's own inevitable death can have the ironic effect of increasing risky behavior that could more quickly lead to that death, if that behavior can serve to enhance self-esteem.

Jonas, Schimel, Greenberg, and Pyszczynski (in press) recently found evidence that mortality salience can also enhance self-esteem striving in a socially valuable way—through helping. One of the most beneficial ways people can feel good about themselves is by helping others. Perhaps this is one reason why religious leaders and psychologists alike so commonly urge people to be helpful to others. This suggests that mortality salience may increase people's desires to be helpful. It is interesting to consider that Charles Dickens, in his well-known tale *A Christmas Carol* (1843/1915), had anticipated this hypothesis. Recall that what really turns Ebenezer Scrooge into an altruistic person is the powerful mortality salience treatment provided by the Ghost of Christmas Future.

To provide a nonfictional test of this idea, Jonas et al. (in press) brought American students into a laboratory, sent them into private cubicles, and manipulated mortality salience as part of a personality assessment study. To ensure that the students had some money they could give to charities, they paid the participants a quarter for each of six questionnaires they filled out. When each participant was finished with the questionnaire, the experimenter explained that the psychology department was participating in efforts to help worthy charities by asking research participants if they would like to give to one of two charities, described in a written brochure. Participants were left in the cubicle to read about the charities privately and then decide whether to put some money in envelopes for each charity. One of the charities was for American poor people and the other was for foreign poor people. Jonas et al. found that the mortality salient participants gave twice as much money to the American charity as did the control participants; however, they gave no more than control participants to the foreign charity. This research shows that mortality salience can indeed encourage helping, but may be limited to charities close to home or those particularly valued by individuals in the context of their worldviews.

ALTERING SELF-RELEVANT COGNITIONS TO MANAGE THE TERROR

In addition to changing behavior to enhance self-esteem following mortality salience, people can also change their perceptions of themselves. One way they can do that is by altering their identifications with aspects of themselves. All of us have aspects of ourselves that serve self-esteem well and others that do not. Thus, for terror management purposes, basketball players should focus on their basketball skills; models, on their appearance; psychotherapists, on their clients who did in fact improve; and scientists, on their publications. On the basis of this idea, in a series of three studies, Goldenberg, McCoy, Pyszczynski, Greenberg, and Solomon (2000) found that after mortality salience, people who feel good about their bodies increase their perception of the body as an important aspect of themselves and people who do not feel good about their bodies will reduce focus on their appearance.

Another way to cognitively bolster self-worth is to alter interpretation of feedback one receives about the self in a self-serving way. A large body of research has shown that people's cognitions about themselves are influenced by self-serving biases in many ways (e.g., Myers, 2002). Dechesne, Janssen, and van Knippenberg (2000b) have recently shown in a set of studies that mortality salience increases such self-serving biases. In one study, after a mortality salience manipulation, Dutch students were randomly given either very positive or neutral (bogus) personality feedback, purportedly based on personality questionnaires filled out earlier. Then they were simply asked how accurate they perceived the feedback to be. Mortality salience had no effect on perceived accuracy of the neutral feedback but led the participants to perceive the positive feedback as especially accurate, presumably to enhance self-esteem.

In a series of recent follow-up studies, Dechesne et al. (2002) found particularly direct evidence that this effect of mortality salience does indeed serve to assuage mortality concerns. In these studies, Dechesne et al. replicated this tendency for people to overrate the accuracy of the positive personality feedback, except if the participants had first been asked to read an article claiming compelling scientific evidence of life after death. As TMT predicts, when people were convinced that they would live beyond their death, the need to enhance self-esteem following a reminder of mortality was reduced.

TERROR MANAGEMENT AND SOCIAL CONNECTIONS

The work on self-esteem striving described so far illustrates a number of ways in which, following mortality salience, people can bolster their sense of self-worth: risk taking, helping, and biasing their identifications with the body and perceptions of feedback about the self. However, a large component of our self-worth is tied up in our group identifications and interpersonal relationships, and so two additional lines of work have looked specifically at the effects of mortality salience on these important sources of social connection.

Group Identifications

A variety of studies have shown that mortality salience generally increases identification with and pride in one's country, university, and gender (e.g., Castano, Yzerbyt, Paladino, & Sacchi, 2002; Dechesne et al., 2000a). For example, Dechesne et al. found that after mortality salience, Dutch participants became more optimistic in their predictions regarding a future soccer match between the Dutch national team and the rival German team. Jonas and Greenberg (2002) recently added to this work by showing that mortality salience increases German participants' positive reactions to the reunification of East and West Germany and their negative reactions to the Euro, which, at the time of the study, was soon to eliminate the cherished national currency, the deutsche mark. This enhanced in-group pride can, of course, take an ugly turn, and recent studies by Greenberg, Schimel, Martens, Pyszczynski, and Solomon (2001) demonstrated that mortality salience can contribute to such manifestations of group pride. In a first study, they simply had White American participants read an essay apparently written by either a White or a Black person expressing racial pride. As expected, these remarks were viewed as more racist when attributed to a White. However, a second study found that with mortality salient, the White was viewed as significantly less racist, and the Black was viewed as somewhat more racist. A third study had mortality salient and control Whites read about a court case in which a White employer discriminated against a Black or a Black employer discriminated against a White. After mortality salience, the White participants were especially sympathetic to the White racist and unsympathetic to the Black racist. The chilling message is that under mortality salient conditions, White Americans become rather sympathetic to other Whites who express racist sentiments.

What happens, however, to group identification when such identification would hamper rather than enhance one's self-esteem? The first study to address this issue examined University of Arizona students' identification with the Arizona Wildcat football team before the fall season and following the team's first game, which they lost to Pac-10 rival Oregon (Dechesne, Greenberg, Arndt, & Schimel, 2000). Before the 1997 season, mortality salience led to increased identification with the football team. However, after the loss, mortality salience led to reduced identification with the football team and a shift toward increased identification with the more successful National Champion Wildcat basketball team. Thus, following mortality salience, group identifications shifted in whatever manner bolstered self-esteem.

More recently, Arndt, Greenberg, Schimel, et al. (in press) demonstrated that these tendencies occur with regard to gender and ethnic identifications, as well as sports allegiances. Ethnic minorities in American culture often live in an atmosphere in which negative stereotypes are prevalent; would mortality salience lead minority group members to disidentify with their own group to protect self-worth? Two studies reported by Arndt et al. indicate that when negative aspects of the group are made salient to members of the group, the answer is yes. In one study, Hispanic students read an article about a Hispanic drug-dealing murderer or a neutral or positive Hispanic. Under the guise of an impression formation and personality study, after a mortality salience manipulation, the students filled out a personality questionnaire, read about a fellow Hispanic student and an Anglo student, and then were asked to give their impressions of these students, using the same personality questionnaire they had previously filled out. Mortality salient Hispanic students who read about the Hispanic drug dealer rated the fellow Hispanic student's personality (but not the Anglo student's) as especially different from their own. Thus, with mortality salience, and a reminder of a negative exemplar of their group, the Hispanic students saw themselves as especially different from a fellow Hispanic.

Dechesne, Janssen, and van Knippenberg (2000a) replicated this basic finding with Dutch students and university identification but also found two factors that determine whether the combination of mortality salience and salient negative aspects of one's group leads to disidentification rather than defense of the group. One was an individual difference—people high in need for structure maintained their identification with the group even under these conditions and defended against the criticism of their university. In contrast, people low in need for structure readily disidentified under the same conditions. Presumably, people high in need for structure invest more of their self-worth in their groups and so tend to stick with their identifications, whereas people low in need for structure seem to rely on more indi-

vidually derived bases of self-worth and therefore flexibly adjust their identifications as needed to protect self-esteem.

The other factor was the perception of the permanency of a particular
identification. Students led to believe that school identification would stay
with them their whole lives maintained and defended their identification,
whereas students led to believe that such identifications are highly change-
able, temporary connections readily disidentified from their school when
mortality was salient and their group was framed negatively. The basic message of this line of work seems to be that although social connections are
important means of terror management, their importance depends on their
value for sustaining the individual's self-worth. Unless a particular social
connection is deeply tied to one's self-worth, people in need of terror management will at least temporarily distance themselves from social connections that reflect negatively on their self-worth.

Close Relationships

Whereas the foregoing work focused on connections to large groups,
many of our central social connections are one on one, with family, friends,
and especially romantic partners. Indeed, Rank (1931/1961) and Becker
(1973) argued that in modern times, romantic partners have become a central basis of terror management because they provide our lives with much of
their meaning and, by loving us, with much of our sense of self-worth. In
support of this idea, Israeli social psychologists Mario Mikulincer, Victor
Florian, and colleagues have recently reported a series of studies providing
evidence for a role of romantic relationships in terror management and have
suggested that the intimate contact they provide quells our anxieties even
beyond their value in providing meaning and self-worth.

In the first set of studies, Mikulincer and Florian (2000) found that
individuals with secure attachment styles, which is roughly two thirds of
people, seemed to use relationships for terror management purposes. Specifically, they found that mortality salience led such individuals to report a
higher desire for intimacy in and higher feelings of commitment to romantic relationships. In addition, they found that following mortality salience,
thinking about commitment to romantic relationships decreased the need
for worldview defense in securely attached individuals. Insecurely attached
individuals, in contrast, exhibit worldview defense in response to mortality
salience, regardless of whether they are thinking about romantic relationships—such relationships do not seem to serve a terror management function effectively for them.

If romantic relationships serve a terror management function, then
when such relationships are threatened, increased death thought accessibility should result. Recent research by Florian et al. (2002) found support for

this hypothesis. An additional set of studies (Taubman Ben-Ari et al., in press) showed that for securely attached individuals, mortality salience increased willingness to initiate social interactions, lowered sensitivity to rejection, and increased perceived interpersonal competence. This last set of studies suggests that people not only take comfort in existing relationships following mortality salience but also become more interested in forming new relationships.

This work fits with some classic social psychological research demonstrating that when people are anxious they seek to affiliate with others, particularly others who are in the same situation. It is also consistent with recent theory and research on the role of attachment in alleviating anxiety (e.g., Collins & Feeney, 2000). However, this new work specifically ties in affiliation needs with mortality concerns and suggests a much broader and deeper desire for social relationships than merely seeking out others in the same shaky boat as oneself.

CONCLUSION

In conjunction with chapter 3, we have now laid out a large body of research supporting hypotheses derived from TMT. Self-esteem has indeed been found to serve an anxiety-buffering function; highly accessible death-related thought activates worldview defenses, often leading to nationalism and derogation of different others. Such thoughts also lead to self-esteem striving through displaying culturally valued attributes and behaviors and by adjusting social connections. For securely attached people, romantic relationships serve a terror management function as well, reducing death-related thought and the need for worldview defense. Research on the processes activated by reminders of death show that death-related thought initially activates relatively direct proximal defenses to quell the immediate conscious concern with death. Once this has been accomplished, individuals employ the distal terror management defenses that have been the primary focus of our theorizing and research. Now that we have reviewed the theoretical analysis and its empirical support, we are ready to apply this analysis specifically to the aftermath of the 9/11 attacks, factors that contributed to the attacks, and possible directions for coping and prevention.

5

BLACK TUESDAY: THE PSYCHOLOGICAL IMPACT OF 9/11

All men live enveloped in whale-lines. All are born with halters round their necks; but it is only when caught in the swift, sudden turn of death, that mortals realize the silent, subtle, ever-present perils of life.
—Herman Melville, *Moby-Dick*, (1851/1986, p. 387)

As we have seen in previous chapters, terror management theory (TMT) asserts that the uniquely human awareness of death, when juxtaposed with the natural inclination toward self-preservation common to all life, renders human beings prone to potentially overwhelming terror that is managed by the construction and maintenance of culture. Culture provides opportunities for individuals to perceive themselves as persons of value in a world of meaning and, in so doing, derive security in this world and symbolic or literal immortality in the next. Empirical support for terror management theory has been obtained from a large body of research demonstrating the anxiety-buffering properties of self-esteem and specific proximal and distal defensive reactions to thoughts of death that are in and outside current conscious awareness. How can TMT help us understand the psychological impact that Americans and many people the world over experienced in response to the events of 9/11?

THE PSYCHOLOGICAL IMPACT OF 9/11

From the perspective of TMT, the 9/11 terrorist attack hit us with a one-two punch of mortality salience coupled with a major attack on our cultural anxiety buffer. First, came a stunning literal blow: Millions of New

Yorkers and hundreds of millions of Americans and billions of others around the world experienced spectacularly vivid and gruesomely horrifying images of death and destruction. We had an otherwise normal day rudely interrupted by the sight of the World Trade Center towers imploding on themselves in quick succession; we simultaneously reeled with the knowledge that the Pentagon was smoldering and another plane had crashed in Pennsylvania, perhaps on its way to the White House; we knew that thousands of people were likely trapped inside and almost certainly doomed to a horrible death or already horribly dead. Then we watched the relentless replays of the planes crashing into the towers, the people jumping from the burning buildings, and the looks of horror on the faces of the rubble-coated survivors. Experiences like these surely rendered our own sheer vulnerability and always potentially imminent mortality profoundly salient in a manner that few other events (e.g., nuclear or genocidal holocausts; massive earthquakes, tidal waves, or having one's planet struck by a giant asteroid) could approximate.

And the literal blow of the horrible scenes of death and carnage was accompanied by a staggering psychological uppercut: the brutal assault on major symbols of the American way of life. The World Trade Center towers were the ultimate tangible representations of American prosperity and economic might. The Pentagon is a universally recognized architectural emblem of the United States' globe-dominating, unassailable-at-home-or-abroad military power. In a matter of moments, one of these symbols had been totally destroyed and the other had been badly damaged—and, to compound the psychological battering, this was accomplished by planes hijacked from American Airlines and United Airlines, two of our country's most respected and reliable air carriers. From the perspective of TMT, people need concrete manifestations of their values and beliefs to serve as a reminder of the power, protection, and security that these more abstract psychological entities provide. The destruction of these cherished symbols severely undermined the functional integrity of the psychological shield that ordinarily enables us to feel secure in a world where the only real certainty in life is death. In so doing, the terrorist attacks surely heightened the explicit and implicit thoughts of death that a secure belief in a cultural worldview typically serves to quell.

The tragic events of 9/11, the subsequent anthrax attacks, the American Airlines plane crash in Queens, and the ongoing threat of additional terrorist activities combined to create a nationwide mortality salience induction that is unparalleled in American history. Many Americans, and especially the residents of New York City and Washington, DC, were, and continue to be, clearly traumatized. For example, Gallup polls indicated (see www.gallup.com) that up to 20% of all Americans knew someone, or knew someone who knew someone, who was missing, hurt, or killed by terrorist attacks on 9/11. This figure is not surprising given Milgram's (1967) classic "small world" finding that the average American has a 0.5 chance of being acquainted with any other randomly chosen American by only two interme-diate acquaintances. In November 2001, 40% of all Americans believed that they or a family member will be the victim of a future terrorist attack; and 74% said they believed such an attack was quite likely in the near future.

People were worried; the specter of death lurked everywhere; no one felt safe, as these reports from people in the New York area make evident (LeDuff, 2001):

> There is a street-corner Santa who works Fifth Avenue at Rockefeller Center with a bell in his hand and a red chimney with a money slot at his side. . . . Mr. De Witt . . . has rung the charity bell for the last 8 years and, predictably, has noticed a subtle yet perceptible change this holiday season. "The normality is not there," Mr. Dewitt said . . . He attributed the change to the post-traumatic stress of Sept. 11. "The parents will not let the hands of their children go," he said. "The kids sense that. It's like water seeping down and the kids feel it. Their reactions to Santa are not natural. There is an anxiety, but the kids can't make the connection. . . . Many times the children don't know what they want at all, and that is strange," Mr. De Witt said. "Usually they have a list." (p. D1)

As Nagourney (2001) notes:

> If there is any business that is booming since Sept. 11, it is the business of writing wills. Starting about 10 days after the collapse of the towers, and continuing ever since, trust and estate lawyers say they have been overwhelmed with requests from people who suddenly want to prepare their wills . . . estate lawyers say the influx is astonishing for its breadth as well as its volume: from people of all ages and economic classes, from married and gay couples and singles, from people with children and without, and from all neighborhoods . . . an implicit, if grudging, acknowledgment of mortality. (pp. A1, D8)

Woodruff (2001) cited the following:

> The number of people requesting pistol permit applications has sky-rocketed since the Sept. 11 attacks, as Capital Region residents reached for guns to help fight off a new sense of vulnerability. . . . "I don't know why," Vic Ferrante, a retired Air National Guard firearms instructor who teaches gun safety. . .said of the apparent increased interest in acquiring guns. "I guess they expect the Afghans to come in by para-chute or something." But mental health experts recognize the phenom-enon—particularly among regular folks who have not experienced combat or carried guns before. It is, they say, part of a craving for com-fort. (pp. A1, A9)

In the language of TMT then, the events of 9/11 and thereafter have produced heightened death accessibility in a large proportion of Ameri-cans—by the one-two punch of a literal confrontation with death and the symbolic attack on our most cherished cultural icons. In fact, social psy-chologist Jamie Arndt (personal communication, 2002) found in the spring of 2002 that exposing University of Missouri students to subliminal images of "9/11" or "WTC" increased the likelihood that they would complete word fragments with death-related words. And given our theoretical and empirically substantiated distinction between proximal defenses in response to explicit thoughts of death, and distal defenses in response to heightened implicit death thoughts, we would expect people to use many aspects of both of these dual defense systems to restore the psychological equanimity disrupted by the potential or actual eruption into awareness of mortality in an animal instinctively disinclined to die.

PROXIMAL REACTIONS TO 9/11

The research presented in chapter 3 indicates that explicit encounters with reminders of death instigate proximal defenses: attempts to push thoughts of one's own mortality from consciousness, either by simply suppressing them through the use of distractions of various sorts, by promises to do whatever it takes to reduce one's vulnerability, or by defensively distorting information to push the problem of death into the distant future, to convince oneself that one has a long and healthy life to look forward to and that accidents and mishaps are problems for others but not for oneself. Most Americans can readily relate to using at least some variants of these tactics in coping with their enhanced feelings of vulnerability brought on by the recent terrorist attacks.

It Can't Happen Here

The first reaction for many was one of simple disbelief: This cannot be happening! Of course this was only a momentary response that was impossible to sustain in light of the very clear evidence coming in from all channels that this really was happening. Another common initial response was to thank our lucky stars that we were not directly and personally involved, that we were not in the World Trade Center, Pentagon, or doomed jets that crashed into those landmarks. Some people found solace in the realization that the terrorists were interested primarily in attacking the seats of governmental, economic, and military power.

Driven to Distraction

Others sought comfort by diverting their attention to other matters, by drinking, gambling, renting videos, watching television, and shopping:

> Almost 3 months after the terrorist attack, New Yorkers are drinking more than ever. . . . The dramatic rise in consumption of alcoholic beverages immediately after Sept. 11 was a nationwide phenomenon. . . .

But nowhere was it more evident than in New York. . . . "At first, people felt a little uneasy and didn't want to appear to be celebrating—now I think there is a certain nervous fatigue that propels people," said Kurt Eckert, the wine director for Jean-Georges Vongerichten's five New York restaurants. (Burros, 2001, pp. F1, F5)

Besides—or perhaps in addition to—alcohol, Blockbuster video rentals surged this fall after a brief dip in mid-September; in Las Vegas, although proceeds from gaming tables dropped, there were steady increases in slot machine income—the only place in a casino where the average person with a bucket of quarters can spend a few hours before (generally) walking away empty handed; prime-time television viewing was up 4% over comparable periods in the past 2 years (Brockes, 2001). At the same time, movie studios postponed the release of movies with terrorist themes, such as Arnold Schwarzenegger's *Collateral Damage*. Schwarzenegger supported this decision, observing in an interview, "You want to release movies that are entertaining for people, with some escapism there" (Miller et al., 2001, p. 72).

And we shopped. At an October 11, 2001, press conference, President George W. Bush responded (in part) to the question " . . . is there anything you can say to Americans who feel helpless to protect themselves?" by stating " . . . the American people have got to go about their business. We cannot let the terrorists achieve the objective of frightening our nation to the point where we don't conduct business, where people don't shop" ("A Nation Challenged," 2001, p. B4). Bush then repeated this advice to the American public a few days later (reported in Carney & Dickerson, 2001): "Well, Mrs. Bush and I want to encourage Americans to go out shopping." But Americans were already thoroughly involved in commercial activity, as evidenced, for example, by Allen's (2001, p. 48) observations:

"When I went to a hardware store the Saturday after the terrorist attacks on New York and Washington, DC, I found the parking lot full. Usually that annoys me, but this time I felt an unexpected surge of pleasure: America was still in business. And the business of most Americans on an early fall afternoon is buying." (p. 48)

Music sales rose domestically and internationally; for example, England's HMV records sales had double-digit growth compared with last fall. According to company chart analyst Gennaro Castaldo, "In an economic slow down, people are less inclined to buy the expensive things, but to cheer themselves up by buying music. . . . They are turning to escapism" (Brockes, 2001, p. 6). Long before 9/11, Becker (1973) had noted our propensity for using such activities in the face of awareness of mortality: "Modern man is drinking and drugging himself out of awareness, or he spends his time shopping, which is the same thing" (p. 284).

Curling Up Like an Armadillo

Another aspect of proximal defense is the attempt to deal with the problem of terror by doing something that can be rationally expected to minimize one's vulnerability. Thus, part of the typical human's response to awareness of his or her ultimate mortality is behavior aimed at forestalling death as much as possible. One obvious example is the widespread tendency to avoid flying. Shunning large crowds; steering clear of national monuments, theme parks, and major internationally televised sporting events (e.g., the Superbowl and the Olympics); and buying latex gloves and gas masks, weapons, and other protective devices are other examples of proximal defense, in which people try to minimize their vulnerability by essentially attempting to outwit the terrorists and avoid becoming fodder for their next attacks.

The massive investigation and hunt for the perpetrators of the 9/11 attacks and the attempts to increase the security of airports, post offices, and government buildings can also be thought of as proximal defensive strategies for ensuring our safety. So, too, can the military actions against the Taliban and other governments that support terrorism. From a TMT perspective, actively thinking about the terrorist attacks would be expected to instigate a broad array of strategies aimed at securing our safety from further atrocities of this type. Certainly the vast majority of Americans and people the world over were doing a great deal of active thinking about the terrorist attacks in the days and weeks after 9/11—to say that the terrorists had gotten our attention is a gross understatement. Unfortunately, some of these strategies, like confiscating nail clippers at airports and searching women's handbags at high school basketball games, amount to inconvenient wastes of time and energy, contributing at best to an illusion of safety. Others may actually impinge on us in more significant ways.

The Undermining of Freedom

Some of the most tragic victims of the terrorist attacks may be the many freedoms that we Americans had come to take for granted in our daily lives. We have it pretty good here, compared with most other places in the world. For the most part, we are able to come and go as we please, with little interference from outside authorities charged with keeping the public safe. Unfortunately, the relative openness and freedom of American society were part of what made us so vulnerable to the terrorist attacks. In a free society, it is relatively easy for people to come and go, and to obtain, transport, and use items that could be used to produce horrific tragedies. One consequence of the recent terrorist attacks is that government agencies are likely to now take a much more active and intrusive role in monitoring our movements in an effort to avert similar tragedies in the future.

Security at airports has been increased massively. Long lines, hand searches of luggage, x-ray inspection of packages, chemical screening of shoes, and bodily pat downs are now an accepted part of air travel. The U.S. Congress acted quickly to heighten the power of law enforcement authorities to conduct clandestine observations, including wiretaps, searches, and other potential invasions of our privacy. Random searches of cars, monitoring of information on the Internet, and more careful scrutiny of foreign visitors are other examples of the steps being taken or proposed to increase our safety and avert the potential for future attacks.

As might be expected, this increase in security and potential reduction in freedoms has sparked a great deal of debate. Some have pointed out that cutting back on the freedoms and privacy that we are accustomed to enjoying is a particularly pernicious form of giving in to the terrorists. Others have countered that our most precious freedom is the freedom to live, and that to ensure this freedom, sacrifices must be made. As in most cases, opinions on this issue are for the most part readily predicted by preexisting ideological preferences that are exaggerated and brought into clearer focus by the awakening of terror that we are all facing these days. Recall the many studies discussed in the previous chapters in which reminders of death led to an exaggeration of preexisting ideological preferences and attitudes.

The majority of Americans seem to be willing to sacrifice at least some freedom and convenience for the sake of safety. People have been remarkably good humored about the longer waits at airport checkpoints and other inconveniences resulting from the heightened watchfulness for signs of new attacks. And public opinion polls reveal that most Americans say they are willing to sacrifice some freedoms in order to beef up security against potential future attacks. For example, in a mid-December 2001 *New York Times*/CBS News Poll (reported by Toner & Elder, 2001), 80% of the American public was in favor of indefinite detention for noncitizens who threatened national security; 70% favored government monitoring of conversations between suspected terrorists and their lawyers; 64% favored giving the president the authority to change rights guaranteed by the Constitution—all of which are tactics that most Americans would surely have balked at before 9/11.

This willingness to sacrifice freedom for the sake of security is interesting in light of the views of Otto Rank, Erich Fromm, Ernest Becker, and many others, who have argued that freedom and security are typically at odds with each other. We have argued elsewhere (Pyszczynski, Greenberg, & Goldenberg, in press) that the same intellectual abilities that allowed our species to become relatively free from reliance on biologically prewired fixed-response patterns create the potential for existential terror, which, in turn, compulsively drives us to live up to internalized cultural values to cope with that potential for terror. The sophistication of our human intellectual capacities makes it possible for us to become relatively self-determined in our actions, but the potential for terror engendered by this intelligence leads us to buy into cultural beliefs and strive to live up to cultural values that severely limit this potential for freedom. Similarly, during the early years of development, the child learns to bring his or her intrinsic impulses under the control of internalized representations of the parents'—and ultimately the culture's—standards of value in exchange for the protection from fear that the parents' love and protection provide. Perhaps it is no surprise, then, that American adults now seem willing to sacrifice freedoms as a means of increasing their safety. After all, if one is not safe, how much freedom can one really have?

One problem, however, with these potentially freedom-threatening safety measures is that they will never be enough to make us completely safe. With domestic acts of terrorism, people do not know who their enemies are until after they attack, and even then, people are often unsure. Sometimes all investigators can do is hope some group publicly takes "credit" for the attack. Terrorists do not walk around American cities wearing turbans, carrying pictures of Osama bin Laden, or chanting slogans such as "Death to the Americans." The success of their efforts depends on their clandestine nature and their knowledge and use of whatever systems we have in place—both we and they know that—and thus we really do not know from whom or where the next attack might be coming.

This uncertainty leaves us in a situation in which, in spite of our best efforts to protect ourselves, we cannot really feel safe or secure. The inscrutable nature of the problem of terror means that vague feelings of vulnerability are likely to linger on the fringes of consciousness, even when we are not actively thinking about death. And it is under precisely these circumstances, heightened implicit death accessibility, that distal worldview defenses are instigated. It is to such defensive reactions that we now turn.

DISTAL REACTIONS TO 9/11

Intensifying the Quest for Meaning and Value

The events of 9/11 clearly undermined the integrity and consequent anxiety-buffering qualities of the cultural worldviews of many Americans and others around the world. How could something like this happen? What does it mean when a few semiliterate malcontents with box cutters can summarily eliminate thousands of people in the strongest, most prosperous and secure country in the world?

Not surprisingly perhaps, people flocked to churches, synagogues, and mosques, seeking answers and trying to restore a sense of meaning and value in a world seemingly gone crazy. A September 21 Gallup Poll found the highest level of church attendance in America since the 1950s. Similar spikes in attendance at formal religious services were recorded in Canada,

100   *IN THE WAKE OF 9/11: THE PSYCHOLOGY OF TERROR*

England, and Australia. And the largest increases in attendees were atheists. Atheists attending religious services tripled between August and November (Lampman, 2001).

Bible sales flourished: Sales increased 45% since 9/11, according to The American Bible Society (Rice, 2001). HarperCollins sold retailers 750,000 copies of *Where Is God When It Hurts?*—over 100,000 more than the book had sold since its original publication in 1978; and sales were brisk for titles such as *When Bad Things Happen to Good People*, *Living a Life That Matters*, and *The Places That Scare You: A Guide to Fearlessness in Difficult Times* (Beyette, 2001). Internet religion also thrived. According to a Pew Internet and American Life Project survey (reported in Lampman, 2001), 28 million Americans (25% of Internet users) visited religious and spiritual Web sites, a 50% increase from a year ago.

In sum, a vast number of Americans and others around the world turned to organized religion (in its traditional and more contemporary forms) as an initial reaction to the traumatic events of 9/11 and thereafter. However, by late December 2001, church and synagogue attendance had generally returned to predisaster levels (for example, see Hoover, 2001; Meineke, 2001), perhaps because of the coincident or subsequent engagement of other distal defensive reactions articulated later.

Intensifying Patriotism and Nationalistic Sentiment

At the same time they sought meaning and security in religious outlets, Americans quickly strove to re-establish their damaged sense of security by reaffirming their faith in the American way of life. Flags literally flew off the shelves and appeared everywhere, on cars, buildings, people's T-shirts, and even their skin in the form of tattoos. Banners, posters, T-shirts, and billboards proclaiming "United we stand," "Proud to be an American," and "God Bless America" seemed to appear everywhere. Corporate logos were quickly retooled in patriotic colors of red, white, and blue. People and groups from all sections of society began to proclaim their solidarity with the victims and their families. Lee Greenwood's hymn to American patriotism, "Proud to Be an American" and Aaron Tippin's "You've Got to Stand for Something" were heard on the airwaves once again, harking back to their dramatic popularity during the Persian Gulf War. Country rock star Charlie Daniels scored a comeback hit with his newly penned tune, "This Ain't No Rag, It's a Flag" (Daniels, 2001):[1]

---

[1]Kienzle (2001) reports that war songs have been a popular American tradition since our country's inception and especially in the 20th century. World War II favorites included "Cowards Over Pearl Harbor," "Get Your Gun and Come Along (We're Fixin' to Kill a Skunk)," "We're Gonna Have to Slap the Dirty Little Jap," and "When the Atom Bomb Fell." The Cold War featured ditties such as "Atomic Power" and "When the Hell Bomb Falls" and celebrated the death of Joseph Stalin with "Stalin Kicked the Bucket."

This ain't no rag, it's a flag
And we don't wear it on our heads . . .
You can crawl back in your hole
You dirty little mole . . .
We're going to hunt you down like a mad dog hound.

More traditional patriotic songs, like "God Bless America," "America the Beautiful," and "The Star-Spangled Banner" were heard everywhere, from children's school rooms to quickly organized benefit concerts to between-innings breaks of the World Series baseball games. The Franklin Mint quickly issued a commemorative George W. Bush coin, with the president depicted in front of a large American flag.

This upsurge in patriotism was also exemplified by the unprecedented levels of support for the government's response to the current crisis. Some public opinion polls showed an unprecedented 94% approval rating for President Bush and his handling of the crisis (Morin & Deane, 2001). The large majority of Americans supported the bombing of Afghanistan, increased security measures at airports, and increased flexibility on the part of police and intelligence agencies in responding to suspected terrorists. Americans seemed to be taking the "United We Stand" slogan seriously and exhibiting higher levels of consensual support for government policies than had been seen in decades.

The increase in patriotism produced by the terrorist attacks was so pervasive that even died-in-the-wool liberals, who previously tended to eschew such blatant displays of their sentiments toward the United States, began unabashedly proclaiming their pride in America. For example, Madonna took the stage at a concert in Los Angeles on 9/14/01 in an American-flag skirt and declared, "God bless America" (Appleford et al., 2001).

Suppressing Dissent

Although the overwhelming majority of Americans supported the various ways in which the government responded to the terrorist attacks, this is certainly not true of everyone. Some questioned the wisdom of our attacks on the Taliban in Afghanistan, arguing that this is likely to further tarnish our image in the Middle East and thus inspire more attacks against the United States and our interests abroad. Others raised concern about harming innocent Afghani civilians, who suffered through the recent war with the Soviet Union and might be best considered additional victims of the Taliban's brutal policies and thus worthy of our protection rather than attack. Some objected to the use of military force under any circumstances, arguing that violence begets violence and that nothing good could possibly result from further bloodshed. Some also pointed to a possible role of the U.S. policy of supporting Islamic fundamentalism in Afghanistan and other places when this helped us in our broader fight against communism in previous decades. On other fronts, many expressed concern about the curtailing of civil liberties as a result of the effort to root out terrorists, bring them to justice, and prevent further attacks. Thus although there was a remarkable level of consensus for current government policies in response to the 9/11 disaster, not every American agreed with these policies.[2]

Our research has shown that when thoughts of death are salient, people generally become less tolerant and more hostile toward those with diverging views. In dozens of experiments, mortality salience has been shown to lead to more negative evaluations of those with different political orientations and attitudes toward a diverse array of subjects. With an issue as central to our worldview and current well-being as how to deal with terrorism, the effects of existential concerns on reactions to dissenters are likely to be especially dramatic.

Consistent with this notion, those who have spoken out against government policies, or even criticized them in minor ways, have become targets of considerable hostility in recent months. Politicians and other public figures who articulated reasons why people in poor Islamic countries might have reason to feel hostile toward the United States (e.g., the bombing of Iraq, presence of U.S. military in locations considered holy by Muslims, U.S. support of wealthy Middle Eastern dictators) received mounds of hate mail peppered with death threats; government officials developed a list of academics who propagated such ideas—imagine dangerous history professors on the loose! When Bill Maher, host of the popular television program *Politically Incorrect*, (on 9/17) said, "We have been the cowards, lobbing cruise missiles from 2,000 miles away. That's cowardly. Staying in the airplane when it hits the building—say what you want about that, it's not cowardly," he came under intense pressure from his network to recant his statements, and local station affiliates throughout the nation threatened to (and seven stations did) stop airing his program. Although the airing of politically

---

[2]See, for example, Barbara Kingsolver's essay "No Glory in Unjust War on the Weak," in which she wrote on 10/14/01:

> I cannot find the glory in this day. When I picked up the newspaper and saw "America Strikes Back!" blazed boastfully across it in letters I swear were 10 inches tall . . . my heart sank. We've answered one terrorist act with another, raining death on the most war-scarred, terrified populace that ever crept to a doorway and looked out. The small plastic boxes of food we also dropped are a travesty. It is reported that these are untouched, of course—Afghanis have spent their lives learning terror of anything hurled at them from the sky. Meanwhile, the genuine food aid on which so many depended for survival has been halted by the war. We've killed whoever was too poor or crippled to flee, plus four humanitarian aid workers who coordinated the removal of land mines from the beleaguered Afghan soil. . . . We need to take a moment's time out to review the monstrous waste of an endless cycle of retaliation. The biggest weapons don't win this one, guys. When there are people on Earth willing to give up their lives in hatred and use our own domestic airplanes as bombs, it's clear that we can't out-technologize them. You can't beat cancer by killing every cell in the body—or you could, I guess, but the point would be lost. This is a war of who can hate the most. There is no limit to that escalation. It will only end when we have the guts to say it really doesn't matter who started it, and begin to try and understand, then alter the forces that generate hatred.

One need not agree entirely with Kingsolver's argument to endorse her conclusion that we need to try to understand and alter the forces that create hatred, and this is a matter we will return to later in this volume.

unpopular attitudes—the basic premise of Maher's program—was considered amusing entertainment before 9/11, the terrorist attacks apparently wiped the smiles off many viewers' faces when alternative views of the issues surrounding these events were raised. Australian boxer Anthony Mundine was stripped of his world ranking by the U.S.-based World Boxing Council after expressing his opinion that America brought the 9/11 attacks on itself (Wellington Newspapers Limited, 2001). A personal friend of one of the authors, who is generally very liberal minded and pacifist oriented but who supports the current war effort, reported nearly coming to blows with a close friend because he could not understand how this person could believe that a pacifist approach to the crisis might possibly be useful.

TMT suggests that hostility toward those with opinions and values divergent from one's own occurs because our attitudes and values are part of the worldview that provides security in the face of existential fear. The mere existence of different points of view raises the possibility that one's own views might be wrong or misguided. To avoid consciously experiencing the sense that their own opinions might be wrong, people disparage the views of the divergent others by questioning their intelligence, knowledge, integrity, or motives. If those who disagree with us are stupid or biased, it enables us to feel secure in the belief that our own opinions are the ones that follow most logically and reasonably from the true state of the world. Thus in times of crisis, dissent is likely to be dealt with harshly.

We have recently gathered experimental evidence that people's existential fears play a role specifically in Americans' reactions to opinions about 9/11. One month after the attacks, Mark Landau and we (Landau, Pyszczynski, Greenberg, & Solomon, 2002) found that reminders of death led American college students, even those who generally feel out of step with the American worldview, to respond more negatively toward a person who suggested that the terrorists had legitimized reasons for doing what they did.

Intensifying Bigotry

People who are merely different are also likely to be dealt with harshly as a result of heightened concerns about mortality. A large body of research (presented in chapter 4) has shown that mortality salience leads to increased prejudice, stereotyping, and bigotry—presumably because the mere existence of those who are different from us is inherently threatening in that it calls into question the absolute validity of our own death-transcending cultural worldview. If there is a literally correct set of beliefs about how the world works and values for how to best act in that world, the existence of those with beliefs and values different from our own implies that someone must be wrong. Given the vital terror management function that our beliefs and values serve for us, you can bet that people will much prefer seeing the other people as wrong and misguided to acknowledging that their own views may be off the mark. Thus, when people are in strong need of protection from anxiety, as has been shown to be the case when they have been reminded of their mortality, their tendencies to stereotype and reject those who are different from themselves are likely to be exaggerated.

Sadly, there is abundant evidence of increased stereotyping, prejudice, and bigotry in the aftermath of the 9/11 terrorist attacks. Many Arab Americans and visitors from Middle Eastern countries have experienced an increased sense of rejection and discrimination in the wake of the bombings. For example (Jacoby, 2001), a mosque in Texas was firebombed, speeding cars rammed mosques in Indiana and Ohio, and death threats were phoned in to the Islamic Center of New England. A New York man tried to run over a Muslim woman in his car, and two Muslim women were beaten at an Illinois college. Not surprisingly, many Islamic Americans reported being afraid to go out on the streets after 9/11, fearful of possibly violent reprisals for the attacks even though they had nothing to do with them. Some have decided that it is simply too dangerous to remain in the United States in the wake of the bombings. Many colleges across the nation have witnessed a drop in enrollment of students of Arabic descent. The American University in Lebanon decided to extend enrollment deadlines to accommodate the many Arab students who have decided to return to places closer to their homelands to avoid the threat of possible persecution in the United States.

This increase in hostility is not limited to targeting people from Arab countries— apparently anyone with darker than average (for Americans) skin who might even remotely resemble an Arab seems to be at risk. People of Hispanic, Chicano, and Native American heritage have all been reported as victims of violence or intimidation in the weeks following the terrorist attacks. One tragic example referred to back in chapter 1 was the shooting of an Indian Sikh gas station owner in Mesa, Arizona. Balbir Singh Sodhi was shot and killed simply because he happened to have dark skin and a beard and was wearing a turban. This was ironic as well as tragic in that the Sikhs of India have long been despised enemies of the Muslims of Pakistan. Fear is an extremely primitive emotion, and very superficial forms of resemblance to the object of people's fear and hostility can be enough to turn one into a target.

Sometimes the fear, anger, and desperate need for understanding resulting from heightened accessibility of death thoughts are directed toward those with no obvious similarities to the perpetrators of the attacks. Recall that research has demonstrated that mortality salience produces especially punitive reactions to moral transgressions—for example, our study in which municipal court judges assigned far greater penalties to an alleged prostitute after a brief reminder of their own deaths (an effect subsequently consistently replicated by other independent researchers). Extrapolating from this research, Donald Judges (1999) argued that excessively punitive reactions to moral transgressions resulting from mortality salience are apt to be especially common in capital cases:

American capital punishment is largely a nonconscious, symbolic defense against the terror that accompanies the awareness of human mortality. This proposition is based on terror management theory's link between fear of death awareness and several phenomena that are relevant to capital punishment: (1) hyperpunitiveness, (2) aggression, and (3) authoritarianism. People tend to increase the level of punishment of and aggression towards values transgressors (e.g., criminals) when an experimental manipulation is imposed (heightened death awareness) that activates the nonconscious defense mechanism of identification with and protection of cultural institutions. (p. 6)

Judges then hypothesized that death sentences for capital crimes have been and will be more common at historical moments when death is especially salient (e.g., wars and economic and political upheaval). Accordingly, we would expect draconian sentences handed out to defendants in criminal proceedings in the near future quite beyond what might be warranted by the nature of the crimes themselves, as compensatory defensive responses to mortality salience. Indeed, over the years, we have been consulted by attorneys a number of times about the impact of mortality salience on juror decision making.

Beyond alleged criminal activities, simply being different or representing divergent values or lifestyles may be enough to incur the wrath of death-denying bigotry. In an interview on *The 700 Club* shortly after 9/11, popular right-wing American evangelist Jerry Falwell declared that we were victimized by these attacks because God was apparently angry with us for deviating from his wishes (Harris, 2001). Said Falwell:

God continues to lift the curtain and allow the enemies of America to give us probably what we deserved. . . the abortionists have got to bear some burden for this because God will not be mocked. And when we destroy 40 million little innocent babies, we make God mad. I really believe that the pagans, and the abortionists, and the feminists, and the gays and the lesbians who are actively trying to make that an alternative lifestyle, the ACLU, People for the American Way—all of them who have tried to secularize America—I point the finger in their face and say, "You helped this happen." (p. C03)

Falwell's comments illustrate how people are likely to draw on their preexisting attitudes and values in their efforts to find meaning in tragedy. Indeed, many other popular figures readily used the tragic events of 9/11 as a jumping off point to espouse their long-standing ideologies. Falwell's comments also show that religiously rationalized bigotry and zealotry are not unique to Islam or any particular denomination. Throughout the history of our species, leaders have used their religious beliefs to justify all sorts of heinous actions and statements. We will have more to say on this topic later in this volume, when we examine the psychological forces that likely lead to terrorist acts and other forms of violence in the name of God.

An Antidote: Calling for Tolerance

Of course, this upswing in bigotry and ethnically directed prejudice and violence reflects the actions of a small minority of Americans. Many others have been outspoken in their calls for increased tolerance and acceptance of those with different religious and ethnic backgrounds. President Bush was exceedingly clear in his September 20, 2001, speech to the nation, that the current crisis and conflict is not with Islam or people of Arab descent and that the perpetrators of the terrorist attacks reflect a minuscule minority of Muslims and Arabs (Jacoby's 2001 report of Bush's remarks):

> President Bush spoke for every decent American when he said that the punks who "take out their anger" on Muslims and Arabs "represent the worst of humankind, and they should be ashamed of that kind of behavior." He made a point of visiting the mosque at the Islamic Center of Washington to drive home the message that attacks on innocent Muslim and Arab-Americans are contemptible, then repeated that message in his speech to Congress. (p. D7)

Simultaneously, church and political leaders throughout the nation called for increased understanding of the Islamic religion and an embracing of diversity and multiethnicity. Many communities witnessed the rather unusual sight of Christian, Jewish, and Islamic clerics meeting together with congregations of people of various religious and political orientations to discuss the tragedy and ways of coping with it. The important point here is that although some people have responded to the terrorist attacks with bigotry and hatred, many others have responded with heightened efforts to embrace and understand those likely to be the targets of such bigotry.

This divergence of responses to the tragic events of 9/11 highlights the role of the individual's core values in determining how people cope with the fear of death. Studies have shown that although reminders of mortality often do lead to increased prejudice, they can actually lead to decreased prejudice among those who are chronically committed to the value of tolerance or among those for whom the value of tolerance has recently been made salient. Fortunately, tolerance of those who are different is one of the principles on which our nation was founded and is accepted, to greater or lesser extents, by most (but unfortunately not all) Americans.

As TMT proposes and the research on mortality salience and self-esteem striving reviewed in chapter 4 has shown, people respond to the heightened salience of that which they fear by working harder to live up to the standards of value to which they are committed. The complexity here is that people are committed to many values, some of which run into direct conflict with others. Our research suggests that responses to mortality salience are likely to be oriented around recently primed or activated standards and values. The terrorist attacks have certainly made a diverse array of thoughts and values salient. Negative antisocial action is likely to be decreased when our more positive values are brought to the forefront. It also seems likely that bigoted prejudiced action might be decreased or averted if the costs of such action—to self and others—are made salient and values that run counter to such action are widely publicized and disseminated. In this light, we applaud President Bush's clear public advocacy of tolerance and believe that it has helped minimize the amount of aggression against Muslims (and those who resemble them) in this country.

Intensifying Altruistic Tendencies

To manage their terror effectively, people want to fulfill their roles as valued contributors to their worldview. Kindness, generosity, and giving to others are obviously highly valued behaviors in our society; they form core values for virtually all religious and ethical systems. By acting altruistically, people reaffirm their value as kind and generous citizens, thereby enhancing their self-esteem, which is much needed as a basis for security and equanimity in times of crisis. Therefore, reminders of mortality do not just arouse defenses that lead to antisocial action; they also intensify positive prosocial action. Recall the research in chapter 4 in which mortality salience increased positive attitudes and actual contributions to valued charities (Jonas, Schimel, Greenberg, & Pyszczynski, in press).

Given this research, it is not surprising that the most common American response to the terrorist attacks was an outpouring of desire to assist the victims in the World Trade Center and Pentagon. Thousands of policemen, firemen, and others rushed to the assistance of those trapped in the buildings, and hundreds died as a consequence of their brave actions. Emergency and medical personnel of all kinds, steel workers, truck drivers, cooks, and others all pitched in to do what they could to help. People came from all over the country to get directly involved in the rescue effort. One man drove a bulldozer over 1000 miles from Minnesota to New York City to get involved. Many others helped in less direct ways. Americans donated millions of dollars to provide for the victims and reconstruction efforts. Similarly, thousands of Americans donated blood to assist in caring for the victims. At usually deserted hospitals and blood banks, would-be donors encountered waits of 4 or more hours and were sometimes told that more people were available to donate blood than the facility was able to process. Some relief agencies ended up with more food, clothing, and other supplies than they could possibly use (see *Newsweek*, 9/24/01, pp. 18–25). Recent evidence reported to us by fellow social psychologist Louis Penner indicates that volunteerism in the U.S. for charitable causes unrelated to the 9/11 attacks also increased in the two weeks after the attacks, although it gradually returned to normal levels over the subsequent three months (L. Penner, personal communication, June 14, 2002).

In the wake of 9/11, these prosocial actions served to reinforce people's security by providing a sense of self-worth. In addition, such helping was also a way of feeling that one was doing something to help in a situation in which one would otherwise feel helpless and impotent. Most Americans wanted to do something in response to the tragedy, and although most of us could not become directly involved in the rescue attempts at Ground Zero, giving money, blood, or useful goods is one thing almost everyone could do. Helping, whether directly related to 9/11 or not, served to bolster both our self-worth and our faith in the goodness and strength of our American worldview.

Increasing the Need for Heroes

The efforts of those who gave aid on and after 9/11 did not go unrecognized. Police and fire personnel, both in the targeted cities and throughout the country, were hailed as heroes, finally getting some much deserved appreciation for their efforts to keep us safe and help us in times of need. Cities and the national media organized events to honor these brave souls. "Infotainment" television programs like 60 *Minutes* and *Dateline* aired segments celebrating the efforts of these and other helpers. Concerts and other entertainment events were scheduled, in which songs such as David Bowie's "Heroes" and Bette Midler's "Wind Beneath My Wings" were dedicated to the helpers. In general, Americans experienced a newfound appreciation for those who protect them and help them in times of need. Similar reactions to the soldiers who were soon dispatched to fight in the War Against Terrorism also occurred.

Especially poignant was the heroic behavior of the passengers and crew on United Airlines Flight 93, who, led by Todd Beamer, Mark Bingham, Rich Guadagno, and CeeCee Lyles, thwarted the hijackers' (presumed) effort to crash their plane into the White House or the Capitol (Breslau, 2001). Rock star and generally liberal-leaning Neil Young was so moved by a *Newsweek* account of the heroic ordeal—in which after reciting the 23rd Psalm while on the phone with GTE Customer Center supervisor Lisa Jefferson, Beamer initiated the attack on the hijackers by saying, "Are you guys ready? Let's roll"—that he immediately penned, recorded, and released (in a noncommercial fashion) the now famous song "Let's Roll" (Weeks, 2001).

All of these uplifting reactions to heroic behavior are, of course, consistent with the large body of research that has shown that reminders of mortality increase the tendency to admire and reward those who heroically uphold and exemplify cultural values. Mortality salience leads people to view positive social actions as more desirable and to recommend larger monetary rewards for those who do good things for others in spite of the risk to their own well-being. Ernest Becker argued in *The Denial of Death* that identifying with heroes enables us to vicariously lift ourselves above our mortal animal origins and again affirm the value and specialness of humankind. The outpouring of admiration for the heroic helpers can be thought of as exemplifying this tendency to identify with heroes in response to reminders of our own finitude.

How Will Individual Americans React to Terror?

In the preceding sections, we outlined a wide variety of ways in which people responded to being reminded of their vulnerability and ultimate mortality. All of the behavior patterns we have discussed have been documented to occur in response to subtle reminders of mortality in laboratory and field studies. All have also been observed in the months following the terrorist attacks on the World Trade Center and Pentagon. It seems highly likely that at least some of these responses brought on by the 9/11 terrorist attacks were proximal and distal defensive reactions to the reminders of our mortality, heightened sense of vulnerability, and uncertainty about whether the American way of life can protect us. Given this diverse array of responses to terror that have been observed in our research and, more recently, in our daily lives, the following questions emerge: Which of the many possible ways of dealing with their fear will people use? Will people become bigoted or helpful? Will they shift in the direction of patriotism or toward a more extreme version of whatever ideology they had previously espoused?

As most readers of this volume realize, it is extremely difficult to predict how any given individual will react to any specific event. Psychological science provides probabilistic estimates of the likelihood of various responses in large groups of people rather than precise certainty with respect to the behavior of particular individuals. Nonetheless, TMT and research do provide some clues to what factors are likely to affect the behavior of individuals.

Like most contemporary thinking about human behavior, TMT conceptualizes the individual as being influenced by a diverse array of forces. The strength or impact of these forces is likely to be affected by a variety of factors. Research suggests that in cases in which multiple forces are impinging on an individual, his or her behavior is often most affected by whatever force is most salient or attention grabbing at any given point in time. Large bodies of research have shown that particular concerns can be made more likely to influence an individual's behavior by simply bringing them to the person's attention—this is typically referred to as *priming* (Bargh, 1996). It also seems that in a world in which many events compete for the individual's attention, recent, vivid, and unusual events seem to grab more attention than others (Tversky & Kahneman, 1973).

In our own research on terror management processes, our mortality salience manipulations could be thought of as procedures that prime the accessibility of death-related thoughts. Nearly 150 separate studies have now shown that priming death-related thoughts can have a clear and predictable effect on people's behavior. The specific direction that these effects take seems to depend on what other factors are currently salient to the individual. If concerns about a particular attitude are salient when thoughts of death become accessible, people's reactions tend to center on that particular attitude. As noted earlier, Greenberg, Simon, et al. (1992) showed that the typical tendency to derogate someone with beliefs contrary to one's own following mortality salience can be reversed by reminding mortality salient individuals of the value of tolerance of different others. A similar effect occurred for people who generally tend to think often about the value of tolerance.

In addition to attitudes, salient standards of self-evaluation can also play a role. If concerns about one's standing on a particular ego-relevant dimension are salient, people tend to respond by bolstering their sense of value on that dimension. In studies that have directly manipulated competing concerns, it has been shown that whatever concern is brought to the forefront is the one likely to be acted on in response to reminders of one's mortality. For example, Simon, Greenberg, Clement, et al. (1997) led students to believe that they were especially different from most others (deviant) or especially similar to most others (conformist). After being reminded of their mortality, those accused of deviance reported that their attitudes on various issues were very similar to those of most people, whereas those accused of conformity reported that their attitudes were very dissimilar to those of most others. Thus, when mortality is salient, people will try to bolster self-worth by shoring up whatever aspects of self seem deficient at the time. This suggests that people's responses to the death-related thoughts engendered by the recent acts of terrorism are likely to vary with situational factors and individual differences that influence the attitudes, values, and concerns that are salient to a particular individual at the time.

Generally speaking, people have strong needs for validation of their worldviews, for self-esteem, and for close interpersonal contact and support. They are likely to respond especially vigorously to anything that threatens the protection that these psychological entities provide. Thus, the behavioral impact of terrorism-engendered existential concerns on any given individual is likely to be centered on whatever else might be happening in that person's life that impinges on his or her protective structures. Social interactions with others are particularly important influences on the effective functioning of these protective structures. People who provide validation of the person's worldview and self-esteem and who provide warmth, affection, and caring are likely to be especially sought after in times like these; those who challenge his or her worldview or self-esteem, or who treat him or her in a cold or rejecting way, are likely to be responded to more harshly than usual.

Events that occur in the world, which are then reported in the media, are likely to be another important determinant of how people react. In times of fear, people have an intensified need for meaning and understanding. This is why so many people find themselves continually tuned to their televisions, radios, or the Internet to keep up with the latest events. As new events unfold, this will, of course, activate new concerns. Terrorist attacks are intended to create fear and chaos; terrorists seem to have an intuitive understanding of the psychological forces at work here and are able to exploit them in a multitude of ways. Thus the threat of new attacks, information about the spread of anthrax, and news of the impact of our military campaign all are factors that will influence how people act, feel, and think about their lives and the people around them.

To summarize, then, individual differences in attitudes, values, personality styles, and vulnerabilities play a critical role in determining how people respond. And, indeed, the diversity of feelings and values that have been activated by the 9/11 bombings has been enormous, ranging from hatred and murder to compassion and self-sacrifice. As has been shown in many studies, reminders of one's mortality tend to channel people to express long-standing values and behavioral proclivities as well as those momentarily salient. Thus, to predict any one individual's reactions, one would need to know a great deal about the person's worldview and bases of self-worth, as well as the situational forces currently prominent in the person's life. However, the common denominator underlying all such actions is the increased need for safety and psychological security that this horrible reminder of our vulnerability has awakened in us all.

HOW SCARED SHOULD WE BE?

How scared should we really be in the wake of the threat that the terrorists pose? Of course, this is an impossible question to answer. Statistically speaking, an individual's chances of dying in a terrorist attack are infinitesimal in comparison with his or her chances of dying of heart disease, of cancer, or in an auto accident. The number of people who died as a result of the 9/11 attacks pales in comparison with those who die annually from any number of causes. This indisputable fact is not, however, particularly comforting at a time like this for two reasons. First, this perspective reminds us of the precarious condition of our lives—in the best of circumstances, the threat of death is all around us. Second, we feel largely protected from these other threats because of the worldviews in which we have been imbedded all our lives; the terrorist attacks were highly vivid threats that are not readily handled by our existing psychological security structures, especially, as we have continually noted, because they have shaken central aspects of our protective worldview along with reminding us directly of our mortality.

Research is fairly clear in showing that dramatic events that are easy to visualize or imagine are seen as more likely to occur than less vivid but statistically more likely ones (Tversky & Kahneman, 1973). The attacks on the World Trade Center and Pentagon were certainly dramatic, and the ongoing media coverage of these events etched vivid, unforgettable images of exactly how these events unfolded in most Americans' minds. Research suggests that the vivid nature of these events is likely to add to people's sense of vulnerability. Clearly, the vast ongoing media coverage of the terrorism-related events makes it exceedingly easy for all of us to imagine scenarios in which we are the victims of terrorism.

Some people live in circumstances that make them especially likely to feel vulnerable. Those living in New York City, Washington, DC, or other large metropolitan areas; those who fly frequently; those who work for the postal service or other agencies involved in the delivery of the mail; and those in many other professions that have been directly involved in the attacks are likely to feel particularly at risk. The fact is that such individuals probably are at greater risk than those living in less populated areas or those working in many other professions. And, of course, those who actually lost loved ones are inevitably the people most hurt by the events. Family members, romantic partners, and friends are important contributors to our psychological security as well as to our capacity to enjoy our lives. Imagine the blow to a small child of losing a parent.

In sum, the events of 9/11 have rendered each of us, like members of Captain Ahab's whaling crew, "caught in the swift, sudden turn of death," and in so doing, forced us all to confront "the silent, subtle, ever-present perils of life." Each of us surely resorted to a complex combination of proximal and distal defenses to restore our sense of value in a world of meaning. Undoubtedly, some of us have coped more successfully than others, and this has much to do with how extensively people's terror management structures were damaged by the losses caused by the events and by the pre-event strength of those structures as well. Psychologists and other mental health care professionals have already encountered many psychological casualties of 9/11. In chapter 6, we discuss some of the types of vulnerabilities that contribute to such difficulties in coping, and then explain how the attacks may have created or exacerbated specific forms of psychological disorder. We will also provide suggestions for improved coping.

6

MANAGING THE TERROR

While the events of Sept. 11 have affected all of us adversely, some people who are mentally ill carry an even extra burden . . . some psychotic patients sadly feel they may have somehow been responsible for 9/11. The disaster . . . has exacerbated the illness of some people with schizophrenia . . . in patients who were on the road to recovery from a bout of depression, the event plunged them back into a depression. . . . Even people who previously suffered no mental stresses are now showing signs.
　　　　　　　—Marilyn Linton, "Feeling Sad? You're Not Alone;
　　　　　Mental Stress After Sept. 11 Has Many People Depressed"
　　　　　　　　　　　　　　　　　　(October 28, 2001, p. 51)

Americans and others around the world were terribly shaken by the tragedy of 9/11. In the previous chapter, we used terror management theory (TMT) to provide an explanation of general reactions to the attacks. In a nutshell, we proposed that dramatic reminders of the fragile nature of human existence and the inevitability of (an always potentially impending) death engendered an especially strong need for the meaning and sense of personal value typically provided by cultural worldviews. And this need was exponentially intensified when the concrete manifestations of the cultural beliefs and values that typically provide the individual with such protection, that is, the World Trade Center and the Pentagon, were concurrently attacked. The fact that the terrorists used our own airplanes as weapons of mass destruction seriously damaged the sense of safety and security previously taken for granted by most Americans, resulting in heightened levels of explicit and implicit accessibility of death-related thoughts. Most people reacted with a host of proximal (e.g., taking effective instrumental actions to minimize danger; willingness to sacrifice personal freedom; taking refuge in distractions such as drinking, watching television, or shopping) and distal (e.g., quests for meaning and value; heightened patriotism; hostility toward outgroup members; altruistic activities; and attraction to heroes)

115

defenses. In so doing, many people have already recovered sufficient psychological equanimity to function adequately on a daily basis.

But not everyone was so lucky; 9/11 had catastrophic psychological consequences for some people with preexisting psychological difficulties, and the disaster has created problems for others who were apparently fine before the tragedy. In this chapter, we consider how inadequate means of coping with existential fears can lead to various sorts of psychopathology and how the events of 9/11 have affected those with previously existing or newly acquired mental illnesses. We also examine how children, who are still in the process of developing their protective "shields" of culturally constructed meaning and value, are likely to have been affected. Finally, we offer a series of suggestions for how psychologists, educators, and other human service professionals might help people cope with the psychic fallout of 9/11 and similar catastrophes we may have to face in the future.

Note that we do not focus on the effects on those adults and children who actually lost loved ones in the attacks. There is already a voluminous literature on effective and dysfunctional coping with personal loss, a topic that has received numerous book length treatments. We would suggest that readers interested in dealing specifically with these tragic consequences of the attacks pursue this literature (e.g., Janoff-Bulman, 1992; Mikulincer & Florian, 1996; Snyder, 2000).

PSYCHOPATHOLOGY AS TERROR MISMANAGEMENT

As Irvin Yalom has pointed out in his book *Existential Psychotherapy* (1980):

> All individuals are confronted with death anxiety; most develop adaptive coping modes—modes that consist of denial-based strategies such as suppression, repression, displacement, belief in personal omnipotence, acceptance of socially sanctioned religious beliefs that "detoxify" death, or personal efforts to overcome death through a wide variety of strategies that aim at achieving symbolic immortality. Either because of extraordinary stress or because of an inadequacy of available defensive strategies, the individual who enters the realm called "patienthood" has found insufficient the universal modes of dealing with death fear and has been driven to extreme modes of defense. These defensive maneuvers, often clumsy modes of dealing with terror, constitute the presenting clinical picture. (pp. 110–111)

The notion that mental illness "is the result of ineffective modes of death transcendence" (Yalom, 1980, p. 28), or "terror mismanagement," (Strachan, Pyszczynski, Greenberg, & Solomon, 2002) has a long history, starting with existential philosophers (e.g., Soren Kierkegaard), psychodynamic theorists (e.g., Otto Rank, Ernest Becker, and Robert Jay Lifton), and practicing psychotherapists (e.g., Victor Frankl, Rollo May, and Irvin Yalom). From this perspective, "average" well-adapted persons are shielded from death anxiety by securely embedding themselves in a culturally constructed conception of reality that provides meaning and by successfully inhabiting social roles and satisfying the standards of value associated with them.

However, some people, *through no fault of their own*, by virtue of either specific biochemical deficiencies or excesses due to genetics, or extreme stresses due to dysfunctional family environments, negative life events, or extreme material deprivation, are unable to quell the rumbling panic engendered by the knowledge of death through the traditional social, shared means of the "average" well-adapted members of their culture. Unable to infuse their lives with meaning and value adequately, they consequently react to existential concerns by adopting dysfunctional patterns of thought and behavior, rendering them victims of mental health problems.

To the extent that this is true, concerns about mortality should be evident in all forms of psychopathology.[1] Accordingly, we briefly describe some major categories of mental illness to explicate the role of mortality concerns in each of them. Along the way, we describe some of our empirical research in support of this analysis and then consider the implications of these notions for therapeutic interventions to minimize the psychological consequences of 9/11.

Schizophrenia

Perhaps the most striking form of psychopathology is schizophrenia. From an existential psychodynamic perspective, the schizophrenic, rather than being securely embedded in his or her own body and the culturally constructed universe shared by those around them, wards off the otherwise unbearable burden of perpetual anxiety by, in Becker's (1973, p. 218) words, "the fantastic ideational system that he fabricates for his own salvation. His feelings of magical omnipotence and immortality are a reaction to the terror of death. . . ." In other words, the schizophrenic literally creates his or her own private universe: (a) unencumbered by bodily demands, "the person may feel out of time, out of space—free floating and *bodiless*" (British Columbia

---

[1]At the risk of being redundant, it is important to note that our assertion that concerns about mortality are common to all forms of psychopathology is not at odds with the notion that specific forms of psychopathology have different inherited or biochemical or social psychological, cultural, or behavioral underpinnings that, in turn, render them differentially responsive to different forms of treatment. What we are claiming is that concerns about death common to all human beings are especially prominent (not consciously, of course) and play a role in the etiology or symptoms of all forms of mental illness—and that recognizing this fact may have practical implications for effective therapeutic intervention.

Schizophrenia Society, 6th ed., January 2000)—the breathing, bleeding, defecating, fornicating body being a perpetual reminder of vulnerability and death; and (b) typically featuring himself or herself as the central heroic character in an immortal position of unlimited power: "They may have grandiose delusions or think they are all-powerful, capable of anything, and invulnerable to danger. They may also have a strong religious drive, or believe they have a personal mission to right the wrongs of the world" (British Columbia Schizophrenia Society, 6th ed., January 2000).

It is not surprising, then, that most schizophrenics vacillate between bouts of overwhelming terror associated with the belief that they are being pursued and persecuted by hostile forces, and rousing displays of power on their part to thwart them. For example, here are some public Internet postings of schizophrenics' delusions and hallucinations from the guest area of http://www.schizophrenia.com. As an anonymous writer (12/98) states:

> When I was psychotic, the main delusion I had was that someone was trying to kill me. I started thinking that it was the mafia, and then everyone I saw on the street became suspicious characters and I managed to work them into my delusions. Pretty soon everyone was out to get me. I wanted to go the police, but thankfully my mother got me to a hospital first. Once in the hospital, any new patient that arrived on the ward, I thought they had been sent there to come and kill me in my sleep.

The mother of D., age 14 (2/99), wrote the following:

> He jumped on a moving train, because all he had in his mind was to get to Oklahoma where his cousin lives. The train people realized that he was on top of a coal car and stopped and told him to run before they called the police. . . . He jumped into the river and in his mind he was going to swim to Oklahoma to see his cousin. He realized the water was too cold, so he got out and took off all his clothes except his boxer shorts and started walking towards a factory. At the factory a security guard called the police and they picked him up. In the police station after they called me, he was talking about the devil made him do it. He said that he had stopped the train with his hand, because he was the son of God. . . . In the hospital . . . one day he thought Roseanne was talking to him through the television. He kept looking at the sun and said that he was getting power from the sun. He thought God was the sun, so he sat staring at the sun a lot of the time.

Eileen (9/99) provides the following account:

> Most of my delusions were paranoid and involved the CIA. . . . I became convinced that I could spot an agent just by looking at him. I was convinced that I was in grave danger because of this "ability" and spent as little time as possible outside my apartment. During the 1980s, I was also extremely paranoid about anyone who was Russian and once dropped a class because my professor was Russian and my nerves could

not stand an entire semester with someone who would surely attempt to recruit me into the KGB. The fact that I had no discernible skills of interest to the KGB did not seem to occur to me at the time.

Schizophrenics are thus, from a "terror mismanagement" perspective, especially prone to devastating terror of death that impels them to construct an imaginary florid idiosyncratic universe in which they are protected from death by virtue of their superhuman powers or close connection to those in possession of such powers.

Phobias and Obsessive–Compulsive Behaviors

An anonymous writer (8/00) supplies the following description on http://www.schizophrenia.com:

> I have recurring fears that someone has stolen my license plate off my car. When this happens I am compelled to check the situation. If I don't check it immediately, I worry until I get around to it. Sometimes, if I can't get to it right away, I find myself in the grasp of a terrible panic attack. There are times, also, when checking it once is not enough. I have had to get out of bed in the middle of the night and cut short shopping excursions because of this. The main fear is that "someone" has taken my tag and blamed me for some hideous crime and told the police that I've removed my tag from my car so no one could report it. Then the police see my car without the tag, and assume the tip is for real. . . . The police, thinking I am a dangerous criminal then have to shoot me. I have to make sure that tag stays on my car.

If schizophrenics combat death anxiety by constructing a vast universe and inflating themselves to superhuman proportions at the center of it, then phobic and obsessive–compulsive individuals assuage the same terror by shrinking their worlds to microscopic and hence manageable proportions. For the phobic individual, potentially overwhelming fear of death, an inescapable abstraction, is converted into fear of something tangible and controllable, for example, spiders, heights, germs, or even license plate theft. For the obsessed, constant preoccupation with recurring thoughts of circumscribed fears maintains focus on potentially controllable threats, thereby averting contemplation of the much larger problem. Compulsive behaviors are, in turn, magic rituals (Freud called them private religions) to stifle death anxiety: the exact performance of a generally mundane, albeit often elaborate, sequence of activities that ensures safety to its practitioners.

But how do we know that concerns about mortality underlie (or exacerbate the symptoms of) schizophrenia, phobias, and obsessive–compulsive behaviors? We did not feel comfortable conducting impactful empirical research with schizophrenics, and we did not have any direct access to such populations. However, in theory, we could have asked schizophrenics to think about death or primed thoughts of death subliminally and then determined whether beliefs of persecution by imagined enemies and consequent delusions of omniscient power and triumph over such evil resulted.

We were, however, recently able to conduct experiments to examine the role of mortality salience on phobic and obsessive–compulsive behaviors. Strachan et al. (2001) investigated the effects of inducing people with phobias and obsessive–compulsive tendencies to contemplate their mortality before exposing them to the objects they fear. In the first study, individuals who were diagnosed with a specific phobia of spiders (via the Specific Phobia portion of the Structured Clinical Interview for *Diagnostic and Statistical Manual of Mental Disorders*, 4th ed. [*DSM-IV*], American Psychiatric Association, 1994; First, Spitzer, Gibbon, & Williams, 1995). Only those who met full *DSM-IV* diagnostic criteria for specific phobia were included in the study. These obsessive–compulsive individuals and control participants with no signs of this disorder were asked open ended questions about either their own death or a neutral topic. They were then exposed to pictures of spiders on a computer screen. Spider-phobic individuals responded to mortality salience by spending less time viewing the pictures of spiders (relative to nonthreatening neutral pictures) and by rating the spiders in the pictures as more dangerous and more likely to attack a human. Nonphobic individuals showed no effect of mortality salience on their response to the spider pictures. Thus, the spider-phobic participants responded to reminders of their mortality by showing even more fear than usual of their phobic object.

In a second study, college students who scored high or low on the Contamination Obsessions and Washing Compulsions (COWC) subscale of the Padua Inventory-Washington State University Revision (PI-WSUR; Burns, Keortge, Formea, & Sternberger, 1996), a measure of obsessive–compulsive tendencies, were induced to think about either their own death or another negative topic (dental pain). Then, under the guise of preparing them for physiological recording, we had their fingers smeared with a gooey electrode paste. When later given the opportunity to wash their hands to remove the electrode paste, the obsessive–compulsive participants who were reminded of their mortality spent more time washing their hands and used more water; nonobsessive–compulsive participants were unaffected by the mortality salience induction. These findings are consistent with the notion that phobic and obsessive–compulsive individuals transform potentially overwhelming anxiety about death into specific and, hence, controllable fears and obsessive–compulsive activities, respectively. In so doing, they "manage" terror somewhat, but this defensive death-denying shrinking of life to an avoidance of spiders or washing of hands is ultimately limiting and unsatisfying. That is why Yalom describes mental illness as clumsy death denial. When people are having difficulty managing their fears with the more typical modes of finding meaning in life and value in themselves, they are likely to focus their largely unconscious existential fears on other, more manageable and ultimately less threatening objects. Focusing their existential fears on relatively trivial problems that can be relatively easily avoided enables people to avoid confrontation with the very real and entirely uncontrollable problem of the inevitability of death. To paraphrase Yalom, it is better to be afraid of *some* thing than to be terrified of *no* thing.

Neuroticism

Although most "normal" people are able to live happy, productive, and relatively anxiety-free lives in spite of their awareness of the fragile and transient nature of human existence, others are not so lucky. These unfortunate souls face their daily lives with fear, anxiety, and a host of other unpleasant emotions (and concurrent lack of many positive emotions) that rob them of the capacity to enjoy their lives, their work, and their relationships with others. Many psychologists refer to this tendency to experience high levels of fear and anxiety in one's daily life as *neuroticism.* Theorists from many different theoretical orientations view neuroticism as a central dimension of personality. It is one of the "Big Five" personality dimensions (Costa & McCrae, 1985) and is one of the three core factors thought to underlie personality by Hans Eysenck (1952). And following a meta-analysis of 137 distinct personality constructs as correlates of subjective well-being, DeNeve and Cooper (1998, p. 197) concluded that level of neuroticism was the "strongest predictor of life satisfaction, happiness, and negative affect."

Although there is a great deal of debate about the origins of neurotic personality tendencies, most contemporary personality theorists agree that neuroticism reflects a stable and pervasive (and at least partially inherited) predisposition toward irritability or emotional responsiveness to aversive events (Watson & Clark, 1984). Granting that inherited differences in sensitivity to stimulation plays an important role in the development of neuroticism, a terror management view of neuroticism focuses on the neurotic's inability to achieve the sense of meaning and personal value necessary to keep core fears under control. Consistent with this notion, Mahoney and Quick (2000) found a positive correlation between neuroticism and alienation from mainstream cultural beliefs (assessed by the Manifest Alienation Measure, Gould, 1969). Pearson and Sheffield (1974) found neuroticism (as assessed by the Eysenck Personality Inventory [EPI], Eysenck & Eysenck, 1969) to be negatively correlated with self-reported purpose in life (as assessed by the Purpose-in-Life Test, Crumbaugh & Maholick, 1964). Moomal (1999) also found neuroticism scores on the EPI to be negatively correlated with the Purpose-in-Life Test and concluded that neurosis constitutes a crisis of meaning and purpose in life. Finally, Maltby and Day (2000) report that neurotics score higher on Abdel-Khalek's (1998) Death Obses sion Scale.[2]

All of these findings suggest that neurotics are inadequately embedded in a world of value and meaning; consequently, they should be especially responsive to reminders of mortality. As Henry Miller states in his book *Sexus* (1965):

> To be sick, to be neurotic, if you like, is to ask for guarantees. The neu rotic is the flounder that lies on the bed of the river, securely settled in the mud, waiting to be speared. For him death is the only certain ty, and the dread of that grim certainty immobilized him in a living death far more horrible than the one he imagines but knows nothing about. (p. 338)

To test this notion empirically, Arndt and Solomon (in press) asked people high and low in neuroticism, as determined by their responses to the EPI, to complete a Desire for Personal Control Scale (Burger & Cooper, 1979) after thinking about death or dental pain. The Desire for Personal Control Scale measures the extent to which people want direct control over their immediate circumstances (e.g., "I prefer a job where I have a lot of con trol over what I do and when I do it"; "I enjoy having control over my own destiny") versus wanting other people to control their affairs (e.g., "Others usually know what's best for me"; "I wish I could push many of life's daily decisions off on someone else"). They predicted and found that although high and low neurotics valued personal control equally after thinking about dental pain, thinking about death increased nonneurotics' desire for per sonal control but decreased high neurotics' desire for personal control. Pre sumably, nonneurotics, securely embedded in their cultural worldviews and confident of their value in it, were able to resort to their own autonomous powers in response to thoughts of death. Neurotics, however, insecure in their faith in both their cultural worldviews and themselves as persons of value in it, responded to thoughts of death by abdicating their own powers and increasing their desire for others to direct their fate.

Another set of studies (Goldenberg, McCoy, Pyszczynski, Greenberg, & Solomon, 2000) tested the notion that neuroticism reflects difficulties man aging anxiety concerning basic existential issues inherent in the human con dition, especially those surrounding death and the human body. From our perspective, sexuality and other aspects of our physical nature are inherently

---

[2]Because these are correlational data, it is impossible to draw causal inferences from them. Perhaps concerns about death cause neurosis by virtue of a consequent inability to acquire meaning and value or an inability to acquire meaning and value cause neurosis by virtue of consequent chronic exposure to heightened death accessibility (or some complex combination of both processes operating simulta neously). The precise nature of the causal connection between neurotics' heightened concerns about death and their inability to sustain a sense of value in a world of meaning is an important area for future inquiry. However, the existing evidence is highly consistent with our general theoretical claim that neurosis is the result of an inability of the person to obtain and maintain a sense of value in a world of meaning in the face of an awareness of the inevitability of one's own demise.

anxiety provoking because they remind us of our creaturely nature—that, at our most basic, we are animals who will eventually die and decay. This is why all cultures imbue sex and the human body with abstract, symbolic, and even spiritual meaning that lifts us above our animal origins and separates us from the rest of the living world. We humans view ourselves as God's special creatures, the crown of creation, or at least the ultimate achievement of a long process of biological evolution, thus emphasizing our mental and spiritual nature as far more significant than our animal side. By imbuing human existence with transcendent spiritual meaning, we distinguish ourselves from the rest of the living world and thus elevate ourselves to a unique and favored position in the universe, one in which we are more than just material beings. Neurotics have difficulty sustaining faith in a system of meaning and value that affords the rest of us this favored position and so should have difficulty with death and with physical behaviors that remind of us of our animality.

Direct support for this view was provided by demonstrating that after being reminded of death, neurotic individuals found the physical aspects of sex especially unpleasant. A second study then found that thinking about the physical aspects of sex caused high but not low neurotic individuals to exhibit an increase in the accessibility of death-related thoughts (Goldenberg et al., 2000). Finally, support for the idea that neurotics' difficulties with sex stem from their difficulty with abstract symbolic meaning was provided by a third study. The heightened death thought accessibility in response to thoughts of physical sex observed among high neurotics in Study 2 was completely eliminated by inducing them to write about romantic love—a very common way that abstract spiritual meaning is attached to sex—before measuring the accessibility of death-related thoughts.

In sum, the studies reported here provide convergent support for the notions that neuroticism reflects a difficulty in finding meaning in one's life and that neurotic tendencies are exacerbated by reminders of death.

Depression

From a "terror mismanagement" perspective (see especially Becker, 1964), people become depressed when deprivation of meaning or value leads to paralyzing inactivity in the service of death denial: Human action grinds to a halt when people become disillusioned and demoralized. Consistent with this notion, research has shown that depressed persons find life less meaningful and purposeful (Crumbaugh, 1968; Emmons, 1992; Kunzendorf & Maguire, 1995) and, conversely, that a belief in a "just" world—a universe in which justice prevails and good things happen to good people and bad things happen to bad people—is associated with lower levels of depression (Ritter, Benson, & Snyder, 1990). Additionally, depressed individuals report higher levels of generally morbid and specifically death-related thoughts (Kunzendorf & McLaughlin, 1988; Wenzlaff, Wegner, & Roper, 1988).

If depressed individuals have tenuous, fragile faith in their cultural worldviews, they should be especially vulnerable and urgently need to fortify their belief in, and commitment to, their culture when confronted with thoughts of their mortality. To test this notion, Simon, Greenberg, Harmon-Jones, Solomon, and Pyszczynski (1996) asked mildly depressed and nondepressed American students (based on responses to the Beck Depression Inventory; Beck, 1987) to think about death or a control topic and then had them evaluate pro- and anti-American targets. In a second study, other mildly depressed and nondepressed students evaluated targets who agreed or disagreed with the students' opinions on the legalization of flag burning, following a mortality salience or control induction. In both studies, mildly depressed participants exhibited especially low defense of their worldview (specifically, derogation of the anti-American target or a person who disagreed with their position regarding flag burning) in the absence of mortality salience. However, after thinking about death, the mildly depressed persons were substantially more negatively inclined toward the anti-American and the person who disagreed with their position on flag burning than either nondepressed participants exposed to mortality salience or mildly depressed participants in the control condition. Thus, when reminded of their own mortality, typically psychologically vulnerable depressed people showed the strongest worldview defense.

Posttraumatic Stress Disorder

Posttraumatic stress disorder (PTSD) is a very extreme reaction to stressful events, usually ones that confront a person with the threat of one's own death or serious bodily injury, or scenes of such events occurring to others. Although criteria for diagnosing PTSD have varied somewhat over the years, *DSM-IV* (American Psychiatric Association, 1994) includes the following symptoms for the assignment of a PTSD diagnosis:

A. The person has been exposed to a traumatic event in which the person experienced, witnessed, or was confronted with an event or events that involved actual or threatened death or serious injury, or a threat to the physical integrity of self or others AND the person's response involved intense fear, helplessness, or horror.

B. The traumatic event is persistently re-experienced in recurrent and intrusive distressing recollections of the event, dreams of the event, acting or feeling as if the traumatic event were recurring, intense psychological distress at exposure to internal or external cues that symbolize or resemble an aspect of the traumatic event, and physiological reactivity on exposure to internal or external cues that symbolize or resemble an aspect of the traumatic event.

C. Persistent avoidance of stimuli associated with the trauma and numbing of general responsiveness, as indicated by (1) efforts to avoid thoughts, feelings, or conversations associated with the trauma, (2) efforts to avoid activities, places, or people that arouse recollections of the trauma, (3) inability to recall an important aspect of the trauma, (4) markedly diminished interest or participation in significant activities, (5) feeling of detachment or estrangement from others, (6) restricted range of affect (e.g., unable to have loving feelings), (7) sense of a foreshortened future (e.g., does not expect to have a career, marriage, children, or a normal life span).

D. Persistent symptoms of increased arousal as indicated by: (1) difficulty falling or staying asleep, (2) irritability or outbursts of anger, (3) difficulty concentrating, (4) hypervigilance, (5) exaggerated startle response.

E. Duration of the disturbance is more than 1 month.

F. The disturbance causes clinically significant distress or impairment in social, occupational, or other important areas of functioning.

PTSD is actually much more common than most people might imagine. One recent survey (Elliott & Briere, 1995) found that 76% of American adults report having been exposed to some sort of extremely stressful event in their lives and that roughly 10% developed PTSD. Another survey (Breslau & Davis, 1992) found that 9% of the population of a large American city suffered from PTSD. Twenty years after the end of the Vietnam War, 15.2% of U.S. soldiers who experienced combat continued to suffer from PTSD. Thousands of people died in the 9/11 terrorist attacks, many more averted death but were nonetheless directly affected by the attacks or had close relations with those who did, and virtually all people worldwide have seen the terrifying scenes of the bombing and its aftermath, most on multiple occasions. The very real possibility of further unspecified attacks keeps these events highly salient for virtually all of us.

Research suggests that PTSD is indeed a rather common reaction to terrorist attacks. McFarlane and de Girolamo (1996) reviewed five published studies of PTSD among victims of terrorist attacks and reported that the rate of PTSD among those directly targeted exceeded 20% of the people studied, with two studies showing rates in excess of 40% (Curran, Bell, Murray, & Loughrey, 1990; Weisaeth, 1993). Perhaps some of the most relevant evidence for understanding how Americans are likely to react to the events of 9/11 comes from studies of Israeli civilians' reactions to the bombings and threat of chemical attack they experienced during the Gulf War in 1991. Initially, Solomon, Laor, and McFarlane (1996) found that fully 80% of those who were evacuated from their houses because of damage sustained in missile attacks reported symptoms consistent with a PTSD diagnosis a week after the attacks; 1 year later, the rate of PTSD symptoms remained at nearly 60% for this group. In another study, Bleich, Shalev, Shoham, and Solomon (1992) examined the 1,059 emergency room admissions from war-related events and found that only 22% of these were due to injuries directly caused by missile attacks or flying debris. The remaining

78% of admissions were the indirect result of fear aroused by the attacks and included 11 deaths (7 from suffocation caused by improper use of gas masks and 4 from fear-induced heart attacks). A quarter of emergency room admissions resulted from physical injuries incurred as people ran for safety in response to warning sirens or needlessly injected themselves with the atropine they were supplied with to ward off the effects of chemical attacks that did not, in fact, materialize. Fifty-one percent of the war-related admissions involved people coming in for treatment of acute psychological distress and anxiety. These findings suggest that the fear aroused by terrorist attacks can produce a broad range of wounds, both physical and psychological, and that PTSD is a common response, especially among those most directly affected by the attacks.

As with most other forms of psychopathology, recent thinking regarding PTSD suggests that both biological and psychological factors combine to make one vulnerable to this disorder in response to exposure to extreme stress or shock. For example, Breslau and Davis (1992; see also McFarlane, 1992) found that having a family history of psychiatric illness increases one's risk for PTSD. More compelling evidence of genetic vulnerability to PTSD was provided by a study of monozygotic twins who fought in Vietnam (Goldberg, True, Eisen, & Henderson, 1990). Research also suggests that pre-existing psychological problems such as depression, anxiety disorders, and neuroticism can also predispose one to exhibit signs of PTSD after exposure to major stressful events (van der Kolk, McFarlane, Weisaeth, 1996). Nonetheless, it is clear that the majority of people who are exposed to extreme stress do not develop PTSD or any other form of psychopathology. The question, then, is what happens in the individual who does succumb to PTSD and other forms of pathological response to extreme stress or threat.

From a "terror mismanagement" perspective, PTSD is the result of a general breakdown in the terror management system that leaves the person unable to cope with the fears to which the traumatic event has given rise. Two features of events seem especially likely to lead to PTSD. First, the event must be so impactful as to confront the individual with the core fear of death that is typically repressed or kept under control through the use of the various coping mechanisms that were discussed in chapter 2. Events that precipitate PTSD arouse terror, extreme amounts of fear that are engendered by a confrontation with a literal threat to one's continued existence. Second, the event must challenge the person's core assumptions or beliefs about the world as a safe and benevolent place, in which one can avoid horrible events and lead a safe and secure life if one simply does the right things.

As Melvin Lerner and his colleagues have shown, people have a need to view the world as a just place where bad things do not happen to good people. Research testing Lerner's "just world hypothesis" has documented the many ways that people adjust their perceptions to maintain their belief in justice in spite of exposure to clear instances of injustice (for a review, see Lerner, 1980; Lerner & Miller, 1978). Such a conception of an orderly and benevolent universe enables people to feel safe and secure as long as they view themselves as good or valuable. It is this deeply rooted, largely unconscious assumption that bad things do not happen to good people that enables self-esteem to provide its anxiety-buffering function. If the world is truly just, then valuable people— that is, people with high levels of self-esteem—would be relatively immune to horrible events. Of course, on a conscious level, most people realize that there is horrible injustice in the world and that bad things do indeed happen to good people. Lerner argues, however, that these rational, conscious beliefs about the existence of injustice are not the psychologically active element in providing people with a sense of security. Rather, it is the implicit assumption of a just world that results from the individual's early experiences of being loved and protected by the parents, when he or she lived up to their standards, that provides the basis for self-esteem and enables people to feel secure.

Acts of random violence and terror in which innocent people are killed or seriously harmed undermine this assumption of an orderly universe and consequently undermine the capacity of self-esteem to make the individual feel safe and secure. We are suggesting, then, that exposure to horrific events in which people suffer randomly and without reason can lead to a collapse of the normal means by which people protect themselves from the frightening aspects of life. When the assumptions on which our security is based are shattered, the normal strategies that we use to maintain security can no longer help us. The unexpected and extreme nature of the events of 9/11 are the sorts of features that are likely to seriously undermine people's assumptive world of safety and security.

This perspective, in turn, suggests that a critical determinant of one's vulnerability to PTSD is the strength and resilience of one's coping system before the traumatic event. The more resilient and flexible one's anxiety-buffering system of meaning, value, and personal connection, the more likely that system will be able to withstand the challenges to it brought on by traumatic events. Although rigid, heavily defended worldviews might provide especially effective protection under normal circumstances, rigidity may not be optimal in facilitating coping with extreme trauma because they may be more "brittle" and thus more likely to fall apart in response to extreme stress or challenge. A worldview and sense of self that are flexible and able to adapt and change in response to new experience and information might be more likely to be able to continue to provide protection in response to extreme events and accommodate the event in ways that maintain anxiety-buffering effectiveness in spite of the confrontation with horror entailed in the traumatic event.

9/11 AND PSYCHOPATHOLOGY

If the foregoing "terror mismanagement" analysis of psychopathology is correct, the events of 9/11 should result in across-the-board increases in all forms of psychopathology as dysfunctional reactions to heightened explicit and implicit accessibility of thoughts of death. And this has indeed been the case, at least in terms of anecdotal evidence (e.g., the quote at the outset of this chapter). Perhaps most obviously, people directly involved in the World Trade Center and Pentagon attacks and the aftermath thereof are showing increased incidences of PTSD—for example, World Trade Center Tower survivor Inez Graham (Jacobs, the *New York Times*, 9/30/01):

> Inez Graham is at war with her memory. She spends most of her days sobbing and afraid, battling images of flames and falling debris and trying to quell the soundtrack of screams in her head. A ringing phone, a plane overhead or a passing truck make her hunker down in fear. She refuses to go outside. She tells friends not to visit and says the smell of smoke, like some unseen phantom, lingers around her home in Newark. She tries to stave off sleep, but when she finally dozes off, the nightmares are always the same. She is back at the World Trade Center, barefoot and breathless, trying to outrun the tidal wave of concrete and glass. But in this version, her daughters are with her, and she cannot save them. "I want the old Inez back," she said, giving in to another round of tears. "But I just can't get that day out of my head." (Section 1B, p. 1)

Less obvious, but completely understandable in light of our analysis, are clear signs of dysfunctional reactions by Americans and others around the world who were not directly involved in the events of 9/11. For example, drug and alcohol abuse has substantially increased since that fateful day ("Substance Abuse up Since 9/11," 2001):

> Drug and alcohol abuse appears to be up in many parts of the country since Sept. 11, especially in New York City and Washington, a survey suggests. "These people are self-medicating because of the stress they feel," said Joseph Califano Jr., president of the Columbia University National Center on Addiction and Substance Abuse, which conducted the survey. "I think we have the beginnings of a self-medicating epidemic." (*Newsday*, New York, 12/7/01, p. A13)

This conclusion was based on a survey of people seeking treatment for drug or alcohol abuse and compulsive gambling. The Columbia survey found treatment for substance abuse increased considerably in New York City and Washington, DC, and in New York State, New Jersey, and Pennsylvania. However, increases were also reported in Alaska, Florida, Georgia, Illinois, Indiana, Kentucky, Mississippi, Nebraska, South Dakota, and Tennessee. Nationally, admissions to treatment facilities rose 10% to 12% since 9/11. Prescriptions for sleeping pills were increased 25% in New York City in late September. Consistent with the Columbia survey, the American Cancer

Society found in another survey in October 2001 (reported in Ochs, 2001) that a quarter of American adults said they had increased, resumed, or started smoking cigarettes, engaging in bad eating habits, and drinking more caffeine or alcohol.

Concurrently, psychologists saw increases in all the forms of psychopathology described earlier (Ochs, 2001):

> "When people are under stress, they resort to their most familiar defense mechanism or reaction patterns," said Florence Kaslow, director of the Florida Couples and Family Institute in West Palm Beach. Kaslow said she is seeing more people in her practice suffering from generalized anxiety disorder. "Those relationships that had problems before Sept. 11 are even under more duress now," she said. "Some people are showing signs of depression and disillusionment, feeling helpless in the face of the unknown," she said. "Others are becoming obsessive–compulsive, trying to impose order and control on a life that seems to have neither. Still others are becoming fatalistic, adopting the attitude that it doesn't matter what they do. . ." (*Newsday*, New York, 12/18/01, p. C4).

Although proper epidemiological studies of incidences of mental illness have yet to be undertaken, existing anecdotal evidence is in general accord with the notion that the events of 9/11 have produced increasing occurrences of all forms of psychopathology. We agree with Florence Kaslow that stress leads people to rely more heavily on their most familiar defensive maneuvers and would argue, in turn, that these patterns are best understood as dysfunctional reactions to heightened death accessibility caused by the events of 9/11 and thereafter.

To the extent that this idea is true, clinicians and epidemiologists should be on the lookout for more frequent encounters with all forms of psychopathology. In addition to the disorders reported earlier, we would expect to see greater amounts of eating disorders, sexual dysfunctions, attention deficit disorders, membership in religious cults and gangs, self-mutilations, and copy-cat criminal or terrorist activities (e.g., 15-year-old Charles Bishop's 1/7/02 deliberate crash of a Cessna plane into a skyscraper in Tampa, Florida, expressing "sympathy" toward Osama bin Laden in a suicide note found in his pocket in the wreckage; Sloan & Peterson, 2002, Feb. 7).

THE IMPACT OF TERROR ON CHILDREN

As Yalom (1980) states:

When behavioral scientists choose to investigate the issue closely, they invariably discover that children are extraordinarily preoccupied with death. Children's concerns about death are pervasive and exert far-reaching influence on their experiential worlds. Death is a great enigma to them, and one of their major developmental tasks is to deal with fears of helplessness and obliteration. . . . Not only are children profoundly concerned with death, but these concerns begin at an earlier age than is generally thought. Children go through an orderly progression of stages in awareness of death and in the methods they use to deal with their fear of death. Children's coping strategies are invariably denial-based: it seems that we do not, perhaps cannot, grow up tolerating the straight facts about existence. (p. 76)

For many people, one of the most upsetting questions that the recent terrorist attacks gives rise to is how all of this is likely to affect our children. Whether we like it or not, all but the very youngest of children who have not yet acquired language are bound to be aware of the events of 9/11. And children's responses to these events are likely to be at least as varied as those of adults, if not more so. For example, Laurance (2001) noted:

Younger children tend to be more literal minded in their responses, recording what happened plainly and bluntly in a way that may some-times seem shocking to adults. Older children tend to adopt a symbolic approach, indicating a more mature reflection on the events. Dr James Thompson, head of the post-traumatic stress disorder clinic at Middlesex Hospital, London, which has treated survivors from disasters, said: "There is an enormous literature on children's drawings after dreadful events. The younger children tend to be absolutely literal and straight-forward. One of the pictures by the New York children shows people falling from a building and quite accurately locates where the fire was. Another shows how the twin towers were hit at different heights. These are factual, accurate drawings—a blunt acknowledgement of what hap-pened." The more detached treatment of the subject by the older chil-dren, using the symbols of the dove of peace and the flag carrying the legend "Fear," were more akin to an adult response to the events. "The key thing is that when a child sees things which are distressing it seems that drawing them and talking about them is a way of processing the event and coming to terms with it and we should probably see it as ben-eficial." . . . Parents should question their children about the events, whether they had witnessed them directly or only seen them on televi-sion. "You should probably ask your children what they think about what they have seen. Kids are generally good at distinguishing reality from fantasy but they can get confused. Some might think they caused the attack on New York or were involved in it. Some might be unsure whether it is over or not." (*The Independent*, London, 9/29/01, p. 3)

Clearly, the child's level of cognitive development and language acqui-sition affects how much he or she understands of what is going on in the world . What is clear to virtually all children, however, is that something very terrible has happened, that many people have died unnecessarily, and that there are people in the world who hate Americans and seem committed to doing us as much harm as possible. If this is a confusing reality with which we as adults have a hard time coming to grips, imagine how much more confusing it must be for young children who lack the understanding of global politics to at least begin to put these events into perspective.

Children seem to vary widely in how interested they are in learning about the current problem we are facing. Whereas some seem to have the same obsessive quest for understanding that is found in many adults, others seem relatively unfazed by the events, seemingly bothered more by the disruption of scheduled events and normal routines than by the tragedies themselves. Educators and those working with children seem to be observing greater interest and upset in response to the event with increasing age.[3] One school psychologist told us of a 10-year-old child whose sleep was disrupted for weeks after the attacks and who seemed to feel responsible for finding a solution to the problems that these events pose for the world. More commonly observed patterns include a vague sense of anxiety and uncertainty about the future, attempts to deny the events or at least minimize one's exposure to information about them, and fears about one's own and one's family's safety. In other words, children seem to be showing the same type of variability in reactions that are observed among adults.

Given the relatively concrete nature of most children's thinking, they are most likely to be primarily concerned with the impact of the 9/11 attacks and possible future attacks on themselves, their families, their friends, and others who play a major role in their lives. More abstract concerns about what this implies for the future, our freedoms, or the global order are likely to be seen primarily among older children and teens. In our own experience of talking with children in places geographically removed from the targets of the attacks, we have gotten the impression that many feel sad and distressed by the events but are greatly comforted by the sense that their own communities are unlikely targets for future attacks. This seems to reflect what most children living in cities that seem relatively low on the list of potential targets for attack have been told by their parents and teachers. Of course, this sense of safety related to distance is also a common source of relief among adults.

---

[3]Florian and Mikulincer (1998) argued that terror management mechanisms should emerge developmentally as children become increasingly aware of the irrevocable nature, and inevitability, of death. Children then become more attached to the cultural worldview as a means of acquiring a sense of meaning and value in order to procure psychological equanimity and begin to defend it accordingly in response to reminders of mortality. In support of this claim, Florian and Mikulincer exposed groups of 7-year-old and 11-year-old children to death salient or control conditions and then obtained a measure of worldview defense. Worldview defense was found in response to mortality salience for the 11-year-old children but not the 7-year-old children, suggesting that terror management mechanisms indeed depend on the development of the concept of death. But it is equally possible that the 7-year-old children had not yet shifted their basis of security from the parents to the larger culture.

The Impact on a Developing Anxiety Buffer

Perhaps the most important long-term concern with respect to the impact of terrorist attacks on children should be centered more on the effect they may have on children's developing sense of emotional security than on specific short-term distress reactions. The psychological structures that provide equanimity and help control anxiety in the face of the frightening possibilities we all face in life develop over the course of childhood and depend heavily on the child's learning to view the world as a safe, orderly, and just place in which to live. Random acts of violence are likely to interfere with the development of a conception of the world as a safe and secure place, a conception that is so essential for anxiety-free functioning. Research has shown that children who are exposed to violence are much more at risk for developing a broad range of psychological problems, all of which can be viewed as related to difficulties in controlling anxiety.

For example, a Swedish study of Chilean refugees (Hjern, Angel, & Hoejer, 1991) whose parents were tortured or persecuted found that 75% had sleep problems, 69% had anxiety problems, 58% displayed defiance, 42% showed signs of depression, and 39% exhibited inappropriately high levels of aggression. An Israeli study of children whose fathers were killed in war (Kaffman & Elizur, 1984) found elevated levels of aggression, discipline problems, and restlessness in one third of the children 2 to 3 years afterward. An American study of 52 Cambodian refugee children who escaped the Pol Pot regime (over half had witnessed homicides; all saw evidence of mass murders) found that 50% had PTSD and most were depressed, withdrawn, and anxious (Kinzie, Sack, Angell, & Manson, 1986; Sack, Angell, Kinzie, & Rath, 1986). Clearly, then, exposure to traumatic events can have a long-term detrimental impact on children's psychological well-being. From a TMT perspective, much of this detrimental impact may result from the influence of such events on the development of the psychological structures that are needed for normal control of anxiety.

On a more positive note, in these and other studies, there are many children who have experienced hellacious trauma and yet continue to function well. Children can be remarkably resilient and many seem able to adapt quite well to extreme stress without obvious negative consequences. A major task for researchers, then, is to understand the factors that promote such resilience. Although in its infancy, the research available thus far (e.g., Cicchetti & Toth, 1997) suggests that resilience to traumatic experiences is enhanced by factors such as (a) secure close attachment to a supportive parent or other adult, (b) a strong bond with a competent prosocially oriented adult from the community, and (c) moderate or higher levels of intelligence, a lack of problems with impulse control or focusing attention (e.g., ADHD), and a lack of family history of mental illness. Note that these are the types of factors we would expect to be helpful given a TMT analysis of how children develop and sustain their equanimity. It seems likely that these factors help the child internalize a secure, socially validated, and compelling worldview that provides meaning and the potential for self-worth.

TMT and the research that is available at this point seem to converge on the conclusion that in order for children to cope effectively with the traumatic effects of the terrorist attacks, they need (a) close affectional bonds with a caring adult; (b) explanations that provide an age-appropriate understanding of the meaning and implications of the events that have transpired since 9/11, an understanding that enables them to view the world nonetheless as basically safe, meaningful, and fair; and (c) opportunities to do things that enable them to feel good about themselves and perhaps to feel that they are contributing in some way to helping solve the problem that we are all facing. Of course, exactly how these needs are met depends a lot on the age, cognitive and social sophistication, and emotional stability of the child in question. Parents and caregivers need to be sensitive to how their children are reacting. Whereas some children may show obvious signs of distress that need to be addressed directly, others may seem relatively unaffected. The research on childhood trauma has demonstrated that some children show externalizing reactions, including hypervigilance, aggression, and other forms of "acting out," and other children engage in internalizing reactions involving withdrawal, passivity, and depression.

Our view is that even those children who seem relatively oblivious to the disaster are likely to have concerns that need to be addressed. Even children who express little direct concern with current events may be troubled by diffuse fears that show up in nightmares, unusual play that symbolically reenacts the disaster, or fantasies. Thus, we would advise that all children be provided an opportunity to talk about these events and that parents, teachers, and other caregivers adjust the explanations and interventions offered to the needs of the specific child in question. Children have told us that they greatly appreciate the time and energy that their parents and teachers put into helping them understand what is going on in the world these days. Some have noted that they feel especially frightened when their parents try to shield them from scary information, because this seems to imply that something really awful might be coming their way. Child care professionals from many disciplines seem to agree that telling children the truth, although not more than they need to know, is ultimately the best way to help them cope with difficult times and events.

GENERAL RECOMMENDATIONS FOR
HELPING PEOPLE COPE WITH 9/11

So what, then, given our existentially psychodynamically oriented "terror mismanagement" account of psychopathology, can psychologists, educators, and other helping professionals do to assist people (children and adults, including ourselves) in coping with the events of 9/11? In the following sections, we focus on three general goals for helping people adjust to the frightening world we are now facing and make some specific suggestions for how these goals might be accomplished.[4]

Providing Social Support and Caring

The most basic, primitive, but nonetheless enduringly effective way of controlling fear seems to be through close meaningful relationships with others. From the earliest days of our lives, we obtained a feeling of safety by clinging to our parents or primary caregivers. These early interpersonal connections are the building grounds from which our more sophisticated means of attaining security through meaning and self-esteem developed as we matured. Thus, the first thing that people need when coping with tragedy and fear of future disasters is close connection with other people.

In the moments after the attacks, people the world over showed an intuitive grasp of this principle by finding others with whom to share their thoughts and feelings about the attacks. Large bodies of research, dating back to Schachter's (1959) pioneering work, have shown that people seek others in times of distress and that contact with others is an effective way of mitigating their distress. Research has shown that the availability of caring contacts with others increases our resistance to both psychological and physical illnesses when we are exposed to stress (Benner & Wrubel, 1989). People with adequate social networks are less prone to develop illnesses and recover more rapidly when they do develop them. Whether one is talking about depression, heart disease, or cancer, the presence of social support is a major force in promoting resilience and facilitating recovery.

---

[4]We do not mean to imply here that an existential psychodynamic approach is the only effective means of therapeutic intervention in general or in specific response to psychopathology induced by the events of 9/11. Rather, we support an eclectic approach currently favored by many clinicians (e.g., Lazarus, 1995; Snyder & Ingram, 2000) in which therapeutic methods are determined by the nature of the problem and the person who possesses it. Some problems are demonstrably more effectively treated with certain methods; for example, antipsychotic medication seems to work better than client-centered therapy for the treatment of schizophrenia, and systematic desensitization seems to be more effective than psychoanalysis for treating phobias (Goisman, 1983). Some problems are more amenable to multiple approaches to treatment, simultaneously or sequentially; for example, depression may be treated with a combination of antidepressants and cognitive therapy, or depression may be treated first with antidepressants and then later with cognitive therapy. Some people respond better to one form of treatment than another; for example, antidepressants are effective for some but not all. Accordingly, the recommendations that we offer here for treatment are not meant to supplant as much as to supplement other approaches to helping those who desire to change.

This finding suggests that in stressful times like these people have an especially strong need for caring, loving contact. This is a time for people to get together and let each other know they care about each other. It is also a time for open discussion and sharing of feelings and ideas. It is a time when family ties may take on even more importance than usual. And it is a time when children are especially in need of love and reassurance from their parents.

Unfortunately, the stresses that many people are now experiencing can, in some cases, lead to irritability and a lack of tolerance. Little things that might normally be interpreted as minor annoyances may be more likely to be blown out of proportion, leading to conflicts that can undermine relationships. Awareness of the heightened potential for irritability might help prevent such misunderstandings. This is a time for tolerance, for giving people the benefit of the doubt, for realizing that many of us are likely to be more susceptible to the minor annoyances that are inherent in any relationship.

How can we facilitate closer, warmer relationships with each other during difficult times such as the present? Helping professionals should urge their clients to make an extra effort to be open and available to the people in their lives, to try a little harder to initiate conversations and expressions of caring. Helping professionals can also model this behavior in the way they relate to those they are trying to help. Teachers and educators can set up classroom activities to facilitate discussion and exchange of feelings and ideas, both about the current crisis and about other issues that are likely to be important to people in a particular milieu. Parents can make special efforts to let their children know just how important they are to them and to facilitate positive interactions within families.

Providing Meaning and Understanding

Another major factor that facilitates coping with tragic events is an ability to find meaning in them. TMT views the ability to find meaning as central to the individual's ability to cope with frightening realities. Meaning for most of what happens in life is provided by the individual's cultural worldview, which offers a framework for understanding the world and our place in it. Finding the meaning in tragic events, like those surrounding the terrorist attacks of 9/11, is, of course, extremely difficult. These events remind us of just how fragile our existence is, and how cruel, unjust, and arbitrary the world can be. Nonetheless, people crave understanding for why and how events like this could happen. And the evidence suggests that finding meaning in tragedy greatly facilitates the individual's ability to cope (e.g., Pennebaker, 1989; Wortman & Silver, 1992).

In chapter 5, we discussed the many ways that the terrorist attacks have led to an increased search for meaning. Of course, the media—television, newspapers, magazines, entertainers, and the like—all play a central role in our coming to an understanding of the crisis we are now facing. People need information to acquire a sense of meaning in today's world. The media constitute our primary source of information, especially about large-scale events of global significance such as these. Thus, people seem drawn to media accounts of the events of 9/11. Many people have become addicted to watching the CNN reports and reading the repeating ribbon of "breaking news" that constantly runs at the bottom of our television screens while commentators and experts expound on their theories of what is going on.

But exposure to the media in times like these can be a double-edged sword. On the one hand, people crave understanding and explanations for the things that have happened to us. They also want to know what might be coming next so they can plan their activities accordingly. Information in times of crisis is essential to the development of understanding. On the other hand, most people can readily assimilate only so much information. And much of the information presented is redundant and not of much real use in helping to make sense out of the many facets of the events with which we are struggling. Thus although some level of exposure to the news regarding terrorist attacks and other crises seems essential in facilitating coping, overexposure to the news can actually overwhelm the individual's ability to cope and can lead to exaggerated feelings of fear and hopelessness.

Even worse, some of the information presented by the media is misleading and can lead to an unfounded exacerbation of fears. For example, e-mail and Internet sites widely disseminated the rumor that major terrorist attacks on shopping malls were planned to occur on or near Halloween 2001. The week before Halloween, *Newsweek* magazine reported that this was a hoax or "urban legend" that should not be taken seriously. Several days before the holiday, the government warned the country that "credible sources" suggested that a new unspecified attack was imminent. Conflicting messages like these can evoke enormous amounts of fear and near panic (Harmon, 2001).

Finding meaning in tragic events like those of 9/11 requires more than mere information. It is what people do with information that gives them a sense of meaning. In one sense, the deaths that occurred as a result of the terrorist attacks are ultimately meaningless, and that is what is so frightening about them. But meaning can be found in these events on a variety of different levels. Different people find solace in different types of meaning.

First, there is a relatively concrete understanding of exactly what happened in New York, Washington, DC, and Pennsylvania on the day of the attacks. Details of what happened, how the attacks were accomplished, who was responsible, and things of that nature are needed to take some of the mystery out of the events. By now, the news media have presented a fairly comprehensive picture of the facts surrounding the events, based on the investigative efforts of the Federal Bureau of Investigation (FBI), Central Intelligence Agency (CIA), Federal Aviation Administration (FAA), State Department, and other agencies around the world. It is natural for people to be curious about the details of major events such as these, and getting a reasonably comprehensive picture of exactly what happened is the first step toward acquiring the understanding and closure needed to help restore one's sense of safety. However, we still lack this type of information about many related fear-arousing events and issues, such as the anthrax mailings, the current plans of the al Qaeda terrorist network, and the possible role played in this and other terrorist attacks by other groups.

But most people do not find a mere list of the facts surrounding the events very satisfying, and few find this very concrete level of understanding sufficient to restore their sense of safety and security. People want to know why this happened, what could have possibly motivated people to sacrifice their own lives in order to wreak such massive destruction and cause so many deaths. People also want to know how religious beliefs can lead to such horrific behavior and consequences. The question on virtually everyone's mind is why the al Qaeda hate us so much. Of course, many other questions about the root causes of the terrorists' hatred of Americans can be broached from historical, economic, political, ethical, and psychological perspectives. In the following chapter, we present our own analysis of the roots of such hatred and violence, from the perspective of TMT.

The human thirst for knowledge of why people behave the way they do has been discussed from many psychological perspectives. In the 1950s, Fritz Heider (e.g., Heider, 1958) laid the groundwork for several decades' worth of research on attribution theory by arguing that to get along in life, people must function as intuitive psychologists and develop theories of why people do the things they do. For Heider, this thirst for understanding was driven largely by pragmatic concerns. If we understand the causes of other people's behavior, we are in a much better position to act effectively in our interactions with others and evoke desirable responses from others and avoid undesirable ones. And even if we cannot control the behavior of others, understanding their motives puts us in a much better position to predict what they will do in the future and thus puts us in a position where we can protect ourselves from the harmful consequences of their actions. If we understand the motives of the terrorists and can predict when and where they are likely to strike next, we can take action to prevent such future attacks or at least minimize their impact. Surely, this pragmatic concern with understanding so as to be in a better position to prevent future acts of terrorism is a big part of the motivation people have for understanding why the terrorists did the things they did. But it is not the only motivation.

As we discussed in chapter 2, a long tradition of existential thinking in psychology posits that people seek meaning in the multitude of complex and varied events they encounter in life because meaning provides security and freedom from anxiety and fear. Ernest Becker, who laid the conceptual groundwork for TMT, argued that the human quest for meaning was the most basic route through which people find safety in the frightening world in which we live. Understanding the motivation behind terrorist acts adds to our understanding of the human condition and helps us understand the long history of hatred and violence that has characterized our species' reign on this planet. Although it may sadden and discourage us, understanding the roots of hatred and violence gives us a perspective that can be applied to our understanding of people in general and of the many other horrific things that people have done and continue to do that cause others to suffer.

Causal theories of human evil and destructiveness are extremely important and can provide a good deal of comfort to us. For many Americans, the events of 9/11 have strengthened their view of America as entirely good and America's enemies as purely evil. But whether the explanations offered are simple or complex, false or accurate, for some people, they have failed to provide the type of understanding and meaning that is craved. Beyond pragmatic or political explanations, most people also need a deeper cosmic meaning, a general sense of how these events fit into the larger scheme of things, perhaps an understanding that finds some good in the horrible events. Becker referred to this sort of meaning as sacred. Such meaning is often frankly religious or spiritual in nature and entails a conception of how we fit into an order of things that stretches beyond what we can observe.

Does such meaning really exist outside people's minds? Many attempts to find cosmic meaning in tragic events clearly reflect wishful thinking, an attempt to put a positive veneer on an otherwise intolerable event. It may be, then, that many types of cosmic meaning are merely illusory. But the human tendency to find good in evil, to "look for the silver lining," may reflect an intuitive experiential form of wisdom that transcends rational thought. Regardless of the literal truthfulness or accuracy of many of the meanings that people extract from tragic events, it may be that such beliefs serve an important psychological function. Taylor and Brown (1988) reviewed a large body of evidence suggesting that positive psychological illusions are associated with high self-esteem and low levels of depression. It may be that by putting a positive "spin" on even the most horrible realities, people are paving the way for their recovery from trauma that has befallen them and for better coping in the future.

What might be even more useful than inventing comforting cosmic meanings in tragedy would be to actively do things that make the event an opportunity for genuine growth. Tragic events have a remarkable capacity to put our ordinary life into a broader perspective, to help us see what is genuinely important to us and to realize the relative unimportance of many of the things that cause us worries and sleepless nights. Events like those that occurred on 9/11 can help us trivialize the trivial. They can also lead to a reexamination of priorities and a reorganization of life goals and aspirations. In the wake of the tragedy, many people found themselves reflecting on just how precious life is, on how much their families and loved ones mean to them, and on what they might be able to do to make their lives better and more meaningful in the future. As one college student described her experience (Sheldon Solomon and Tom Pyszczynski personal communications, November, 2001) :

> My gratitude for each moment has swelled. My understanding of myself and how I fit in this existence has made a beautiful leap forward. Yeah, the world may seem more "scary" and unpredictable, but I am more the person I want to be, due to the reminder that we, indeed, live in a precarious and life-threatening world. The human existence is a glorious opportunity and journey. I am thankful that I am mentally healthy enough to play and discover my thoughts and soul. (This is why I have decided to go on to school.) I will spend my time helping people acquire the mental health necessary to study their world and discover the beautiful gifts of friendship and love.

An interesting finding is that our own laboratory research using mildly depressed individuals suggests that even a small reminder of mortality can be beneficial in increasing the perceived meaningfulness of life. Specifically, Simon, Arndt, Greenberg, Pyszczynski, and Solomon (1998) replicated Study 1 conducted by Simon et al. (1996), which we described earlier in this chapter, but added a condition in which the participants could not evaluate the pro- and anti-American essays. As in the earlier study, depressed individuals reminded of death exhibited especially high worldview defense when given the opportunity to do so. At the end of this study, though, Simon et al. (1998) had participants fill out Kunzendorf's No Meaning Scale (Kunzendorf & Maguire, 1995; Kunzendorf, Moran, & Gray, 1995), which assesses how much meaning a person sees in life. For example, one item asks for level of agreement with the following statement: "Life has no meaning or purpose." Depressed participants reported that life was less meaningful than did nondepressed individuals in all conditions except one—when the depressed individuals were reminded of mortality and allowed to evaluate the pro- and anti-American essays, they reported viewing life to be just as meaningful as their nondepressed counterparts did. Thus, the combination of mortality salience and an opportunity to defend their worldview enhanced the meaningfulness of life to those usually deficient in meaning. Similarly, the terrorist attacks, when combined with reaffirmations of the values of the American worldview, may have enhanced the perceived meaningfulness of life in some people formerly lacking such meaning.

Irvin Yalom (1980) argued that a confrontation with death and tragedy has the *potential* to be a liberating and growth-enhancing experience. This is not to say that everyone who encounters death and tragedy inevitably uses such events as a springboard for growth, but that the potential for such growth is there if the individual is able to take advantage of it. In a clinical interview study of 70 patients facing potentially life-threatening cancer diagnoses, Spiegel, Bloom, and Yalom (1981) reported that many showed some signs of growth and emotional development as a result of this experience. Some of the more common effects reported by patients who showed such improvement included the following:

1. A rearrangement of life's priorities: a trivializing of the trivial
2. A sense of liberation: being able to choose not to do those things that they do not wish to do
3. An enhanced sense of living in the immediate present, rather than postponing life until retirement or some other point in the future
4. A vivid appreciation of the elemental facts of life: the changing seasons, the wind, falling leaves, the last Christmas, and so forth
5. Deeper communication with loved ones than before the crisis
6. Fewer interpersonal fears, less concern about rejection, greater willingness to take risks than before the crisis

Thus, therapists, educators, parents, and spiritual leaders can help people use the recent tragic events as an occasion for reevaluating their priorities in life and, as in the case of the student quoted earlier, coming to a greater appreciation of the wonderful opportunities that exist in life. The recent terrorist attacks have seemed to put people in a reflective mode, and this may provide an opening for people to strengthen their resolve to make their lives meaningful and worthwhile, to take advantage of the opportunities that are out there for them, and to create opportunities to improve their lives wherever possible. This massive reminder of the fragile and temporary nature of human existence can also be used to motivate people to take action to turn their hopes and dreams into realities. Although many people have ideas about what they *could* do to make their lives better, confrontation with tragedy can be used to motivate people to take at least the initial steps toward actually accomplishing their goals. And there are concrete signs that some people with psychological difficulties have reacted to the events of 9/11 in this fashion, as noted by Monmaney in his article entitled "Response to Terror" (2001):

> Several therapists said they have observed a phenomenon that may surprise the nonexpert: Some patients long disturbed by free-floating anxiety or self-doubt say they are less troubled. Gary Emery, a Los Angeles-based cognitive therapist who espouses swift treatments of depression and other disorders, said some of his clients have suddenly improved. "It put everything in perspective and their own problems seemed less serious," he said. "The cause of many emotional problems is patients turning inward, and these events forced people to turn outward."
>
> Also, the devastation and terrible losses have probably awakened in many people an often dormant appreciation for life. "People may actually have some gratitude that they didn't have before," he said. (Part A, Part 1, p. 1.)

Providing Opportunities for Heroism and Self-Esteem Building

TMT suggests that existential fears are kept at bay by maintaining a healthy level of self-esteem, by viewing oneself as a person of value who is making an enduring contribution to a world filled with meaning. Large bodies of research, summarized in chapters 3 and 4, have documented the anxiety-buffering properties of self-esteem and the use of self-esteem bolstering in response to reminders of death. This work suggests that another important direction for helping people cope with the tragedies of 9/11 is to aid them in feeling good about themselves, that is, to help them maintain and maximize their self-esteem.

From a TMT perspective, self-esteem is acquired by viewing oneself as living up to the cultural standards of value that one has internalized and made one's own. When we live up to our standards for what is good and valuable in life, we feel good about ourselves and become less prone to experiencing debilitating anxiety. On the most basic level, helping professionals can assist people acquire self-esteem by helping them discover their many positive qualities and the many things they do that exemplify these qualities. We can all help each other by being a little more generous with our praise and compliments and a little more tolerant of others when they do things that fall short of our expectations or hopes for them.

Perhaps more useful in times of specific crises, therapists, parents, and helping professionals can help people think of things they can do to help others who are less fortunate than themselves.[5] Doing good things for others and helping make the world a better place to live reflect standards of value that are held in the highest esteem by virtually all religions and systems of ethics and that have been internalized, to a greater or lesser extent, by virtually all people. When people help others, they are actually helping themselves by increasing their self-esteem and, therefore, their resistance and resilience in the face of threat. Fortunately, a broad range of social institutions and organizations, from the American Red Cross, to local churches and schools, to pop radio stations and MTV, have all suggested ways in which people can help. Making donations, volunteering one's time and skills, and even simply spending time listening to those in distress provide the triple benefits of providing something useful to others, shifting focus from one's own concerns, and boosting one's own sense of personal value.

---

[5]The classic Kurosawa film *Ikira* (1952) provides an excellent example of someone attaining a sense of self-worth and security through this type of altruistic act. The title character, a midlevel government bureaucrat, is diagnosed with terminal stomach cancer. His initial reaction is to "party hardy." But this hedonistic response leaves a void, which he eventually fills by helping to get funding for transforming a swamp into a park for children.

CONCLUSION

In sum, our work suggests a number of important directions we as individuals, practitioners, and a society can take in helping people cope with the 9/11 attacks and with the possibilities of further terrorism in the future. We can all contribute to social support and caring and can provide opportunities for enhanced self-worth, increased understanding, and personal growth. However, one of the toughest things for Americans to understand is how people can hate us so much and be willing to sacrifice their own lives to kill us. We believe that TMT provides the most compelling answers to these questions available and so can contribute to the type of understanding for which people are searching. By doing so, the theory also suggests some long-range approaches not only to helping us better cope with terrorism but also to lessening the likelihood that such acts will occur in the future. Chapters 7 and 8 tackle these complex matters.

7

THE ROOTS OF ISLAMIC TERRORISM

> We calculated in advance the number of casualties from the enemy who would be killed . . . I was the most optimistic of them all . . . due to my experience in this field. . . . They were overjoyed when the first plane hit the building, so I said to them: be patient.
>
> —Osama bin Laden, from the videotape captured by the American military in Afghanistan, broadcast by CNN (December 13, 2001)

> Everybody praises what you did, the great action you did, which first and foremost by the grace of Allah. This is the guidance of Allah and the blessed fruit of jihad. . . . A plane crashing into a tall building was out of anyone's imagination. This was a great job. He [Mohammed Atta, leader of the terrorist group who carried out the attacks] was one of the pious men in the organization. He became a martyr. Allah bless his soul . . . Allah be praised.
>
> —Sheik Ali Saeed al-Ghamdi, former theology instructor and colleague of bin Laden, from the same videotape, broadcast by CNN (December 13, 2001)

Chapter 5 showed how our terror management work could be used to understand people's reactions to the events of 9/11, and chapter 6 offered recommendations for how people can better cope with the realities of terrorism in the 21st century. Although mortality is a fact of each of our lives, terrorism need not be. So another approach to ameliorating the problem of terrorism is to try to get rid of it. Anxiety, depression, disease, car accidents, other forms of violence, and daily hassles would still be with us, but at least we would have one less threat to fear, and an especially pernicious one at that. Of course, this is the expressed goal of the American government—to find bin Laden and his terrorist network, and put them, as well as other terrorist cells throughout the globe, out of commission.

However, to eliminate terrorism fully, we need more than just overt and covert military action and espionage—we also need a psychological understanding of the causes of terrorism. We believe that terror management theory (TMT) is particularly well suited for providing such a psychological analysis of terrorism. We now present this analysis, focusing primarily on anti-American terrorism by Islamic extremists in the Middle East. Then, in chapter 8, we will use this analysis to suggest strategies for working toward the exceedingly difficult goal of eliminating such terrorism.

The question on everyone's minds in the days after the 9/11 bombing was, why would someone do such a thing? Why do they hate us and want to destroy us? How could religious leaders take joy in the killing of so many people and tell their followers that it is their *sacred duty* to kill Americans? Seeing news reports depicting scenes of Palestinian and Pakistani women and children celebrating the devastation wrought by the bombing, hearing of thousands of Muslims from around the world rushing to join the Jihad and of the widespread support for the terrorists' actions from many corners of the Islamic world, caused many people to wonder, what is really going on here? As we have argued, people need an understanding of the events that happen in the world around them, both to provide guidelines for how to act effectively and to provide the soothing balm of security that meaning and understanding provides for us. Shocking events, like those of 9/11, challenge our comprehension of how the world works, leaving us especially hungry for explanations to restore psychological equanimity.

By now, everyone has surely heard numerous theories about why so many people in the Islamic world are hostile toward the United States; most of them are based on two diametrically antithetical notions. One perspective embraced by many Americans is that Islamic terrorists are evil people who hate us because we are good and they are evil. And if it is not pure evil in the hearts of those who hate us, then we view them as brain-washed pawns carrying out the diabolical plans of their evil leaders, who themselves are under the sway of a cruel and tyrannical religion. This kind of response is not surprising, given decades of research in social psychology documenting the *fundamental attribution error* (Ross, 1977). Our first tendency in explaining behavior of any kind, especially in individualistic cultures like that of the United States, is to make dispositional attributions for people's behavior, while not adequately adjusting those attributions in light of situational factors. For many people, these were the first explanations to come to mind; for some, explanations of this type seem to be enough.

Others, both here and abroad, took a second but equally simple-minded approach to explaining the roots of the current atrocities. We had it coming! Some asserted that American foreign policy, driven by greed and the lust for ever-expanding influence and power, wreaked havoc throughout the Middle East and led to the justifiable rage that motivated the suicide bombers to pilot the jets they hijacked into the Word Trade Center and Pentagon. Some American religious leaders portrayed the attacks as retribution for our own moral lapses here at home. As Pat Robertson noted on *The 700 Club* (9/13/01):

> We have allowed rampant secularism and occult to be broadcast on television. . . . We have insulted God at the highest levels of our government. And, then we say "Why does this happen?" It is happening because God Almighty is lifting His protection from us.

Many people throughout the Middle East suspected that the Central Intelligence Agency (CIA) or the Israeli Massad master-minded the attacks to provide an excuse for further violence committed against peace-loving Muslims. We have also heard similar theories expounded by liberal Americans at cocktail parties; for example, to build an oil pipeline through Afghanistan, we needed to take over that country; so to give us a pretext for doing so, the wealthy oil cartel that truly runs the world funded Islamic terrorists to provide the provocation for us to attack. People who adopted this explanation of the events were, of course also quick to detail President Bush's connection to the oil industry and to recount the many ways that capitalistic greed has influenced U.S. foreign and domestic policies over the past century.

It is easy to see why people would be attracted to such conspiratorial accounts of the motives behind the bombings. They provide us with a straightforward, orderly conception of recent events that preserves our faith in our culture as good and perhaps incapable of doing wrong—or of our culture as inherently evil and incapable of doing good. In either case, they tend to follow directly from one's preexisting beliefs, values, and ideologies. For example, on viewing the captured videotape of Osama bin Laden expressing his joy that the destruction wrought by the 9/11 bombings had exceeded even his most "optimistic" calculations, U.S. Senator Richard Shelby (R-Alabama) commented, "I don't see how any rational person could come away thinking, anywhere in the world, that Osama bin Laden had nothing to do with the 9/11 events." Similarly, Senator Kay Bailey Hutchinson (R-Texas) commented, "That clinches it for the world." However, many of those who supported bin Laden before the release of the tape had markedly different interpretations of the same video. Jordanian political analyst Labib Kamhawi said, "This does not prove that bin Laden was responsible for the September 11 attack; maybe it reflects wishful thinking for what happened or praising the attacks." Italian Islamic leader Ali Abu Shawa responded to the tape by saying, "I had the sensation that it wasn't bin Laden. Maybe it was a stand-in or an actor" (all quotes from *New York Times* 2001, December 14). Our point is that these kinds of explanations for events (i.e., "the terrorists are evil and we're good," or "we had it coming") have more to do with maintaining one's ideology than a thoughtful attempt to understand the roots of the problem. Such accounts may provide meaning and comfort—and may even contain a glimmer of truth—but they are unlikely to provide much help in understanding the causes of a complex and multifaceted conflict like the one we are currently facing.

More sophisticated theories as to why the United States is hated throughout much of the Islamic world have also been proposed. Many commentators and pundits have delineated how various factors have combined to provoke the hostility of the masses, leading people to be willing to die to help destroy our nation. Virtually everyone who has made a serious attempt to comprehend the conflict in the Middle East has acknowledged that this is a very complex problem, with roots in history, economics, social deprivation, religion, and ideology. Many of the ideas advanced by experts shed useful light on the problem, and some may be essential for developing constructive solutions. We believe, however, that a psychological analysis of the roots of Islamic rage can provide the integrative framework for understanding how the many forces that have led us to where we are today fit together. As Herbert Marcuse (1955) argued, explanations for collective behavior are inevitably incomplete unless they show how broad social forces affect and are affected by the psychological forces that motivate individual action. Such a psychological analysis should facilitate formulating and implementing constructive solutions to the problem. With these goals in mind, we turn now to a terror management analysis of international terrorism. Although we focus primarily on the roots of hatred toward the United States by many people in the Islamic world, we believe this analysis can also inform our understanding of terrorist action in general.

TERROR MANAGEMENT AND ETHNOPOLITICAL HATRED AND VIOLENCE

As Bernard Lewis states in his article entitled "The Roots of Muslim Rage" (1990):

> Islam is one of the world's great religions. . .Islam has brought comfort and peace of mind to countless millions of men and women. It has given dignity and meaning to drab and impoverished lives. It has taught people of different races to live in brotherhood and people of different creeds to live side by side in reasonable tolerance. It inspired a great civilization in which others besides Muslims lived creative and useful lives and which, by its achievement, enriched the whole world. But Islam, like other religions, has also known periods when it inspired in some of its followers a mood of hatred and violence. It is our misfortune that part, although by no means all or even most, of the Muslim world is now going through such a period, and that much, although again not all, of that hatred is directed against us. (p. 48)

One of the most unsettling contradictions of the human condition is that the very institutions that provide security and comfort and inspire some of the most noble acts of human kindness, altruism, and heroism can also inspire unrestrained hatred, vicious cruelty, and mass murder. In the above-mentioned passage, Bernard Lewis notes the irony that some forms of the Islamic religion have been a positive force in countless lives but other forms of Islam play an active role in breeding hatred and violence toward Western civilization in general and the United States in particular. This ironic connection between a people's source of meaning and inspiration and the instigation to evil actions is in no way unique to Islam. The history of humankind can be viewed as an ongoing struggle between competing religious and secular ideologies that, on the one hand, have provided security for those who accept them but, on the other, have inspired violence against those who do not. The Christian Crusades of the 11th to 13th centuries provide a clear example of a time when the religion that now dominates Europe and the Americas led its followers to travel great distances to commit horrible acts of cruelty against Muslims and Jews in the name of their God.

Is Religion the Root of the Problem?

Then, as now, devout believers were willing to sacrifice their lives to rid the world of those who failed to accept their god. Then, as now, religious extremists viewed themselves as virtuously fighting the good fight, serving their god by killing those who were different. Some have suggested that the core problem in most human conflict is religious belief itself. For example, respected evolutionary theorist Richard Dawkins, writing in the *Manchester Guardian* on 9/15/01, suggested that belief in an afterlife is primarily responsible for the willingness of terrorists to sacrifice their lives in the service of their cause. And TMT provides the most parsimonious account of why people believe in such afterlives—to quell the terror engendered by the knowledge of the inevitability of death and the haunting suspicion that it represents absolute annihilation. Dawkins has a point in that the promise of martyrdom and a rendezvous with 72 virgin brides clearly contributed to the hijackers' willingness to commit suicide for the cause.

However, Dawkins' vilification of religion is far too sweeping, as this passage indicates:

> I am trying to call attention to the elephant in the room that everybody is too polite—or too devout—to notice: religion, and specifically the devaluing effect that religion has on human life. I don't mean devaluing the life of others (though it can do that too), but devaluing one's own life. Religion teaches the dangerous nonsense that death is not the end. . . . To fill a world with religion, or religions of the Abrahamic kind, is like littering the streets with loaded guns. Do not be surprised if they are used.

Similarly, in his fine book *The Broken Connection: On Death and the Continuity of Life*, psychiatric historian Robert Jay Lifton (1979/1983) argued that literal immortality beliefs are very dangerous, whereas symbolic immortality ideologies are essential and far less likely to lead to evil consequences.

Positions like these are rather popular in academic circles and can be seen in the writings of Sigmund Freud as well. However, they are unquestionably wrong and reflect an inadequate grasp of both history and psychology. Although we agree that belief in an afterlife can indeed sometimes lead people to devalue the only real life they know and lash out at others, it can also inspire the cherishing of life and acts of courage in the pursuit of noble causes. The Christians who helped Jews escape the Nazis in various cities in Europe, the Hindus whose nonviolent protests led to the establishment of India as a free and independent nation, and the people of many religions who fought for the civil rights of African Americans in the United States in the 1960s are just a few examples of people inspired by religious faith to risk and give their lives for the welfare of others. And recent research conducted in the Netherlands by Mark Dechesne and colleagues (Dechesne et al., 2002) demonstrated that increasing people's belief in an afterlife can militate against harmful forms of worldview defense. For example, in one study, following mortality salience, increasing American participants' beliefs in life after death reduced their tendency to derogate a critic of America.

Additionally, the most horrible genocidal atrocities of the past century and, indeed, in recorded history, Hitler's Holocaust in Central Europe, Stalin's purge of non-Communists in the former Soviet Union and Eastern Bloc, and the Khmer Rouge's killing fields in Cambodia (which currently holds the record for the largest number of human casualties) were all perpetrated in the name of atheistic ideologies that made no provisions for an afterlife and were sometimes directed at eliminating those who believed in an afterlife. What more compelling evidence could there be that it is misguided to point the finger of blame for this or other humanly perpetrated atrocities at religion per se or at the belief in some form of life after death? TMT asserts that religion and beliefs in literal immortality serve essential psychological functions, but so do symbolic immortality ideologies; both modes of death transcendence have been extensively involved in the genesis of human cruelty. However, neither is, in and of itself, the real problem.

In fact, all wars are fought by people who are in many ways just like ourselves, who see themselves as part of a virtuous struggle to promote good and banish the world of evil. Those who fight without such conviction are unlikely to make the sacrifices to be successful and are likely to be riddled by anxiety and guilt. Those who are willing to risk their lives for a cause are inevitably convinced of the righteousness and intrinsic value of that cause, whether their cause is sanctioned by a deistic or secular ideology. As we have argued throughout this volume, both religious and secular ideologies are part of human nature and fulfill important psychological needs. Put simply, people all over the world need something to believe in—they always have and always will. How is it, then, that ideologies that have the potential to do so much good for people so often end up leading to such cruelty and evil?

The Need for Terror Management as the Root of the Problem

From the perspective of TMT, the root cause of man's inhumanity to man is the existential contradiction into which we are all born: We are animals with an instinctive desire for life with enough intelligence to know that we will someday die. The potential for terror this knowledge creates leads us to seek shelter in the form of cultural worldviews that give life meaning and permanence, give us the opportunity to view ourselves as valuable, and provide some hope of transcending death. Whether these anxiety-buffering worldviews are religious or secular, they ultimately serve the same psychological function of protecting us from the "rumble of panic" that lies beneath the surface and that energizes our quest for meaning in life and value in ourselves.

Over the time our species has inhabited this planet, many wildly divergent cultural worldviews have come and gone. Our propensity to think and explore has been an ongoing challenge to existing worldviews, and there has been a perpetual tension between the security provided by existing systems of belief and the implications of both new scientific knowledge (e.g., Darwin's theory of evolution and the evidence for it) and new knowledge of alternative worldviews. These types of new knowledge push our worldviews in new directions, sometimes undermine their anxiety-buffering value, and occasionally lead to their downfall.

The protection against anxiety that cultural worldviews provide is very fragile. To accomplish their function, they require constant validation. Because no belief system can be verified in any absolute sense, we rely heavily on social consensus to maintain faith that our conception of reality is in fact correct. Whether we acknowledge it or not, those who disagree with our conceptions of reality undercut our faith in these beliefs and threaten to release the anxiety from which our conceptions shield us, thus undermining the promise of literal or symbolic immortality afforded by them. This anxiety drives the hostility and hatred we often feel toward those who view the world differently than we do. As we discussed in chapter 2, humankind has developed a variety of ways of reducing the threat posed by those who are different—from simple derogation to attempts at converting them to the "truth" of our conception to the all too common response of trying to annihilate them, thereby removing the threat posed by their divergent beliefs once and for all.

Although annihilation of those who are different from us occurs more often than anyone would wish, it is far from the most common response. Most people do live side by side with those with diametrically opposed worldviews and do so with relative peace and equanimity. Although they may not like it, they seem to be able to tolerate this diversity, perhaps by employing a variety of psychological tactics to defuse the threat posed by the different set of beliefs and values. Probably the most common response is to simply view the others as misguided, unenlightened, or too stupid, uninformed, or brainwashed to see through the facade of unreasonable faith that ties them to their delusory belief system; and perhaps to wish silently that someday, somehow, they will see the light and come to view the world from our own far superior perspective. This, of course, is hardly a socially constructive solution, because it tends to build walls between people and undermine their ability to communicate with each other in an open and honest way. But we suspect it plays a much bigger role in defusing the threat posed by diverging beliefs than most people would be willing to admit: "If only the 'other guy' had the benefit of my wisdom, knowledge, and perspective, surely he would see the error of his beliefs and accept the 'truth' as I know it."

For people convinced of the truth of their own beliefs, taking action to change the beliefs of those who do not share their beliefs, or even ridding the world of such dangerously misguided people, can seem to be the right thing to do. After all, if we know how the world works and the other people do not, should not these others be allowed to benefit from our wisdom? It is difficult to overestimate the allure of "helping" others by encouraging them to adopt our beliefs and practices. Despite the liberal desire to accept and perhaps even celebrate diversity, if we really know the truth, why not help others see it? Again, although many explicitly endorse a worldview that recognizes all people's right to believe whatever they want—this is, indeed, part of the American constitution and a central component of the American worldview—it can be exceedingly difficult *not* to intervene and attempt to change beliefs and attitudes that deviate from our own when we are strongly convinced of the superiority of our own perspective.

Consider the case of medical and agricultural practices. When we hear reports of people in the underdeveloped world dying of illness and starvation because their traditional tribal methods of medicine and farming are ineffective in a drought or disease-ridden environment, and we know ways of using modern technology to solve these problems, it seems morally imperative to help them see the light so they can reap the benefits of our more advanced technology. Anyone with even an ounce of concern for the welfare of others would be hard pressed *not* to try to bring our superior knowledge to bear to solve the crisis that the less fortunate occupants of the less developed world are facing. Our point here is not to assert whether or not such impulses are warranted or lead primarily to good or bad consequences. Rather, we are using this scenario to illustrate that there are often good intentions behind the strong desire people feel to change the practices of others they see as misguided and whom they believe can be helped by adopting one's own more enlightened perspective.

Now consider the case of a person who fervently believes that he or she has the benefit of knowing the truth about God or which form of social or economic organization is ultimately best for humankind. Throughout history, both distant and recent, there have been many cases of such "wisdom"—from Christian missionaries' desire to save the souls of the "savage godless people" who inhabited Africa and the Americas, to Hitler's vision of a pure Aryan race, to Stalin's utopian hopes for a Communist world order—where the future good of the many was seen as more important than the current needs and desires of the misguided and unfortunate few. From such a perspective, it does indeed seem to become one's "sacred duty" to take action to help others see the light. Usually, it is easy for the true believer to see the benefits to the others' eternal souls or the world's peace, prosperity, and well-being as more than justifying whatever actions must be taken to help bring about a better world order. Sacrifices must be made; some people may have to suffer, but it is all in the interest of a greater good. Most of us recoil at such reasoning when presented in the context of Hitler's Nazi ideology or Stalin's plan for world Communism. Clearly, all efforts to spread an ideology are not equally moral—judgments can and, we believe, should be made based on the content of the worldview and the consequences of its implementation. But the motivations fueling all of these movements, whether morally righteous or reprehensible, are essentially the same—to be part of an enduring, meaningful, self-worth–providing, and death transcendence–providing belief system.

Some may object that knowledge gained through scientific inquiry is different. Science is based on empirical observation; it has safeguards built into it that reduce bias and push toward a more objective answer to questions about how the world works. And one need only look at the fruits of a scientific approach in terms of reducing disease, improving agriculture, and generally raising our standard of living to argue that knowledge gained from science is somehow better—or at least has a better track record of being useful. We certainly agree that a scientific approach to understanding the world has some powerful advantages over other approaches; indeed, it is the one we use ourselves. But there are two important counterpoints. First, science has contributed to its share of aversive consequences, from Hiroshima and Chernobyl to technology leading to rampant pollution and the depletion of the ozone layer. Second, from the perspective of believers in any ideology, scientific or otherwise, their own particular conception of reality is inevitably going to be seen as better, and the benefits that would accrue to others, were they to accept their perspective, will seem obvious. Thus, from the perspective of the believer in any worldview, be it sacred or secular, taking action to bring nonbelievers into the fold is likely to be seen as reflecting pure and altruistic motives.

However, as the research reviewed in chapter 3 has shown, other psychological forces are at work here as well. Most notable are the threat to the security provided by our own worldviews by those with different conceptions and the increased security and perhaps sense of heroic altruistic goodness that come from helping others see the light. Our point is that what appears to the proselytizer as an act of virtue or kindness is likely to be rooted in deeper existential motives for the security provided by ever-increasing consensus for one's own worldview.

Things get even nastier when a cultural ideology explicitly directs people to go out and help others see the error of their ways and help them see the light of truth that shines through one's own worldview. From the perspective of many belief systems, it is indeed one's sacred duty to help others see the light, and this is formally encoded within the belief system. From evangelical Christianity to Stalinist Communism to fundamentalist Islam, part of the mission of the group is to bring everyone in the world into the fold, ultimately in the service of creating a utopia or heaven on earth. When a worldview explicitly values the active conversion of others to the fold, the individual follower is able to acquire self-esteem, grace, or a general sense of fulfilling one's duty by going out and trying to convince the rest of the world that their views are dangerously mistaken. In such cases, changing the beliefs or behavior of those who are different not only restores faith in one's own worldview but also helps establish oneself as a valuable contributor to that worldview—that is, it provides self-esteem and, in some cases, increased hope of a heavenly reward. Converting others thereby becomes an act of heroism, a pathway to salvation for the proselytizer.

The ultimate danger to others comes when one's worldview explicitly teaches that those who are different are so dangerous as to make their continued existence a serious threat to the well being of the ingroup and perhaps even the world as a whole. Sadly, this extreme reaction to those who are different has been a common feature of many ideologies throughout history. In the Spanish Inquisition, the Catholic Church "saved the souls" of heretics by burning them at the stake. During the early years of the colonization of North America, puritanical Christians in New England burned witches as a way of freeing them from the evil spirits that occupied their bodies. Sixty years ago, Adolph Hitler was able to mobilize much of the German population to participate in or at least tacitly condone his "final solution" to the "Jewish problem" in the death camps of Auschwitz and Buchenwald. And today, some Muslim leaders teach that it is the duty of the faithful to fight infidels—that is, non-Muslims—wherever they may be found. Since 1988, in a Fatwah declaring Jihad against America, Osama bin Laden declared it the sacred duty of all Muslims to kill Americans (Barr & Peterson, 2001):

> The ruling to kill the Americans and their allies—civilians and military—is an individual duty for every Muslim who can do it in any country in which it is possible to do it. . . . This is in accordance with the words of Almighty God. . . . We—with God's help—call on every Muslim who believes in God and wishes to be rewarded to comply with God's order to kill the Americans and plunder their money wherever and whenever they find it. We also call on Muslim ulema, leaders, youths, and soldiers to launch the raid on Satan's U.S troops and the devil's supporters allying with them, and to displace those who are behind them so that they may learn a lesson. (p. 32)

Such injunctions go beyond simply inciting violence and hatred; they make it sinful or evil *not* to hate and to allow others to live in peace.

The essence of the terror management view of ethnopolitical violence is that the mere existence of those who are different poses a threat to the individual's faith in the absolute validity and correctness of his or her own perspective on reality. This threat undermines the protection against deep existential fears that our worldviews provide. Derogating different others, working to convert them to one's own worldview, and in some cases doing battle to eliminate them from the face of the earth and thus help create a more perfect world can thus become a heroic, self-esteem–enhancing, and salvation-assuring virtuous activity that adds further protection to the defensive shield that we all need to survive in a world where the only real certainly is our inevitable demise.

Fortunately, not everyone responds to his or her existential dilemma by becoming hateful and violent toward others. Although we have argued that the roots of hatred and hostility toward those who are different can be found in the threat they pose to our own beliefs and values, and that religions sometimes actively promote efforts to change or eliminate those with different worldviews, most religions also actively discourage such behavior and teach love and kindness toward those who are different. For example, in spite of the many cases of Christian aggression against those with different beliefs, loving thy neighbor, acceptance of those who are different, and peace and goodwill toward all people have been central tenets of the Christian faith since its inception. Similarly, despite the recent calls for Jihad and holy war on the part of some Muslims, the Koran explicitly forbids taking the life of others or oneself except for just cause:

> If anyone slew a person—unless it be for murder or spreading mischief in the land—it would be as if he slew the whole people. And if anyone saved a life, it would be as if he saved the life of the whole people. (Chapter 5, Verse 32)

> Come, I will tell you what your Lord has made binding on you . . . that you shall not commit foul sins, whether openly or in secret; and that you shall not kill—for that is forbidden by Allah—except for a just cause. (Chapter 6, Verse 149)

We suspect that these injunctions against unjustified violence may have developed to stem the tendency to respond with disdain and hostility toward those who are different, a tendency that seems inherent in the way people maintain faith in their worldviews. The problem, then, is not religion per se but, rather, the human difficulty in coping with the threat posed to the protection against existential fear provided by our own cultural beliefs and values.

Given that love and hatred, tolerance and bigotry, and peace and war have all characterized the existence of virtually all religious and ideological groups at various periods in history, the question becomes what tips the balance from one side to the other? What pushes people away from tolerance in the direction of hatred? Our empirical work suggests a number of factors that can tip the balance. The mortality salience research we reviewed in chapters 3, 4, and 6 shows that individuals who subscribe to worldviews that emphasize the importance of tolerance do not derogate different others when thoughts of tolerance are in or close to consciousness—even when mortality is salient. People with high self-esteem also are less prone to derogating different others when mortality is salient. In contrast, people who have authoritarian tendencies, who are low in self-esteem, and who experience a preponderance of negative affective states (such as neurotics and depressives) react to mortality salience with especially strong worldview defense.

In sum, people who are most likely to lash out at different others are those who subscribe to narrow, rigid worldviews that do not value tolerance, and those prone to low self-esteem and negative affective states. This is especially likely when such people are living under conditions of heightened mortality salience, as in war-torn, starving, or disease-ridden regions of the world. This empirically based description turns out to be a good general characterization of the types of people who commit acts of terrorism. Of course, this psychological analysis must be supplemented with historical and political analyses to explain the precise nature and determinants of contemporary Islamic terrorism. So let us now focus on this specific question: What leads some people in today's Islamic world to be so angry and hostile toward the United States as to be willing to sacrifice their own lives to lash out at the Western world?

TERROR MANAGEMENT AND ISLAMIC TERRORISM

Terrorism is one particular type of violence among many others. We should not forget about ordinary murder, rape, assassination, military conflicts, and genocidal extermination efforts. In fact, terrorism has been responsible for only a minute fraction of the bloodshed that has occurred over the course of history. But it is a type of violence of particular concern in the world today, not only because of the American tragedies and lingering insecurities caused by the events of 9/11 but also because of its role in continually blocking compromise peace efforts in the Middle East and elsewhere and because of the attacks on the Indian Parliament on December 13, 2001, by Pakistani Islamic militants (Jones, 2001, December 29), which recently almost led to all-out war between two nuclear-armed nations. Terrorism is different from other forms of violence in several important ways. It is almost always a surprise attack carried out by a single individual or small group of individuals and conducted to enact revenge or spread feelings of terror among a large group of people. The attacks are often directed at random targets, but as we know, they are also often directed at politically important targets. What leads to such acts?

Let us begin by suggesting that terrorism is a response to a perceived grievance from people who are in a position of physical—that is, political, economic, or military—weakness. If everything were going well, then even the most ardent adherent to the most extreme ideological creed would be in no position to grouse. Despite the threat to one's worldview posed by competing visions of reality, an effectively functioning cultural system would provide enough meaning and personal value for people to be able to bear the threat posed by alternative worldviews in less destructive ways. Although virtually all people have a need to defuse the threat posed by alternative worldviews in some way, it is only when one is unable to get one's physical and psychological needs met within the context of one's own worldview that blatant hostility and violence toward those who are different are likely to come to the forefront. And if one were coming from a position of strength, one would presumably use the political, economic, or military powers at one's disposal to remedy the currently problematic situation. Although there may be conflicts, and these conflicts may be violent, people resort to the random or surprise killing of typically innocent outgroup members to create terror throughout the outgroup, primarily when they lack the power to address their grievances in more straightforward ways. Thus, terrorism is the product of extremely difficult life circumstances in a group of people who perceive that they lack the physical, political, or military power to solve their problems in other ways. Those who support terrorism may truly feel that it is their only chance for improving their lot in life and that of their group.

But terrorists are psychological weaklings, too. As Erich Fromm, in *The Anatomy of Human Destructiveness* (1973), and Ernest Becker, in *Escape From Evil* (1975), pointed out, destructive people lack not only the physical power to exert their will without hurting others but also the psychological and intellectual fortitude to develop a constructive alternative to existing conditions. Random or targeted killing of innocent civilians is unlikely to be an effective means of bringing about constructive social or cultural change. It does, however, often hamper efforts to develop compromise solutions to intergroup conflicts.

The history of previous terrorist activities shows that, in the vast majority of cases, such actions tend to lead to a strong backlash and undermine whatever support a cause might have had hopes of acquiring from those in power. It also tends to lead to forceful action to eliminate the threat that terrorists pose to the rest of us. This certainly seems to be the case with the conflict sparked by 9/11. As we write, the Taliban government of Afghanistan that provided support and shelter for the al Qaeda terrorist organization responsible for the 9/11 attacks has been violently removed from power, and Osama bin Laden and the al Qaeda terrorist network are clearly on the run and may well be near the point of extinction. Terrorist action is the recourse of those who are unable to develop more constructive means of solving their problems. It is the result of a failing economic and political system that is unable to meet the needs of its constituents. Because of this breakdown, the populace is unable to muster the psychological resources necessary to develop strategies more likely to bring about effective social change.

The Middle East has been embroiled in terrorism for most of the 20th century and all of the 21st so far. Despite the riches that an oil-based economy have brought to the wealthy elite and royal families in some Middle Eastern countries, the standard of living for the average person in much of the Islamic world is among the lowest on the planet. These economic woes are made worse by the affluent lifestyles enjoyed by the tiny percentage of their countrymen—usually those coming from elite families with close ties to the government—who have been able to capitalize on the oil industry. To note just one example, at the age of 25, one wealthy prince in Saudi Arabia was able to spend $300 million on an opulent palace and shortly thereafter received a $1 billion commission on the kingdom's telephone contract with AT&T (Zakaria, 2001). When such conspicuous affluence is juxtaposed against the abject poverty of the masses, discontent is the likely result.

To make matters worse, the wealthy ruling families have, for the most part, enforced highly restrictive regimes that deny their citizens even the most basic civil rights. Writing in *Newsweek*, Fareed Zakaria (2001) and Samuel P. Huntington (2002, January), prominent experts on Middle Eastern politics, both suggested that Islamic fundamentalism arose partly because it provided the only voice able to speak out against corrupt regimes. For example, the revolution in Iran that toppled the wealthy Shah's regime and brought a fundamentalist Shiite Islamic government headed by the Ayatollah Khomeini was successful largely because it was able to mobilize the masses through religion. And religious fervor is the one force that the powerful elite seems unable to counter effectively, perhaps because religion serves death transcendence so directly and provides the promise of something better in a next life for those doing so poorly, from both a material and a psychological perspective, in this one.

Ironically, it also appears that some Middle East governments, most notably the Saudi Arabian royal family, have provided strong support to Islamic fundamentalist groups, such as the extremely puritanical Wahhabi sect. This is one of the most extreme militant versions of Islam currently popular both in the Middle East and in the rest of the world. For example, a Wahhabi textbook that is required reading in all 10th-grade Saudi classrooms, teaches students, "it is compulsory for Muslims to be loyal to each other and to consider the infidels their enemies" (cited in Zakaria, 2001). By pouring both economic and political support into militant Wahhabism, the Saudi rulers obtain spiritual legitimization for their government and avert the potential for the rage of the impoverished masses to be turned against them in the form of internal struggle. Thus, although Islam has in some cases been used to speak out against the inequality and social injustices present in many Middle Eastern countries, it is increasingly being co-opted by the financial support that the ruling families are able to provide it.

The Scapegoating of America

As Osama bin Laden stated in an interview on *Frontline* (5/1998):

Our battle against the Americans is far greater than our battle was against the Russians. . . .They have attacked Islam and its most significant sacrosanct symbols. . . . We anticipate a black future for America.

What the radical Islamic clerics seem to be doing is turning the Western world into a scapegoat for the various troubles that face their followers. This is not to say that Western and particularly American policies have the interest of the Islamic people in mind. American economic and political interests have long dictated our policy, both in the Middle East and throughout the world, and people worldwide are rightly suspicious of our motives and often resentful of our use of economic incentives and military might to achieve our objectives. We will return to the role that U.S. foreign policy has played in the growing conflict shortly. But for now, we simply wish to point out that by turning America into "The Great Satan," the radical Islamic sects have redirected rage that might well have been focused elsewhere in the absence of having the Western world to blame for all the woes of the world. Future fanatics begin to locate their problems as resulting from the mere existence of their supposed enemy, above and beyond the actual political, economic, and military conditions that prevail at the moment or have existed in the past. Bernard Lewis (1990) observed the following:

At times this hatred goes beyond hostility to specific interests or actions or policies or even countries and becomes a rejection of Western civilization as such, not only what it does but also what it is, and the principles and values that it practices and professes. These are indeed seen as innately evil, and those who promote or accept them as the "enemies of God." (p. 48)

It is quite easy to see how a wealthy secular country that seems to be moving away from the traditional moral values that are held in high esteem in the Middle East but are now viewed as outmoded by many Americans can be easily vilified. The glitzy, materialistic, sexually open American way of life is indeed quite alien to traditional Islamic values, as it is to fundamentalist Christian values. As we have argued repeatedly in this volume, ways of life different from one's own threaten the existential protection that one's culture provides. This is all the more likely to be the case when those espousing the different values and living according to different principles and ethics appear to be highly successful and prosperous, as we Americans are clearly seen in comparison to almost all of the rest of the world. From the American movies and pop songs that dominate the entertainment industry, to the American companies that dominate the world economy, to the American military that is now unrivaled as the supreme force in the new millenium, our nation dominates the world scene. And much of what we do with this dominant position is alien to traditional Islamic values. The fact that there is some inherent appeal to material wealth and sexual openness, and that behavior reflecting the American lifestyle dominates the world news and entertainment media, no doubt adds to the threat that such alien values pose to the traditional way of life in Middle Eastern countries.

The Threat of Modernity to Fundamentalist Ideologies

Francis Fukuyama (2002), among many other political commentators, has argued that it is not so much America per se that is threatening to the Islamic world, but the modernization and secular rule that dominates the Western world, of which the United States is the prime representative. Modernization and secularization are also what Christian fundamentalists in the United States have been railing against for years. Secular values, sexual liberation, equal rights for women, and explicit acceptance of those who do not share one's religious beliefs have all been raised by American fundamentalists as threats to the way of life they hold dear. And in America, just as in the Middle East, fundamentalist Christian groups decry the corrupt ways of the modern Western world and long for a return to an older, more traditional way of life. It is not just the Muslims who object to the values— or as they would put it, lack of values—that currently dominate contemporary Western culture. Pat Robertson made the following statement in *New York Magazine* (1986):

> The people who have come into (our) institutions (today) are primarily termites. They are into destroying institutions that have been built by Christians, whether it is universities, governments, our own traditions, that we have. . . . The termites are in charge now, and that is not the way it ought to be, and the time has arrived for a godly fumigation. (p. 24)

Modernity, the ongoing march of ideas and the changes in lifestyle that they bring about, has always been a threat to the dominant social order. The human propensity to increase our understanding of the world by integrating new information and experiences with existing beliefs and psychological structures inevitably pushes us toward new ways of thinking and understanding that often run counter to older traditional views. The history of ideas can be viewed as an ongoing struggle between new insights and long-standing conceptions. The conflicts posed by new ways of thinking are often extremely heated and sometimes violent. The ideas of Copernicus, Galileo, Darwin, and Freud were all hotly contested, not only within scientific circles but also, more broadly, within the culture at large, because they challenged comfortable existing ways of understanding the world that had long functioned to provide security to the society. Authorities often try desperately to suppress such new ideas, censoring them when possible, and sometimes going so far as to threaten to eliminate those who espouse them. Fortunately, ideas that fit well with empirical reality are difficult to keep under wraps. Although repressive forces may hold them back for some time, the practical advantages they provide tend to lead them to ultimately resurface and eventually be worked into the cultural mainstream.

It is tempting to suggest that rigidity and resistance to new ideas are exclusively products of right-wing ideologies. However, this is not always the case. For example, the leftist former Soviet Union was extremely intolerant of dissent, deviance, and new ideas. Just as the Taliban banned Western music in Afghanistan, the Soviet Communists suppressed the modern music of composers such as Shostakovich (Cross & Ewen, 1969). Thus, the problems of fundamentalism, rigidity, and intolerance are not matters of right versus left but matters of the specific content of worldviews and individual propensities (whether due to personality or circumstances) toward clinging to those worldviews in narrow, rigid ways.

This discussion leads to two important questions. First, what specifically do Islamic fundamentalists find so abhorrent in the modern Western world? Second, what accounts for the appeal of Islamic fundamentalism? The short answer to the first question is, a lot! As noted earlier, the Western emphasis on materialism, wealth, sexual openness, women's rights, and individual freedom can be readily seen as incompatible with traditional Islamic ways. Although these factors are of clear importance, Francis Fukuyama (2002) recently suggested that the Islamic disaffection with America and the West goes even deeper than this and reflects core Western values that make these more superficial departures from traditional morality possible:

> The Islamic world . . . celebrated September 11 because it humbled a society that they believed was at its base corrupt. This corruption was not just a matter of sexual permissiveness, homosexuality, and women's rights as they exist in the West, but stemmed in their view from secularism itself. What they hate is that the state in Western societies should be dedicated to religious tolerance and pluralism rather than to serving religious truth. (p. 46)

In many parts of the Islamic world, where the ultimate goal of a society is seen as serving God, a highly visible, successful, and dominant culture that is based on separating religion from politics is threatening because it makes possible, and indeed legitimizes, all of the more specific "abominations against God" they find so objectionable.

Note that this separation of church and state, and the deviations from traditional morality that such separation makes possible, is also a sore point for many religious conservatives within the United States. The stated objective of our own Christian Coalition is to establish—or in their view, reestablish—the United States as a Christian nation, guided by the rule of the Christian Bible. The popularity of this movement in the United States increased dramatically in response to the economic difficulties of the late 1970s and early 1980s and the threats to American pride posed by our virtual defeat in Vietnam and the changing social mores brought about by the cultural revolution of the 1960s. We suggest that rapid cultural change in which traditional values are challenged by the popularity of a newer, alternative, more liberal set of values, coupled with economic and political setbacks, often pave the way for fundamentalist cries for a return to traditional values. As Pat Robertson notes in his book entitled *The New World Order* (1991): "How can there be peace when drunkards, drug dealers, communists, atheists, New Age worshippers of Satan, secular humanists, oppressive dictators, greedy money-changers, revolutionary assassins, adulterers, and homosexuals are on top?" (p. 227)

Fukuyama argues that although many countries all over the world are offended by American materialism and our flaunting of traditional values, segments of the Islamic world are especially enraged by our modernity because the primary source of support for the impoverished masses there has been radical Islamic sects, who, in addition to helping meet the people's needs for food, medical help, and spiritual comfort, have also adamantly promoted the doctrine that the primary function of the state should be to serve God. In countries like Iran and Afghanistan (while under rule by the Taliban), where Islamic clerics have indeed become the leaders of government and where Western-style hedonism is anathema and punishable in some cases by death, strict Islamic Law has become the order of the day. In other countries, like Saudi Arabia, where the government has maintained power in part by providing support to fundamentalist sects like the Wahhabis, the daily affairs of the average person are more affected by proclamations made from the mosque than they are by the precepts of the royal families. From Fukuyama's perspective, the struggle we face, at least as it has been framed by the radical Islamic clerics, is a potentially apocalyptic battle between believers and nonbelievers, between the forces of good (them) and evil (us).

It is important to point out again that nothing inherent in the Islamic faith makes a secular, tolerant, pluralistic society unworkable—just as nothing in the Christian faith makes secularism and tolerance inevitable. The history of Christian domination of European government and the current waves of Christian fundamentalists who hope to turn the United States into a thoroughly Christian nation should quickly dispel such illusions. Jerry Falwell's stand is clear in the following quotation from a sermon entitled "A National Rebirth Needed" (2000):

> In spite of all these outward worldly signs of our national success, we are actually on the brink of destruction, and if we don't awaken now, it will be too late. . . . We have never been so prosperous. Yet, we have never

been so secular and pagan. We are becoming both amoral and immoral. We are making secularism our national religion.

So some Christians despise secularity and diversity. And many Muslims have no such qualms. Indeed, Muslims lived side by side with Christians, Jews, and Hindus, in relative peace and harmony, throughout most of the reign of the Ottoman Empire (Collins & Lapierre, 1972). Many Middle Eastern states, starting with Nassar's Egypt, actively embraced modernity, secularism, and at least limited democracy; today's Turkey is an example of an Islamic country that has continued to have at least moderate success as a modern secular state (Zakaria, 2001). We are arguing that it is the current confluence of political, economic, and, ultimately, psychological forces that has led large segments of the Islamic world to seek solace in fundamentalist theocracies that view modernism and secularism as inherently evil.

The Nature and Allure of Fundamentalism

Why is modern secularism, both here and in the Middle East, so antithetical to fundamentalism? We think a big part of the problem is that fundamentalists of all religious persuasions take the teachings of their religion in an absolute literal way. For a fundamentalist, if it is in the Bible, Talmud, or Koran, it must be literally true, down to the smallest detail. The problem with such literal interpretations of ancient sacred texts is that all such books were written millennia ago, in a language and style specific to a time, place, and indeed world, different from our own. Many sacred texts were written within a cultural context that used metaphor to communicate ideas that were too abstract and complex to be easily carried by straightforward literal text. This is especially apparent in Jesus' parables, as transmitted in the New Testament of the Christian Bible. The story of the Good Samaritan, for example, was clearly intended to convey a message about kindness and altruism rather than to recount the actual deeds of a person traveling the roads near ancient Jerusalem. Indeed, one of the hallmarks of the Abrahamic religions, from which Judaism, Christianity, and Islam all descended, is the movement away from worshipping tangible objects and idols, such as the Biblical Golden Calf, toward faith based on more abstract concepts that transcend the physical. In Protestant theologian Paul Tillich's (1959/1964) words:

> Religion opens up the depth of man's spiritual life which is usually covered by the dust of our daily life and the noise of our secular work. It gives us the experience of the Holy, of something which is untouchable, awe-inspiring, an ultimate meaning, the source of ultimate courage. This is the glory of what we call religion. (p. 9)

In other words, in Tillich's view, religious writings give voice to deep spiritual thoughts and feelings that cannot be easily (if at all) expressed by logical, rational discourse.

Tillich argued that it is important for believers to understand that religious symbols are just that, symbols, and should not be taken literally. If religious teachings are understood as a means of transmitting powerful truths about the human condition rather than literal recounting of history and concrete plans for practical action, then faith in one's spiritual world would not be undermined by the mere existence of alternative beliefs. For Tillich (1959/1964), religion becomes dangerous when adherents take their symbols literally, and in so doing become intolerant of anyone who does not share them: "But beside its [religion's] glory lies its shame. It makes its myths and doctrines, its rites and laws, into ultimates and persecutes those who do not subject themselves to it" (p. 9). If the teachings of one's sacred texts are viewed as literally and concretely true, then all other teachings become a threat to one's own. However, if one's religious teachings are taken in the symbolic context in which they were intended, this opens the door for peaceful coexistence and harmony among those who worship different gods or who do not worship any gods at all. We believe that the greatest danger of fundamentalism is the insistence on one literal truth—which happens to be the one that each individual fundamentalist sect espouses—with the consequent need to show the wrongness of any and all other systems of belief.

But perhaps such insistence on literal truth of all details is necessary for many or most people to acquire the psychological benefits that religious faith provides. People no doubt have an easier time understanding and finding meaning in concrete stories that are interpreted in a literal manner. Otto Rank argued that people need concrete manifestations of the more abstract conceptions of reality and value that they use to forge their existential protection. Flags, crosses, crescents, and stars are all used to symbolize something grander and more abstract than these particular objects and shapes, but people seem to find sacred value in the objects themselves. As discussed in chapter 3, our research has demonstrated the terror management function that such objects serve by showing that reminders of mortality increase people's distress when using cultural icons in a way counter to cultural norms.

Although the Judaism of Abraham forbade the worship of tangible physical objects, the Biblical story of Moses' dismay on discovering his people worshipping a golden calf when they were terrified of being lost in the desert suggests that people may be especially prone to long for concrete physical manifestations of their deity when they are most afraid. For individual terror management purposes, there is no doubt that absolute belief in the rightness of an unambiguous, meaning-providing, death-transcending worldview is preferable. To live with doubt about the basis of meaning and value in one's life is to live with tenuous equanimity. Yet it seems that one of the concomitants of the development of modern thought is the increasing movement away from a literal interpretation of religious dogma toward a more abstract and symbolic conception. It is interesting that this more abstract symbolic orientation seems to have characterized some Eastern religions, such as some forms of Buddhism, for many centuries. But most peoples of the world have had a hard time living within a relativistic abstract meaning system. People judged by psychologists as high in authoritarianism are particularly prone to clinging to concrete and rigid belief systems (e.g., Adorno, Frenkel-Brunswick, Levinson, & Sanford, 1950). Although people differ individually in these propensities, it also seems clear that economic and psychological threats move people toward authoritarian worldviews (Sales, 1973).

Of course, as noted earlier, the problem of international terrorism cannot be reduced to any one individual cause or root. Religious fundamentalism exists in many parts of the world, including the United States, where terrorist activity in the form of attacks against random civilians with the intention of inspiring panic in the masses is extremely rare—although Christian fundamentalist attacks on abortion clinics and their personnel do occur. Many segments of the world's population may feel threatened by modernism and American economic wealth and military might, but the vast majority do not consider us an enemy that must be destroyed. And although terrorism is not unique to the Islamic world, it is disproportionately found there. Writing in *Newsweek*, Samuel P. Huntington (2002, January) pointed out, "In one inventory of *The Economist*, Muslims were responsible for 11 and possibly 12 of 16 major acts of international terrorism between 1983 and 2000" (this obviously excludes many state-sponsored acts of violence around the globe). Thus we need to consider additional forces that are at work in creating the Middle Eastern powder keg that exploded on 9/11 here in the United States.

THE UNITED STATES' ROLE IN THE MIDDLE EAST

To this point, our discussion of the multitude of psychological, economic, and political forces that combined to produce the current crisis and ultimately led up to the terrorist bombings of 9/11 may seem to have conveniently avoided discussion of any possible role played by American foreign policy. It may appear that we are blind to the effect that American policies in the Middle East may have had in generating the hatred that led to the violence perpetrated against us. That is not the case. We have no doubt that American foreign policy has done a great deal to incite anger toward us, and we do not wish to downplay the role that our foreign policy has played in contributing to the current crisis. To say that American foreign policy is at least in part responsible for the hatred that many Arabs and Muslims feel toward the United States is not to say that our policies in any way justify terrorism or murder. Nor is it necessary to make moral judgments about such policies. It is quite possible that actions taken with all the best intentions could backfire and lead to resentment and even hatred. For understanding the roots of the current hostility toward Americans, the morality of U.S. policies is less important than understanding how they are perceived by the people who are affected by them. We turn now to a consideration of the role of U.S. foreign policy in generating the rage that led to the events of 9/11.

If you were to ask an Islamic terrorist what the United States has done wrong, what we have done to justify the extreme actions that bin Laden and associates have taken against us, he or she would no doubt produce a litany of offenses that our government has perpetrated against the Islamic world. Probably the major issues that would come up would be our ongoing support for Israel; our continued embargo and military strikes against Iraq; our lust for the resources locked up underground throughout the Middle East, for example, oil; our support of "corrupt regimes"; and the way we have thrown around our financial and military support to maximize our own economic well-being with little or no consideration of what this implies for the people living in these resource-rich but otherwise underdeveloped countries. We turn now to a consideration of each of these issues.

American Support of Israel

Much of the conflict in the Middle East is often framed in terms of the ongoing struggle between Israel and the Palestinian people. Many Arabs and Muslims view the United States' military and economic support of Israel as support for an illegitimate occupation of Arab lands. In the Fatwah urging Jihad against Americans (from *Al-Quds al-'Arabi*, 1998), bin Laden and his associates point to the U.S. support for the state of Israel as a direct act of hostility toward the Islamic world:

> If the Americans' aim behind these wars are religious and economic, the aim is also to serve the Jews' petty state and divert attention from its occupation of Jerusalem and murder of Muslims there. The best proof of this is their eagerness to destroy Iraq, the strongest neighboring Arab state, and their endeavor to fragment all the states of the region . . . into paper statelets and through their disunion and weakness guarantee Israel's continued survival and the continuation of the brutal crusade occupation of the Peninsula.

From the perspectives of many Arabs, Israel is occupying land that belongs to the Palestinian people and has no right to exist. The many years of declared and undeclared war between Israel and its neighboring Arab states reflect their competing claims for the same land. American support of Israel has made the United States an enemy of those who are enemies of Israel.

The truth is that although both Jews, who before the establishment of Israel, had last controlled this area in AD 70 , and Muslims living in the area have long-standing ties to Palestine, this piece of land has long been controlled by powerful outside forces, including Assyria, Babylon, Egypt, Greece, Rome, and the Ottoman Empire (Collins & Lapierre, 1972). Before the establishment of Israel in 1948, it had been controlled by the British, who had taken it over from the Ottoman Empire at the close of World War I. It was only in the middle of the 20th century that the land became nationalized. Of course, the problem is that both Jewish and Islamic people have legitimate historical claims to the land. This small area contains religious and historical sites considered sacred to Islam, Judaism, and Christianity. Perhaps this should not be surprising, because all three of these major faiths evolved in this same tiny region of the world. Because of their history in this region, all three of these religions make claims to the area, most importantly to Jerusalem, a holy city for all. Perhaps because Christianity has spread so thoroughly across Europe, the Americas, and the rest of the world, there is somewhat less urgency to the Christian claim for this territory. Thus, the primary conflict is between the states of Israel and Palestine, descendants of people who have inhabited these lands since ancient times.

The modern nation of Israel was first established in 1948 as part of a United Nations charter to give the beleaguered Jewish people a homeland after they suffered the horrors of the Holocaust in Nazi Germany and other parts of Central Europe. The Zionist movement, which fought for the establishment of an independent state, goes back somewhat further to roughly 1890. And this movement itself, of course, was an echo of long-standing longings of the Jewish people for a return to the Promised Land of their ancestors (Collins & Lapierre, 1972). Given the prejudice and hostility that Jews have suffered for more than 1,000 years while being dispersed throughout the largely Christian areas of Europe and Asia, many prominent Jewish intellectuals argued for the establishment of Israel as an independent state, back in the cradle of Jewish civilization, which had been inhabited primarily by nomadic Arab groups for the past 1,000 years. Although there had been discussion of the establishment of a Jewish homeland in the Middle East for several decades, the devastation Hitler's Nazis wrought on the Jews of Europe led to a swelling of support for the formal establishment of the Israeli state. The problem, of course, was that other people also lived in these territories and an already fierce fight (replete with acts of terrorism) for the treasured territories intensified greatly once the British ceded control of the area and Israel was officially created. Progress has often been made toward a stabilizing compromise solution that could lead to peace and serve everyone, including us in America—everyone except for those who deny one side or the other's right to exist at all. The Palestinian radical groups who hold this extremist position have continually used terrorist attacks precisely to disrupt progress toward such a solution. Among those truly interested in a mutually acceptable compromise, the most difficult sticking point beyond the continual flare-ups of bloodshed remains Jerusalem, for which both groups have ancient claims (from Collins & Lapierre, 1972, p. 7). These problems were evident even in the songs of the exiled children of Israel, sung by the waters of Babylon, Psalm 137:

How shall we sing the Lord's song in a strange land?
If I forget thee, O Jerusalem, let my right hand forget her cunning.
If I do not remember thee, let my tongue cleave to the roof of my mouth;
If I prefer not Jerusalem above my highest joys.

And it is also echoed in the Hadith, the sayings of the Prophet Mohammed:

O Jerusalem, the choice of Allah of all his lands! In it are the chosen of his servants. From it the earth was stretched forth and from it shall it be rolled up like a scroll. The dew which descends upon Jerusalem is a remedy from every sickness because it is from the gardens of Paradise.

American Economic and Military Policy in the Middle East

In addition to objecting to our relatively consistent support of Israel in its ongoing struggle with its Middle Eastern neighbors, the Fatwa, commanding Muslims to "kill Americans," states two other major grievances, both related to U.S. foreign policy in the Middle East. First, bin Laden and associates are incensed by the presence of American military forces in Saudi Arabia and other parts of the region (bin Laden, 1998):

For over seven years the United States has been occupying the lands of Islam in the holiest of places, the Arabian Peninsula, plundering its riches, dictating to its rulers, humiliating its people, terrifying its neighbors and turning its bases in the Peninsula into a spearhead through which to fight the neighboring Muslim peoples.

Second, the Fatwa views the American-led war against Iraq as further evidence of our malevolence toward the Muslim world and justification for the holy war they wish to wage against our country (from Al-Quds al-'Arabi, 1998):

The best proof of this is the Americans' continuing aggression against the Iraqi people using the Peninsula as a staging post, even though all its rulers are against their territories being used to that end, still they are helpless. . .despite the great devastation inflicted on the Iraqi people by the crusader-Zionist alliance, and despite the huge number of those killed, in excess of 1 million . . . despite all this, the Americans are once again trying to repeat the horrific massacres, as though they are not content with the protracted blockade imposed after the ferocious war or the fragmentation and devastation.

In general, then, the al Qaeda terrorists view American foreign policy in the Middle East as fundamentally evil, selfish, and blasphemous toward Muslim holy sites and intent on destroying Iraq and fractionating the Islamic world. Some of the grievances lodged by bin Laden and his ilk are fueled by anti-Semitism, some by antimodernity; some may have elements of validity.

Regardless of whether they are valid or not, the perception of these grievances as just among many Muslims in the Middle East is a problem for everyone. Clearly, many forces are at work determining U.S. policies in the Middle East. American political support for the right of Israel to exist and economic interest in the plentiful oil that is found in many Middle Eastern countries have undoubtedly been the prime forces behind our policies in the region. Our support of and alliances with the rulers of the countries richest in oil serve both the economic well-being of American companies that are involved in the refining and distribution of Middle Eastern oil and the availability of a steady supply of oil to American consumers at prices well below those found in the rest of the industrialized world. Many people viewed the enthusiasm with which the United States came to the aid of Kuwait when it was invaded by Iraq and the ongoing attempts to minimize Iraqi military power as signs of our concern for keeping the oil flowing our way at low prices from our Middle Eastern allies. Certainly, a case can be made that American foreign policy, in the Middle East and the world over, is overly influenced by our short-term economic interests.

Another factor often cited as playing a critical role in American foreign policy in the Middle East is the strategic value of the bases we have established in various locations there for our military (see e.g., Kosterlitz, 2001). The Middle East is at the crossroads between Asia, Europe, and Africa. Thus, the presence of American military bases in the region provides a major strategic advantage, giving us the potential to launch military campaigns in many different directions. This was clearly of great importance during the Cold War years, when it seemed necessary to be ready to counter the threat of feared Soviet military activities. Given the instability in many countries on all three of these adjoining continents, military bases in the various Middle Eastern countries with which we are allied continue to be a valuable asset. From this perspective, the claim that American foreign policy in the Middle East is driven by strategic military concerns is also a valid one.

Of course, it is natural that a nation's foreign policies foremost serve the needs of its own people. What fundamentalists and others in the Islamic world object to is that we have pursued our economic and military interests throughout the Middle East with relatively little concern for the impact of our policies on the people living there. These objectives have led us to support corrupt monarchies and dictatorships that have done little to address the needs of their own people. And these same economic and military interests have led us to bring military troops into areas that are considered holy by the Islamic religion and to take military action against Iraq, which has indeed led to the deaths of many innocent people. These policies and actions have led to the inference by many Muslims that our government and people are hostile to Arabs and Muslims. In referring to Great Britain and the United States in a November 1996 interview for *Nida'ul Islam*, bin Laden noted, "It is well known that the policies of these two countries bear the greatest enmity toward the Islamic world." The fact that our country's dominant religion is Christianity, which at many points in its history has been actively hostile toward Islam, adds to this perception. And as discussed previously in this chapter, the flaunting of materialism, sexuality, and women's rights, which seem to run counter to Islamic values, provides further grist for the argument that the United States must be hostile toward Islam.

Although it is undeniable that economic and military concerns play a major role in U.S. policies in the Middle East, and that humanitarian concerns have often taken a back seat, we doubt that a core hatred and malevolence toward Muslims has been responsible for American foreign policy in the region. If this were the case, why would the United States have committed its armed forces to defend the Muslim people in Bosnia and Kosovo in the former Yugoslavia? Historically, the United States has also supported a variety of other Islamic countries, such as Kuwait and Somalia, against outside aggressors of various sorts. In addition, millions of Muslims have immigrated to the United States and have been able to live here in peace and thrive under the same rights and protections granted to all legal aliens and citizens. Although the Israelis are indeed close allies with the United States and we have supplied them with military and economic aid, over the years we have also supplied such aid to Islamic countries, such as Afghanistan, Iran, and even Iraq.

Moreover, dating back at least to Henry Kissinger's work in the Nixon administration of the 1970s, the U.S. government has tried a variety of tactics to bring the Israeli and Palestinian people together in negotiations aimed at creating a workable and lasting solution to the conflict that has existed between these groups for so long. Although the motives behind American foreign policy in the Middle East certainly do reflect a concern for our own economic and military well-being, and it is certainly true that *some* Americans are indeed prejudiced against Arabs and Muslims (and virtually any other group that is different from their view of the prototypical American), we seriously doubt that hatred of Arab and Islamic people plays a major role in determining American foreign policy in the region.

CONCLUSION: WHERE DO WE GO FROM HERE?

We return to the question that opened this chapter—why do so many Arabs and Muslims have hostility toward America? We can sum it up this way. Part of the reason is the preaching of Islamic extremists, like Osama bin Laden and others, who are convinced of our malevolence and whose own political agenda is advanced by depicting Americans as hateful devils intent on the destruction of Islam. There, as here and everywhere else, the attitudes of the masses are strongly influenced by the words of their leaders, their clerics, and the media—but only if these words fit their psychological needs. The various psychological forces discussed earlier in this chapter have led to a discontent, anxiety, restlessness, and, most important, need for meaning and value that has been satisfied in large part by focusing on a great repository of evil—or scapegoat—on which to blame the people's troubles. The United States, with its secular values, relaxing of traditional morals, economic wealth, and military might, seems an ideal candidate for being held responsible for the various woes that have befallen the people of the Islamic world. Indeed, who else has the power to have wreaked such havoc and caused such dismay? Only an extremely powerful country could have such a large impact, and today the United States is unrivaled as the most powerful nation in the world.

Although we believe that an interrelated set of psychological forces lead many people in the Islamic world to dislike the United States, we also believe that American foreign policies do indeed bear some of the responsibility for the hostility and suspicion that many people in the less developed world feel toward us. One could argue that the United States is well within its rights to pursue advantageous deals with those who control the flow of oil in the Middle East and to place military bases in Arab countries that permit us to do so (to protect our allies against malevolent forces in the region and nearby). One can also make the case that the United States had other concerns in addition to simple greed and a lust for oil that led us to go to war with Iraq in the early 1990s. However, we believe it imperative that our government work harder to understand the impact that such policies have among the disaffected people in the region. Although economic and military advantages are legitimate reasons to pursue particular foreign policies, they should not be the *only* ones. If we as a nation truly do believe that freedom and prosperity are basic rights of all people, these rights must extend to people all over the world, not just within our own borders. We should do this for moral reasons but also because doing all that we can to ensure the freedom, prosperity, and opportunity of people all over the world is ultimately in our own best interest. Indeed, it may well be the best way possible to meet our long-term goals for economic growth and a stable, peaceable world, for ourselves and for others. Poverty and a lack of a sense of meaning and value lead to a need to participate in a heroic triumph over evil, and this need ultimately can lead to acts of violence such as those perpetrated against us on 9/11. If people were getting their material *and* psychological needs met, they would have little inclination to hate and destroy. Doing all that we can to help the people of the Middle East achieve peace and prosperity is ultimately in our own best interest.

Of course, we are far from the first to suggest this (e.g., Huntington, 2002; Zakaria, 2001), and, to some extent, such thinking has played a role in U.S. foreign policy for many years. Although strategic military and economic concerns certainly played a role in our involvement in the Gulf War with Iraq of the early 1990s, so, too, did a concern with the welfare of the people of Kuwait, who were invaded by the Iraqis, the rights of the long-persecuted Kurdish people within Iraq, and ongoing military build up and manufacture of weapons of mass destruction by the Saddam Hussein regime. The fact that for years some governments within the Middle East have actively sponsored terrorist attacks against Israeli and American military and civilians has certainly been another factor in determining our policies toward these nations. We simply suggest that our government needs to be more far sighted, be more sensitive to the worldviews and well-being of the people of the region, and take more factors into account when making critical decisions about our relationship with the various nations in the Islamic world.

The Middle Eastern conflict has been one of the most intractable in all of history. But greater attention needs to be paid to the psychological needs of the people embroiled in this conflict, and we hope that our work helps illuminate these psychological needs. People need to sustain faith in a meaningful worldview and, based on that worldview, to be able to establish an enduring self-worth and a sense of death transcendence—that one is more than just an animal doomed to absolute annihilation. Fundamentalist doctrines are appealing sources to fulfill these terror management needs, particularly when secular, material bases of self-worth and a sense of valued participation in the larger global scene are highly limited. Strategies need to be developed to help the people in this region meet their needs so that they will be less prone to the insecurities and resentments that lead them toward rigid worldviews that advocate the destruction of others. Like every other thinking person on the planet, we realize that this is a daunting task—this is why "solving the problems in the Middle East" is so often jokingly used as a metaphor for an impossible dream. But it is imperative that we work toward this goal, no matter how impossible it may seem to achieve. Our survival, and that of the world, may depend on it. In the next chapter, we use the foregoing analysis to make some suggestions that might be helpful in moving us toward lasting peace.

8

GIVING PEACE A CHANCE

This is the great moral that Albert Camus drew from our demonic times, when he expressed the moving hope that a day would come when each person would proclaim in his own fashion the superiority of being wrong without killing than being right in the quiet of the charnel house.
—Ernest Becker, *Escape From Evil* (1975, p. 145)

Now that we have explored how terror management theory (TMT), in combination with a consideration of important historical, political, and economic factors, can shed light on the causes of the international terrorism currently plaguing our nation, we can offer some suggestions for ameliorating this problem. Although rooted in very different specific concerns and played out in very different ways, the anger, hostility, and fear felt by people involved with terrorism result, we believe, from the same basic underlying psychological dynamic we all share. Both those who resort to terrorism and those who are the victims of it are responding to potent threats to the psychological structures that provide the psychological security that makes possible a satisfying life in the frightening world in which we reside. We have reviewed a large body of evidence from rigorously controlled psychological research that supports our contentions that humans need conceptions of the world and their place in it to help manage concerns about mortality. These conceptions in turn contribute to the genesis of hostility toward those who subscribe to alternative worldviews. And we have explained how this work illuminates an important facet of the clash between the Western and Islamic worlds. However, for our ideas about the causes of terrorism to have any real value, they must be useful in suggesting some ways of bringing about a more peaceful and stable state of affairs in the Middle East and the world at large.

We should say at the outset that finding a solution to the problems that led to the bombing of the World Trade Center and Pentagon is a daunting task that many have faced before, with the occasional limited success and then an inevitable series of frustrating setbacks. The roots of the problems run extremely deep and entail issues of great importance to the hearts and souls of the people living in the war-torn Middle East. Attempts to resolve the crisis, therefore, require solutions that similarly reach out to the hearts and souls of those involved and meet the frustrated needs that have for so long bred hatred and distrust. We believe that this is precisely the situation for which a psychological analysis can be most productively used to complement other (e.g., political, economic, sociological, and theological) approaches to these problems.

A terror management analysis is based on the idea that to control our basic fears all humans must find enduring ways of embedding themselves within humanly created meaning systems that offer bases of self-worth and a sense that we are more than just animals doomed only to die and decay. The particular cultures within which we are socialized provide these psychological bases of security for each of us. Intergroup conflict results from worldviews that are easily threatened by alternative belief systems and by worldviews that portray other groups as evil and prescribe destruction of such groups as a lofty basis for self-worth and death transcendence. And this is precisely what we have in the case of fundamentalist worldviews in general and Islamic terrorist worldviews in particular.

From this perspective, then, one thing we need to do to achieve lasting peace is to facilitate some changes in these worldviews. If such worldviews could be shifted toward tolerance and toward more constructive and attainable bases of self-worth and death transcendence, this problem truly could go away, or at least be vastly abridged. Much easier said then done, no doubt. One thing we have learned from our own empirical work is that what makes people cling most tightly to their current worldviews and behave most negatively toward those with alternative views is heightened mortality salience. Thus, another key to ameliorating the current conflicts and facilitating worldview change is to reduce mortality salience in places where it has been all too salient—another tall order. Our analysis thus suggests two extremely challenging goals. The big question is, how can we progress toward achieving them?

If a potential solution is to have any chance of success, it must start with a basic respect for the beliefs and values of all those involved. It also must entail more than starry-eyed ideals and calls for better understanding, more tolerance, and universal love and acceptance for all. It must be practical and take into account the realities and complexities of the situations as they exist in the real world. It must go further than catch phrases and inspiring slogans and must provide concrete tangible suggestions for how to bring about the desired end-states. In this spirit, we offer a series of suggestions, both for general objectives that need to be pursued to help move the region toward stability and peace and for some specific strategies on how these more abstract objectives might be achieved. Of course, our expertise is in psychological understanding of human social behavior, not in foreign policy, economics, political science, and diplomacy. So our suggestions, which necessarily intersect with these domains, should be taken as guidelines based on our psychological analysis that would require the expertise of others for refinement and implementation.

MEETING THE NEEDS OF THE PEOPLE

We have argued that the Middle East is currently such a powder keg because the needs of the people residing there are not being met. As Abraham Maslow (1970) taught us, people have a variety of hierarchically organized needs, from physical needs for the basic requisites for continued life, to psychological needs for security, and ultimately toward the even more abstract needs for self-expression and growth. Maslow believed that the more basic needs for biological sustenance must be met before people become concerned about psychological security and that, similarly, security needs must be met before growth motives become a major focus. Although we doubt that policy makers have consciously attempted to apply Maslow's need hierarchy in their attempts to engender peace in the Middle East, this line of thinking seems to dominate most existing strategies for solution. The emphasis seems to be on first trying to stop the fighting, thereby ensuring the people's physical survival, and then fostering economic growth or, more commonly, providing financial aid to meet people's other physical needs.

Although we agree that the fighting must be stopped and people's basic physical needs for sustenance must be met, this is only the beginning of a solution to the problems that lead to terrorist violence. From the perspective of TMT, people's more abstract needs for meaning and value must also be addressed if there is to be any real hope for peace in this or any other region. Man does not live by bread alone; the deeply religious nature of the present conflict attests to this ancient wisdom. And attempts to stop the violence solely through military measures are likely to breed only more contempt and further violence. The renewed deadly clashes between Israeli and Palestinian forces in the winter and spring of 2002 have provided continued demonstrations of this basic fact. The violent attacks by both sides seem to have served only to reinforce all parties' belief in the malevolence and evil of their opponents, leading to further violence and an escalating cycle of reprisals. The clearest effect of violent actions by both sides, whether they be in the form of suicide bombers or military invasion, seems to be that of verifying the embattled parties' view of each other as hateful inhuman monsters with a deep, unquenchable thirst for the blood of one's own people.

A lasting end to the violence that has long plagued the Middle East and recently spilled over into our own country requires that the unmet psychological needs that have given rise to violence be satisfied. Although poverty and economic frustration must certainly be reduced if a plan for peace is to have any hope of success, the more abstract psychological needs for meaning and value that provide the individual with the security necessary to face life in our dangerous universe are also of vital importance. Meaning systems in which those on the other side are seen as repositories of all-encompassing evil must be changed in order to give peace even the faintest chance of blossoming.

As we argued in the previous chapter, threats posed by modernity and Western values also play a big role in the disdain and rage that many Muslims feel toward the Western world and their own corrupt governments that they believe are kept in power by Western governments. When the core values of one's culture are being threatened, it becomes exceedingly difficult to obtain meaning and self-esteem within that cultural context. Poverty and the absence of opportunity within the economic marketplace make heroism within the context of a radical religious worldview seem like the only option for feeling valuable that is available to many young people living in this region. Both economic needs for a decent standard of living and psychological needs for obtaining meaning and value within the context of one's culture must be met if there is to be any hope of achieving a stable peace in the Middle East.

Although these are monumental tasks, we believe them to be highly interrelated. Economic security would reduce the threat posed by alternative cultural beliefs, and an ability to achieve a sense of personal value without resorting to radical extremism would facilitate economic growth and financial security. Indeed, all of the needs that we discuss are intimately intertwined. Just as deficits in one area exacerbate the negative impact of problems in the others, so, too, would gains in one area facilitate movement toward meeting people's needs in other areas. Just as the current situation can be viewed as a vicious cycle of interrelated problems spinning out of control, so, too, can our suggestions for peace be viewed as a set of interrelated steps, each of which will make progress in other needed areas all the more likely.

ENHANCING MEANING AND REDUCING THE THREAT OF ALTERNATIVE WORLDVIEWS

From a TMT perspective, the more secure one's faith in one's own cultural worldview, and the more one is able to get a sense of personal value from one's worldview, the less threatening alternative conceptions of reality become. We have already noted the importance of economic development in helping people achieve a sense of value without having to resort to extreme acts such as martyrdom through terrorist attacks. What needs to be accomplished to reduce further the outrage that many Muslims feel about the lifestyles practiced in the Western world is to develop other ways of attaining meaning and value within the Islamic cultural context that do not require a denouncement of the West. In essence, we are arguing that steps need to be taken to encourage tolerance of divergent belief systems, and that before such tolerance is likely to emerge, alternative means of achieving security within the context of the Islamic worldview must be provided for the people.

First of all, it is essential that Muslims all over the world be made to feel that their lifestyle is respected and valued by people of other faiths and of no faith. Missionary activities to try to convince Muslims that their beliefs are wrong and that they would do better by converting to other faiths (whether religious or secular) are clearly counterproductive in that they communicate a fundamental incompatibility of Christianity, Judaism, and the Western world with the Islamic faith. In other words, if we want to encourage tolerance and acceptance of diversity within the Islamic world, we must first demonstrate our own tolerance and acceptance of the religious and cultural beliefs valued by Muslims.

This is no simple task. Just as many of the humanistic, capitalistic, and modernistic values practiced in the West are abhorrent to many Muslims, so too are the harsh traditional religious values preached by Islamic fundamentalists abhorrent to many people in the West. Traditional Islamic justice, treatment of women, and the low value placed on the rights of the individual are diametrically opposed to modern Western values. This poses a major ethical dilemma: To what extent should we tolerate and implicitly condone practices that run counter to our own deeply held values? Of course, this is the same dilemma that people in the Islamic world face when contemplating the godless and "decadent" lifestyles commonly practiced in the Western world. A fine line must be walked here, and some tolerance for practices that we find objectionable ultimately may be the best way to bring about change. Although we should not condone violations of basic human rights, neither should we be too adamant in our demands for immediate change in these very sensitive areas. Again, we are suggesting that what is needed is a long-term strategy to bring about constructive social change that will make long-term peace in the Middle East a possibility. Perhaps the ultimate question here is whether Islam is, in fact, compatible with modern Western values.

We, and many Muslims all over the world, believe that it is or at least that it can be. As noted earlier, although there are verses in the Koran that condone and even promote violence and intolerance, there are also verses that promote a general respect for all life and equal rights for all. It is not

Islam, per se, that is incompatible with Western values and human rights, but the radical fundamentalist versions of Islam that have currently taken hold of parts of the Middle East. As we have noted in previous chapters, intolerant fundamentalist Islam has much in common with the intolerant fundamentalist Christianity promoted by Jerry Falwell and Pat Robertson in the United States and strands of Orthodox Judaism promoted by some groups in Israel. Fortunately, there are more liberal versions of each of these religions that are highly committed to the peaceful coexistence of all. Thus, what needs to be countered is intolerance and fundamentalism rather than any particular religion.

A major step toward this goal would be getting the moderate Islamic world involved in the quest for peace. Just as the radical Islamic clerics preach Jihad and intolerance, so, too, could the more moderate clerics take a more active role in promoting peace, love, and tolerance. The Koran could certainly be quoted to support such moderate views:

> Let there be no compulsion in religion. (Chapter 2, Verse 256)

> We made you into nations and tribes so that you may know one another. (Chapter 9, Verse 13)

The message needs to get out that Allah is not really impressed by murder and suicide bombers and that those with different beliefs are not necessarily and inherently one's enemy, as preached by many of the fundamentalist sects.

This message is unlikely to be effective if it comes from Americans or Europeans, or from people who are not deeply committed to the Islamic faith. Decades of research on basic communication and persuasion processes teach us that people are more persuaded by messages when they are presented by similar others from their own group, especially when these voices are credible, charismatic experts on the subject in question (e.g., Hovland, Janis, & Kelley, 1953). Messages extolling the core Islamic values of peace and brotherhood for all need to come from respected Muslim leaders, be sincere and heartfelt, and be communicated in a way that is respectful to traditional values but clear in proposing an alternative to hatred and intolerance. Although some moderate Muslim clerics and world leaders have indeed spoken up against terrorism, intolerance, and hatred, these voices need to become stronger and more numerous. The mosques and airwaves throughout much of the Middle East are currently dominated by radical mullahs preaching Jihad and praising the actions of bin Laden and his associates (Zakaria, 2001).

These angry voices must be countered with the voices of reason and compassion. Although moderate Islamic leaders and various Arab authors have expressed a disdain for terrorism and a desire to promote peaceful coexistence, they have also expressed fear of the consequences they might suffer from angry radical fundamentalists. This threat is quite real. The most widely known example is the Ayatollah Khomeini's decree of a death sentence for Salman Rushdie in response to publication of his *The Satanic Verses* (1989). What is less well known is that although Rushdie has been able to survive despite this threat, others involved in the publication of translations and excerpts of this book have not been so fortunate (Stephan, 2002). In 1991, Hitoshi Igarashi of Japan was stabbed for translating the work but survived. In 1993, William Nygaard of Norway was shot to death for the same act, and Turk Aziz Nesin escaped a mob attack after publishing excerpts from the book. In addition, evidence suggests that members of the militant Islamic group al-Gama'a al-Islamiyya were responsible for a knife attack on Egyptian author and Nobel Laureate Naguib Mafouz, who survived, and the 1992 fatal shooting of a well-known Egyptian humanist writer, Farag Foda, who was critical of militant Islamic groups (Khadurri, 1999; also see Viorst, 1998).

Our point is that extolling human rights or peaceful coexistence in many parts of the Near and Middle East can be an extremely dangerous thing to do. Any measures that can be taken to spread the value of freedom of speech and condemnation of the idea that murder of those who express views different from one's own is justifiable would facilitate the possibility of open dialogue among people in these regions.

One message that needs to be conveyed is that a more moderate and peaceful version of Islam is both more in accordance with the teachings of Mohammed and also very much in the best interests of the people throughout the Muslim world. Moderate Islamic leaders must show the people that peaceful solutions to current problems are more consistent with the true meaning of Islam. And an important task for U.S. foreign policy is to reinforce the view that moderate nonviolent Islam is indeed in the best interest of the people of this region.

Extolling the Value of a Liberal Education

One traditional Islamic value that could be of use in promoting greater tolerance and openness toward the rest of the world is that of education and learning. For millennia, the Middle Eastern world has put great value on knowledge and scholarship. When Europe was plunged into the Dark Ages, from AD 476 to 1000, the arts, literature, and sciences flourished in the Middle East. A multitude of great advances in science and mathematics that have had a lasting effect on Western civilization were made by Middle Eastern thinkers of this era. For example, this region produced such mathematical advances as algebra and the concept of zero.

There are several ways that education can be of value in improving the lives of the people in the Middle East and defusing the anger and hostility that seem to be reaching a boiling point in the region. First, education is important in preparing people for jobs that would promote economic and technological progress, which would ultimately help the Islamic world compete in the global economic marketplace. In addition, education can play a major role in planting the seeds of tolerance that are necessary to promote peaceful coexistence among the many different ethnic and religious groups within the region. Research has clearly shown a strong correlation between level of education and acceptance of liberal values of tolerance and human rights (Altemeyer, 1988). The more one knows about the diversity of cultures and lifestyles that exist in our world, the less threatened one is likely to be by those who view the world differently from oneself. Emphasizing the long-standing Islamic value of learning and scholarship might provide another path toward showing how Islam can indeed be compatible with a modern scientific world.

However, educational systems inevitably reflect the worldview of the culture in which they are based, both explicitly and implicitly. Although a Western-style liberal education would likely increase sympathy for Western ways, the type of education currently provided in some Middle Eastern countries may do quite the opposite. At present, many young people in the Near and Middle East are educated primarily in fundamentalist *madrasas*, or religious schools, which are often controlled by radical mullahs who preach the militant teachings of Muhammad bin Abd al-Wahab, which encourage Jihad against nonbelievers. In an October 19, 2001, article in the *New York Times*, author Neil Macfarquhar argues that the public school education in much of the Middle East actively promotes negative attitudes toward the West and may be a breeding ground for potential terrorists:

> The textbook for one of the five religion classes required of all 10th graders in Saudi public high schools tackles the complicated issue of who good Muslims should befriend. After examining a number of scriptures that warn of the dangers of having Christian and Jewish friends, the lesson concludes: "It is compulsory for the Muslims to be loyal to each other and to consider the infidels their enemy." That extremist, anti-Western worldview has gradually pervaded the Saudi education system. . . . "If you review the curriculum in Saudi Arabia, you would see that it promotes any kind of extremist views of Islam, even in the eyes of very devout Muslims," said Abdul Khadir Tash, the editor of *Al Bilad* newspaper. This extremism, born of the local, puritanical Wahabi brand of Islam, constrains life here, shaping the way people live and the way Saudi Arabia greets the world. The United States seeks to build a coalition against terror with the kingdom, long a Western business and military ally, and yet the country has revealed itself as the source of the very ideology confronting America in the battle against terrorism. (p. B1)

Some Saudis believe that these anti-Western views help bin Laden and other extremists find recruits for future terrorist attacks because they mold the imperfectly formed religious creed of young, easily influenced men and convince them that their faith condones violence against non-Muslims.

These schools do little to prepare young people for careers and earning a living. Each year, tens of thousands of young Saudis emerge from the *madrasas* with an education that leaves them unqualified for work—an estimated 50,000 per year cannot find jobs. With half the 14 million native population younger than age 25, some estimates say unemployment among the youngest job seekers is as high as 30%. "They exploit some of the half-educated people and uneducated people and they give them the illusion that this is the real Islam," said Adnan Khalil Basha, secretary general of the International Islamic Relief Organization (Macfarquhar, 2001).

Thus, education can do more harm than good if it promotes disdain, distrust, and violence against other groups of people. Combine such an education with young unemployed men lacking ways to feel that their lives are meaningful and that they are valuable, and the attraction of joining the great cause of defending the Islamic world from the American and Israeli infidels is no surprise. A more open-minded approach to education is sorely needed throughout the region, one that provides job skills and promotes modernism and tolerance and that views Islam as compatible with modern democracy and peaceful coexistence with people of all faiths and cultures.

Moving Away From Political Repression

Part of the appeal of radically militant Islam is that it provides a voice of hope against the repressive monarchies and dictatorships that rule much of the Middle East. An annual survey of world governments recently released by New York's Freedom House reported that whereas 75% of the world's governments are rated as "free" or "partly free," only 28% percent of Middle Eastern governments could be rated as such (Huntington, 2002). Whereas the worldwide trend has been toward a general increase in freedom over the past 20 years, the presence of freedom and civil rights has been gradually eroding over the same period in the Middle East. Even in Africa, which is often thought of as dominated by corrupt and repressive regimes, 60% of nations were rated as currently free or partially free. To the extent that a lack of basic human rights fuels some of the rage that Islamic fundamentalists have turned against the United States, using our influence to push these governments toward greater freedom and human rights could be a useful step toward defusing this rage. Given that many of these governments are the recipients of rather large amounts of U.S. economic and military aid, making such aid contingent on improving human rights could provide the leverage that is needed to encourage such change.

It is of interest that in a recent *Newsweek* article, Fareed Zakaria (2001) pointed out that the Middle East is the one place in the world where the U.S. government has been reluctant to push existing regimes in the direction of increased human rights and democracy. He suggested that the problem is that, given the current volatile situation in this region, democracy is seen as more dangerous than a monarchy or dictatorship that is friendly to U.S. interests. As Zakaria put it,

> [Although] America's allies in the Middle East are autocratic, corrupt, and heavy-handed . . . they are still more liberal, tolerant, and pluralistic than what would likely replace them. If elections had been held last month in Saudi Arabia with King Faud and Osama bin Laden on the ballot, I would not bet too heavily on His Royal Highness's fortunes. (p. 24)

The point is that given the popularity of radical Islamic factions in today's Middle East, democratic elections might well bring such regimes into power, leading to repressive theocracies like those of the Taliban in Afghanistan and the Ayatollah's in Iran. Thus, it is fear of an even worse alternative that has prevented U.S. foreign policy from pushing for democratic reform and, rather, led to continued support for the corrupt and oppressive governments with which we are currently allied.

Like most of the other problems fueling the Middle East conflict, this, too, is a difficult one. Zakaria suggests that in spite of the possibility that radical Islamic leaders would gain more power if civil liberties and individual rights were increased in currently oppressive Arab nations, a gradual increase in the extent of power given to them would ultimately be beneficial. An increase in civil rights could get things moving in the direction of a more open and, eventually, democratic, society. Francis Fukuyama (2001) points out that Iran, which has been under strict Islamic theocratic rule for 23 years, has been showing increasing signs of dissatisfaction with Islamic rule and slow but steady moves toward democracy and normalization of relations with the United States and the West. As Fukuyama (2001) put it,

> "Islamic theocracy is something that appeals to people in the abstract. Those who have actually had to live under such regimes . . . have experienced stifling dictatorships whose leaders are more clueless than most on how to overcome problems of poverty and stagnation." (p. 48)

Zakaria (2001) echoes this view, suggesting that although Islamic ideologues are clearly adept at promising their people a better, more righteous future, once they assume the role of civil leaders and are forced to face the realities of the economic and social ills with which their nations are afflicted, the appeal of their ideologies will quickly wear thin.

The plight of theocratic rule by the Taliban in Afghanistan is another prime example of what happens when religious fundamentalists take over government functions. Although Afghanistan has a long history of war, poverty, and social problems before the Taliban came to power, compared with the state they were in just before the 9/11 terrorist attack on the

United States, cities like Kabul looked like bubbling modern metropolises. In the wake of the Taliban era, human rights, health, economic well-being, and general quality of life in Afghanistan were among the worst of any country on earth. Of course, today, the streets of many Afghan cities are littered with the rubble produced by the military campaign recently conducted there to push the Taliban from power and bring bin Laden and his al Qaeda colleagues to justice. The Taliban's militant anti-Western policies, including the support of Osama bin Laden and al Qaeda, can be seen as directly responsible for the downfall of their regime.

The point is that in both Iran and Afghanistan, Islamic theocracies may have held initial appeal for their people, but this appeal quickly faded when the ideologues were forced to come to grips with the ordinary problems of life. The same general pattern has been repeated over the past century, with many ideologically appealing ideas ultimately leading to dictatorial governments that trample human rights and ignore the needs of their people. From Hitler's Germany to the Soviet Union to South Africa, these governments eventually were replaced by more democratic institutions, although only after causing very great harm. In each of these cases, totalitarian regimes that were initially popular with at least some of their people were toppled when their policies ran afoul of the ideals of the broader international community.

Thus, we agree with Zakaria and others who have argued that the potential long-term benefits to be reaped from increasing freedom and civil rights throughout the Muslim world are likely to exceed by far the relatively short-term risks of even more repressive fundamentalist regimes coming into power. And with increasing rights would likely come economic development, as foreign investors become more willing to expend capital, hopefully ultimately increasing the standard of living for the majority of the people in the region. The multitude of problems that have led to the current crisis all feed on each other; similarly, the resolution of each of these problems should facilitate the resolution of the others.

The movement toward democracy and liberalization of human rights policies would need to be gradual and might benefit from support and assistance from nations having more experience with democratic rule. Moderate political leaders, with the support of moderate Islamic clergy, would do well to underscore the difficulties produced by the Islamic theocracies of Iran and Afghanistan. Just as the radical Islamic movement has gotten its message out through the mosques and news media throughout the region, so, too, must a more moderate Arab culture reach its people with this message. And the key message should be that a movement toward democratic rule, cooperation with the West, and tolerance and peaceful coexistence is both more compatible with the teachings of Islam than the fundamentalist radical alternative and also in the best interest of the common people. Despite the difficulties in getting the masses to take this message seriously, it is crucially important that the message be sent.

THE OPPORTUNITY OF A NEW AFGHANISTAN

In spite of the harshness of previous Taliban rule in Afghanistan—actually perhaps because of this harshness—Afghanistan might provide an ideal opportunity to show what a more liberal democratic government in the Middle East could accomplish. The Taliban came to power both because they had the military power to oust their rivals and because of the meaning and value they provided for the people, first by helping defeat the Soviet Union and driving them from their country and then by offering a religious ideology that gave life meaning and provided the hope of a better world to come after this one. The Taliban fell from power because it took its Islamic mission too far, first by repressing virtually all individual rights of the people, even to the extent of outlawing music and casual conversations between women and unrelated men, and second, by supporting the destructive al Qaeda network that was responsible for so many terrorist acts over the past decade. Whereas the latter actions of the Taliban provoked the United States and much of the rest of the world to take unified military action to drive the Taliban from power, the repressive policies of the Taliban led many of the people of Afghanistan to accept the presence of foreign military forces and the destruction that this entailed because it provided the hope of a better future. It is incumbent on us, now, to help provide the people of Afghanistan with the better future for which they have so long hoped.

We are suggesting that the United States and our allies take advantage of the current opportunity to help establish a modern secular state in Afghanistan that respects and values the people's Islamic heritage but is modeled after the liberal democracies that exist in the world's more prosperous nations. Of course, what took hundreds of years to evolve in the United States and Europe cannot be expected to emerge overnight, especially in a country with such a long history of conflict and autocratic rule. Nonetheless, the United States and our allies can provide powerful incentives and assistance to help move the new Afghanistan in the direction of democracy and human rights. The current multiethnic provisional government seems a step in the right direction. Now seems a good time to begin using our influence to show the Afghan people the advantages of participatory democracy and basic human rights.

Note that we are suggesting that this is a task for the United States *and* her allies. Just as the war against the terrorist-supporting Taliban was facilitated by a broad international coalition, so too the building of a well-functioning modern democratic Afghan state would be facilitated by broad-based international support. Unilateral incentives and suggestions from the United States would undoubtedly be viewed as yet another instance of American imperialism and would likely lead to resentment and rejection. Advice and support from a broader coalition, perhaps involving the United Nations or NATO, seems likely to have a better chance of success. Of course, the decision about which form the new Afghanistan will take must ultimately be left up to the people of Afghanistan—that is the nature of democracy, and people do sometimes support leaders and initiatives that ultimately turn out to work against their own best interests. It would be up to the Western world to show the advantages of a modern secular government to the Afghan people, perhaps using the disaster created by the Taliban as a strong bit of evidence in support of this cause.

BRIDGING THE GAP BETWEEN ISLAM AND SECULAR DEMOCRACY

As we have argued throughout this volume, there is nothing inherently incompatible between the Islamic religion and modern secular democracy. Turkey is an Islamic nation with at least a moderate level of success in blending Islam with democratic rule, and human rights there are at the highest level of anywhere in the Islamic world. As we pointed out in the previous chapter, perhaps the most fundamental obstacle to the development of modern democracy in the Middle East—besides the greed and lust for power of the monarchs and dictators currently in control of most of the region—is the belief that the function of the state is to lead the people in doing the wishes of God. If the aim of the state is to do the will of God, this is easily translated into the view that the best people to rule and set policy are clerics and religious leaders, who have a direct line to the wishes of the Almighty. At some point in their history, virtually all the great civilizations of the world have been under theocratic rule. It is probably no coincidence that virtually all of these civilizations have moved away from rule by religious leaders and have drawn a relatively clear line between the functions of church and state. Throughout human history, the belief that one's nation is doing the will of God has been associated with all manners of social evil and destructiveness, from the Crusades of the Middle Ages to our own subjugation and near-extermination of the native people living in the Americas when the Europeans began the colonization of what was then the "New World." When one sees one's nation as having a direct line to God and as having the mission of performing the sacred duty of "helping" the rest of the world see the light, one has a ready-made rationalization for all manner of trampling on the rights of those who are different (McNeill, 1999). Those living in secular democracies are far from immune to this sort of thing, but at least secular democracies provide checks and balances that make it difficult to use rationalizations about the will of one's god to justify atrocities against those who worship a different god or no god at all.

Of course, people all over the world are drawn strongly to religious belief systems. Although some countries, like the Soviet Union and China,

have tried to suppress religious beliefs, such suppression has never been successful in the long run (McNeill, 1999). No matter how hard a government
tries to suppress religion, people always seem to find ways of expressing their
basic psychological need for death transcendence and contact with an ethereal world greater than the one we actually inhabit. And religious beliefs
have typically played an important role in the creation of the beliefs and
values around which secular democracies are oriented. Given the vital role
that the Islamic faith has played in the history and daily lives of the people
of the Middle Eastern world, it seems critical that a role for Islam be found
in the laws and ethical systems that guide the secular democracies that we
believe would help move this region of the world forward and away from the
spirit of externally projected Jihad that seems to dominate much of the
thinking there.

Ideally, Islamic principles could form the system of ethical principles
that guide a secular Arab state, much as Christian and Judaic principles form
the underlying ideology that guides the secular governments in countries
like the United States and Israel. Although occasional conflicts between
religious and secular values seem inevitable, most modern countries seem
able to work these difficulties out to the satisfaction of all but the most
diehard proponents of religion and secularism.

FACING THE PALESTINIAN QUESTION

In bin Laden's most recent attempts to justify his terrorist campaign
against the United States, he continually referred to our support of Israel
and Israel's opposition to the establishment of an independent Palestinian
state as major points of contention responsible for the current wave of terrorism. This was part of the original Fatwah declaring war against the United
States, and it has long been a sore point throughout the Arab world. Of
course, the conflict over Palestine is an ancient one that has proven to be
perhaps the most intractable of all the disputes faced by the modern world.
Both sides seem to deny the right of the other to even exist. The debate over
ownership of this rather small piece of prime real estate has led to a series of
full-scale wars and a seemingly unceasing flow of violence and terrorism
directed against those on both sides of this debate. Countless thousands of
people have been killed as part of this struggle, and its continued explosive-
ness has ignited violence the world over, including the recent terrorist
attacks against the United States.

Clearly, something needs to be done to resolve this conflict in a way
that grants sovereign rule to both Israel and a Palestinian state. Sadly,
although many plans for peace have been proposed over the past several
decades, and some have been accepted at least in principle by the leaders of
both sides, none have led to the lasting peace that has proven so elusive in

this region. Hatred and distrust among these groups run very deeply indeed, and extreme elements on both sides seem determined to see the total annihilation of the group toward which they have projected so much hostility. The experience of past attempts at peaceful coexistence suggests that although diplomatic agreements between governments are difficult to come by, such negotiations can at least lead to *plans* for peace. The more difficult task is to get the people of the region to accept these peace initiatives and, in some cases, simply to accept the right of the other group to exist.

ELIMINATING TERRORISM AS A VIABLE TACTIC FOR PROMOTING SOCIAL CHANGE

It seems that one of the most daunting obstacles to a peaceful resolution to the Palestinian-Israeli conflict is the recurrence of terrorist violence, which time after time has brought the peace process to a grinding halt. The irony here is that the terrorists claim that Israel's occupation of Jerusalem and the West Bank are major injustices that leave them no recourse other than terrorist action. But it seems that terrorist violence is a big part—although certainly not all—of what prevents Israel from being more receptive to ceding territory to a Palestinian state in a way that might provide a solution to the conflict that would be acceptable to the majority of Palestinians. Once again, terrorism is used as a strategy for bringing about desired social change, and this use of terrorism stands as a major obstacle to social change that might otherwise be quite feasible. And once again, the many forces that feed the hatred and hostility in the Middle East are feeding into each other, creating a vicious cycle that seems nearly impossible to break.

The cessation of terrorism would be of great help, but Israel could do some things as well, like eliminating territorial expansion through the building of new settlements in the disputed territories. Israel may also want to consider relocation of those areas in some existing settlements in exchange for the possibility of a lasting peace. Compromise solutions require trust, respect, and sacrifice by both sides. Both groups need to realize that temporary inconveniences and economic and territorial concessions are far better alternatives than perpetual violence and terror. We recommend that interested readers consider the work of Harvard social psychologist Herb Kelman (1987, 1997, 1998), who has been studying strategies for resolving this conflict for more than two decades.

Throughout this chapter, we have focused on various strategies for eliminating terrorism: economic growth so that the people's physical and biological needs can be better met, widespread informational campaigns aimed at promoting the value of tolerance and peaceful coexistence, support for education and the more positive prosocial values that are inherent in

Islamic tradition and theology, establishment of functioning secular democracies that guarantee fundamental human rights for all, and resolution of the various specific grievances, something that will become easier as each of the other strategies begins to take hold. All of these objectives can serve as part of a multifaceted strategy to eliminate terrorism.

Unfortunately, the continued existence of terrorism itself stands as an obstacle to meeting any of these goals. It is extremely difficult, if not impossible, to promote peaceful coexistence, trust, democracy, civil rights, and tolerance in a world where random violence is rampant. In addition, as our work very clearly shows, conditions that heighten mortality salience promote clinging to existing worldviews and lashing out at those with different ones. Thus, in addition to the steps outlined to decrease the impetus for terrorist action, direct and forceful steps must be taken to reduce the imminent threat of terrorist acts. Although it may seem tautological to suggest that terrorism must be reduced so that we can implement steps to reduce future terrorism, it is analogous to common treatment approaches for severe depression or psychotic episodes. First, one alleviates the imminent problem with drugs; once that is accomplished, therapy to gain further improvement and protect against further episodes is more likely to be effective.

A first step in this direction might be a multinational condemnation of terrorism in all its forms, with an accompanying promise from each nation to do all it can to stop terrorists from using its land as a base from which to operate and a genuine effort on the part of all to arrest and prosecute terrorists, whatever their political or religious orientations. In the wake of 9/11, virtually all the governments in the world, even those that have previously provided direct sponsorship of terrorists, have condemned terrorism in general and the recent attacks on the United States in particular. After the large-scale military action against the Taliban in Afghanistan of recent months, no government seems willing to openly offer refuge to bin Laden, the al Qaeda, or other terrorist organizations. For example, Somalia, which has previously been viewed as a potential haven for terrorists and a place to which bin Laden and associates might be likely to flee, formally stated that it would not offer safe haven to bin Laden and al Qaeda (Guardian Home Pages, 2001). It seems the time is right for a major international treaty that outlaws terrorist activity and the harboring of terrorist organizations within one's borders and promises swift and effective attempts to apprehend and punish terrorists wherever they strike.

The immorality of terrorist violence against innocent civilians seems self-evident to most people in the world, and this is likely to be enough to get most world leaders to support such a multinational agreement. Of course, this "moral majority" does not include everyone, and it is the people who do not particularly object to terrorism as a form of political protest who most need to be brought into the fold of those supporting an antiterrorist resolution. In such cases, economic and political pressure will need to be applied to make it clear that supporting terrorism is in *no one's* best individual or national interest. A good deal of momentum seems to have already been built in this direction. Economic boycotts, international isolation, and financial incentives might all be useful in getting nations to agree to outlaw terrorism and vigorously prosecute those who practice it. As a last resort, and as a very strong negative incentive, the sort of military action recently taken against the Taliban in Afghanistan could also be used as a way of convincing national leaders that terrorism is incompatible with the best interests of their nations. Although this last strategy risks fanning the fire, and almost always leads to the spilling of more innocent blood, we have seen time and time again that when terrorism pushes a nation too far, violent responses are likely to occur. In such cases, one can only hope that military responses are measured and targeted toward those truly contributing to the terrorist acts.

CONCLUSION

Terrorism results from the interaction of a wide range of social, political, ideological, and psychological forces. TMT and research illuminate the psychological aspects of the problem. People need a worldview that provides a basis of self-worth and death transcendence, and they need to feel that they are contributing to some great cause—a heroic triumph over evil. And these needs are especially potent when mortality is salient, as it often is in the various flashpoints in the Middle East. Based on this analysis, the following two general goals must be met. First, through whatever methods are possible, we need to reduce the salience of mortality. Second, we need to help the people of the Middle East currently relying on extreme fundamentalist belief systems to shift to bases of meaning and self-worth that do not portray other groups as repositories of evil whom it is one's duty to eradicate.

Of course, just as no single factor can be reasonably viewed as *the* preeminent root cause of terrorism, so, too, is no single remedial step likely to be effective in accomplishing these goals and eliminating this most vexing problem. We have suggested a variety of steps that we believe would be useful in reducing the likelihood of further terrorist violence. But in order for any of these steps to be effective, additional steps in other domains need to be taken. A solution to the crisis we are currently facing will require an interaction of peace-building steps, each one facilitating the success of the others.

9

IN THE WAKE OF 9/11:
RISING ABOVE THE TERROR

Whatever man does on this planet has to be done in the lived truth of the terror of creation, of the grotesque, of the rumble of panic underneath everything. Otherwise it is false. . . . A project as grand as the scientific-mythical construction of victory over human limitation is not something that can be programmed by science . . . it comes from the masses of men sweating within the nightmare of creation. . . . Who knows what form the forward momentum of life will take in the time ahead or what use it will make of our anguished searching.
—Ernest Becker, *The Denial of Death* (1973, pp. 283–285)

When we were asked to write this book to explore the causes and consequences of the terrorist bombings on 9/11 from the perspective of terror management theory (TMT), we were excited to do so, in part perhaps because it provided us with a way of personally coming to terms with the tragedy and doing something in response to it. Like many Americans, we were overwhelmed by the events and felt a need to understand how and why something like this could occur and to think of ways similar events might be prevented from happening in the future. And, like many Americans, we wanted to do something to help. This, in a sense, is our effort to "do the right thing" in our own small way. We hope that our ideas and research will be of value to academic and clinical psychologists and to other interested readers and that those in the political sphere can productively use our analysis of the psychological underpinnings of human motivation to inform the development and implementation of effective political policies.

Before proceeding with a brief recap and some final thoughts, we should acknowledge the limitations of our terror management treatment of the aftermath of 9/11—especially for those of you who skipped our preface. We hope that this book is of some value, but we realize that it will be useful only if it is fortified by knowledge and insights from other sources. We have approached these issues from one particular perspective, and although we think it is an important one typically overlooked by people in the media, academics, and practitioners, we realize that multiple sources are needed to grapple fully with matters of this magnitude. Our ideas about personal coping with tragedy and threat need to be supplemented with the knowledge and expertise offered by psychiatrists, clinical psychologists, and grief counselors. Our analysis of the causes of terrorism and the conflicts that fuel it need to be enhanced by knowledge offered by foreign policy and Middle East experts, historians, and religious scholars. In addition, within academia, a variety of perspectives other than our own, from cognitive, personality, and social psychology, and from sociology, anthropology, and political science as well, can be fruitfully applied to understanding aspects of terrorism such as perception of risk, and determinants of stereotyping, aggression, and social identification. We hope there will be plenty of forums for these other worthy voices to be heard.

A RECAP

TMT posits that human beings' highly sophisticated cognitive capabilities render us aware of the utter fragility of life and the absolute inevitability of death. This awareness engenders the potential for overwhelming terror—terror that is assuaged through the construction and maintenance of culture: humanly constructed beliefs about the nature of reality that confer symbolic or literal immortality by providing a sense that one is a person of value in a world of meaning. Because cultural worldviews are social constructions rather than absolute mirrors of reality, they require social consensus for sustenance and are easily undermined by the existence of alternative conceptions of reality. Consequently, the mere existence of others with different cultural worldviews is threatening. Additionally, because cultural worldviews are symbolic solutions to the very physical problem of death, and no symbol is ultimately sufficiently powerful to overcome death, residual unconscious anxiety is often projected onto scapegoats designated as all-encompassing repositories of evil. We then tend to respond to scapegoats, or those who are merely different, by derogation, efforts to convince them to dispose of their beliefs and adopt ours instead, or exterminating them entirely to restore the death-denying psychological equanimity normally provided by confident allegiance to one's own cultural worldview. From this perspective, then, prejudice and ethnic strife of all sorts, including terrorism, are ultimately the results, at least in part, of humankind's psychological inability to tolerate the existence of others who do not subscribe to their death-denying cultural constructions.

Empirical support for TMT has been obtained in more than 150 studies conducted by independent researchers in at least nine countries. Research has demonstrated the anxiety-buffering properties of self-esteem and shown that dispositionally high or momentarily elevated self-esteem reduces defensive reactions to reminders of death. Research has also established that subtle reminders of death produce increased clinging to and defense of one's cultural worldview. These tendencies include the following: greater affection for similar others or those who uphold cherished cultural values and greater hostility toward different others or those who violate cherished cultural values, heightened discomfort when handling cherished cultural icons in a disrespectful fashion, sitting closer to a person who shares one's culture and farther away from a foreigner, and increased physical aggression toward someone critical of one's cherished beliefs. Additional studies revealed some important individual differences that moderate the effects of mortality salience on worldview defense. Specifically, people who have high self-esteem (dispositional or situational), who hold liberal worldviews that stress tolerance (or for whom the value of tolerance has been primed), or who are securely attached are less prone to disparage those who are different from themselves following a mortality salience induction.

Subsequent research led to a more detailed understanding of the cognitive processes that underlie the effects of death-related thoughts on human behavior and led us to make a distinction between the proximal and distal defenses that occur, respectively, in response to conscious and unconscious concerns about death. When mortality is made salient, direct rational *proximal* psychological defenses are activated to reduce conscious awareness of death, by instrumental responses to avert an actual threat or psychological defenses to remove the troubling material from current awareness, such as distracting oneself from the problem, denying vulnerability to the threat, or emphasizing the temporal remoteness of the problem. Once the problem of death is out of focal attention but still highly accessible, terror management concerns are addressed by *distal* defenses, by bolstering faith in the worldview (e.g., by derogation of those who violate or challenge one's worldview and enhanced regard for those who validate the worldview) or by enhanced self-esteem striving (e.g., behaving altruistically if being helpful is an important aspect of one's self-concept). Heightened accessibility of death thoughts seems to be a necessary and sufficient condition for the production of mortality salience effects. Worldview defense and self-esteem bolstering serve to reduce the accessibility of death-related thoughts and in so doing avert the potential to experience terror. The findings thereby confirm the role of cultural worldviews and self-esteem in terror management processes.

IN THE WAKE OF 9/11

TMT and research provide a conceptual framework for making sense of Americans' reactions to the events of 9/11. The attacks on the World Trade Center and the Pentagon constituted an extremely potent and enduring mortality salience induction: literally, by witnessing the horrifying death of thousands of people like ourselves, and symbolically, by the destruction of our most cherished military and economic symbols. We documented the proximal and distal reactions to heightened mortality salience that parallel those obtained in our empirical studies. Proximally, after brief unsuccessful efforts to deny that anything serious had occurred, people went to enormous lengths to distract themselves from the tragedy—by drinking, gambling, renting videos, watching television, and shopping. Simultaneously, many Americans avoided public places, such as airports, bridges, tunnels, sky-scrapers, government buildings, and sports facilities—where additional ter-rorist activities might be undertaken. Distal reactions included intensified quests for meaning and value, as evidenced by soaring Bible sales and church and synagogue attendance, pervasive and vivid displays of American patri-otism, highly emotional suppression of political dissent and intensified hos-tility toward anti-American opinions and Muslims in general, and efforts to bolster self-esteem through a variety of altruistic responses and identifica-tion with the heroic reactions of others (e.g., the especially courageous actions of the passengers on the plane that crashed in Pennsylvania instead of into the White House or Capitol).

Concerns about mortality play a significant role in the etiology of a variety of forms of psychopathology, including schizophrenia, neuroticism, depression, obsessive-compulsive disorder (OCD), and posttraumatic stress disorder (PTSD). Not surprisingly, then, there were across-the-board increases in many forms of psychopathology following 9/11 as well as ele-vated levels of drug and alcohol abuse and compulsive gambling. To help people manage the terror engendered by the events of 9/11, in chapters 5 and 6 we proposed a number of broad suggestions to practicing clinicians, includ-ing providing social support and caring, meaning and understanding, and opportunities for acquiring self-esteem and behaving in a heroic fashion.

TMT is also highly relevant to understanding the psychological under-pinnings of the hatred of, and aggression toward, Western civilization in gen-eral and the United States in particular that is currently sweeping many parts of the Islamic world. Recall the basic terror management tenet that the mere existence of those who are different poses a threat to people's faith in the absolute validity and correctness of their own perspectives on reality. This threat undermines the protection against deep existential fears that our world-views provide. Derogating different others, working to convert them to one's own worldview, and eliminating them from the face of the earth, thereby cre-ating a more "perfect" world, can thus become a heroic, self-esteem–enhancing, and salvation-assuring virtuous activity that adds further protection to the defensive shield that we all need to survive in a world where the only real cer-tainly is our inevitable demise. With regard to the clash between radical Islamic fundamentalists and the West, this general tendency is exponentially exaggerated by a host of historical factors (e.g., the Crusades) and current political and economic circumstances.

This analysis leads to some general suggestions for peaceful resolution of problems in the Middle East and reducing the appeal of terrorism against the United States. These include measures to help the people in the region meet their material needs and to provide greater opportunities to acquire meaning and value in the context of nondestructive forms of Islam (and other religious and secular ideologies as well). Movement toward this latter goal can be facilitated by encouraging nonfundamentalist forms of religion that are not hostile to alternative worldviews, extolling the virtue of education and democracy, and emphasizing the compatibility of Islam and secular society.

AS WE COMPLETE THIS BOOK . . .

Sadly, as we complete this volume in June 2002, the world is just as terrifying, maybe more so, than in the days and weeks after 9/11. Israel and Palestine continue trading punches in an escalating cycle of senseless violence: Palestinian suicide bombers have killed, maimed, and terrorized many civilians in Israel; Israeli incursions into Palestinian territories and displays of brutal force there have led to the death of even more Palestinians and have done little to stem the tide of suicide bombers. Time and again, targeted killings of Palestinian militants are, in turn, avenged by additional suicide bombers (Dempsey et al., 2002). India and Pakistan have mobilized their armies for a possible nuclear confrontation over Kashmir. In India, Muslims firebombed a train and incinerated 58 Hindu activists heading to build a temple on the ground where a mosque once stood (until torn to the ground by a handful of Hindu fanatics); Hindus retaliated by roasting hundreds of Muslims alive in their homes and businesses (Watson, 2002). Al Qaeda operative Richard Reid allegedly tried to blow up his foot, himself, and the American Airlines plane he was on; al Qaeda sympathizers subsequently beheaded *Wall Street Journal* reporter Daniel Pearl when he tried to investigate Reid's connections to radical Islam (Drogin & Mohan, 2002). Synagogues in France and Belgium have been firebombed (Williams, 2002). In Afghanistan, leaflets distributed by Taliban and al Quaeda supporters are offering $50,000 for dead Westerners and $100,000 for live ones (presumably not for long, given Daniel Pearl's fate; Filkins, 2002).

The Good Guy–Bad Guy Mentality

In conflicts between groups of all sorts, members of each group inevitably think they are the good guys and the members of the other group are the bad guys. This is certainly a barrier to coming to a peaceful resolution and is certainly the case in the Israeli-Palestinian conflict. However, third parties with vested interests in a peaceful resolution *must* try to avoid this type of thinking. Clearly, many in the Muslim world think the Palestinians are the good guys and the Israelis (and Americans) are the bad guys, and that adds fuel to the fire. Many people in the United States have a similar black-and-white view of the conflict. In general, political conservatives and those with ties to Israel view Israel as a much deserved homeland for the Jewish people, as a strong democratic ally in a region otherwise dominated by autocratic regimes with anti-Western worldviews, and as a great contributor to secular progress in the sciences and arts (listen, for example, to Michael Savage's syndicated radio talk show, "The Savage Nation"). They argue that American support of Israel is essential for Israel's survival and of great strategic value to the United States. They also often portray the Palestinians as bloodthirsty terrorists with a medieval worldview bent on the destruction of Israel.

Many political liberals in the United States (and Europe), on the other hand, seem to portray Israel as the bad guy—a racist nation brutally engaging in a campaign of ethnic cleansing and genocide against the beleaguered Palestinian people. A variety of American media outlets and historians seem to take this perspective, which often involves the idea that the U.S. government is also a bad guy in this, unfairly favoring Israel and engaging in policies in the Middle East that justify hatred of America. We argue that *both* of these viewpoints are far too biased and simplistic to capture the subtleties and complexities of the current situation. Such black-and-white thinking is highly counterproductive.

Like many Americans, we believe that terrorist attacks are acts of mass murder that are never justified. This view stands in sharp contrast to the views of some Arab leaders like Saddam Hussein who view Islamic terrorists as heroic martyrs, worthy of honor and great financial reward for their families (Dickey, 2002; Yacoub, 2002). Policies such as those of Hussein send exactly the wrong message, both morally and pragmatically. We believe that such terrorism and support for it have interfered with peaceful resolution of conflicts all over the globe.

However, we also think it is undeniable that, as in most intergroup conflicts, both the Israelis and the Palestinians have committed atrocities and both sides have many legitimate grievances. But harping on these negative aspects continues to widen the gap between the groups; most people in both groups, from their own perspectives, want what all humans want— secure homelands where they can live peaceful, prosperous, and meaningful lives in which they can feel a sense of personal and collective value. Neither group is purely evil or purely good; presumably within each group there are mainly decent people and a minority prone to evil actions. The answer lies not in accusations, taking sides, and focusing on past transgressions but in recognizing the legitimacy of these human needs and focusing on the concrete disagreements over territory and policies that must be resolved politically to establish secure homelands for both groups.

Conflicts with substantial histories, whether interpersonal or intergroup, can be resolved only by wiping the slate clean, by starting where things are now—today—and then moving forward. The parties involved are unlikely to forget the past bloodshed and may never be able to forgive it, but they must let go of it as the driving force for their current actions, which must be focused on a future in which the needs of all people for security, meaning, and value can be met—even if it means negotiating with people who have contributed to the blood spilling of the past. Of course, this is much easier said than done, but these are possible goals if relentlessly and earnestly worked toward—look at what has happened in the past decade in South Africa and Northern Ireland, lands in which bigotry and terrorism have given way to peaceful coexistence and resolution of long-standing and very bitter intergroup conflicts toward better, more peaceful futures for both groups. Here is hoping one day soon we will be able to say the same about the Middle East.

CONCLUSION: HANDLING THE TERROR WITHIN US ALL

Clearly, there are no easy answers to the current political problems that exist in so many corners of our planet. We know that we have not seen the end of terrorism or of the many other forms of violence that have pervaded the historical record and continue to this day to be staples of our daily news. In the face of these facts, rather than give in to hopelessness, we should unquestionably continue to do what we can to reduce the prevalence of "man's inhumanity to man." However, we each have a limited time on this earth; and so, at the individual level, we suggest that the more pertinent matter is how to do what we can to help others while making the best of our own lives.

No one is psychologically equipped to handle all the miseries of the more than 6 billion people out there; the best we can hope for is to be able to deal with the problems within our own sphere of family and friends. People who lose that perspective and get too caught up in these tragedies around the globe are doomed to live out lives of misery and bitterness themselves, and if that is what we all should do, we could ironically relax about the death all around us, because the dead would be better off than the living. After all, death is only bad if life is good.

If we do not appreciate our lives when we are in decent health and life circumstances, then when *can* life be appreciated? And yet we live under constant threat and with the knowledge that eventually life will deteriorate for us and end completely. In this respect, we are all living within a tough situation and all deserving of compassion. Those who fail to make the best of their lives while things are good are making a foolish error. But even greater errors are committed by those who lash out at others to avenge their fate or who try to cope by hiding behind narrow belief systems that prescribe suffering and death to others. All the evils that people perpetrate can be viewed as products of terror management errors stemming from fear and weakness. This is not to say that we should not hold people responsible for these errors; we should, because if we do not, we will most likely all end up victimized by them.

Embedding Ourselves Safely Within Belief

We are all more or less safely embedded in our own belief systems. These belief systems may be religious or secular, but they all function to imbue us with an ultimately fictitious sense that our lives have unshakable meaning and that we have enduring value. Becker (1973) put it this way:

> Civilized society is a hopeful protest that science, money, and goods make man count more than any other animal. . . . It doesn't matter whether the cultural system is frankly magical, religious, and primitive, or secular, scientific, and civilized. It is still a mythical hero system in which people serve in order to feel of primary value, of cosmic special-ness, of ultimate usefulness to creation, of unshakeable meaning. (p. 5)

Of course, some of us feel our lives are meaningful and valuable, and some of us do not. And this plays an enormous role in our satisfaction with life and in our mental health; we would venture to say this plays a more impor-tant role than almost any other factor. When a person has lost all sense of meaning and value, he or she either falls into a deep depression or desper-ately lashes out at the world. This is what the killers who took the lives of 13 of their fellow students at Columbine High School, in Littleton, Col-orado, did. Consider the posthumous testimony of Eric Harris (Vaughn & Klack, 1999):

> By now, it's over. If you are reading this, my mission is complete. I have finished revolutionizing the neoeuphoric infliction of my internal ter-ror. Your children who have ridiculed me, who have chosen not to accept me, who have treated me like I am not worth their time are dead. THEY ARE FUCKING DEAD.

Stripped of all sense of meaning or value, left only with terror, these two teenagers took it out on everyone around them. Why live if we are just worthless, purposeless animals, doomed only to die and decay?

Consequently, some humanly created system of meaning and value is utterly necessary. The question then becomes which such system would be maximally beneficial to those within it while least harmful to those outside it. Unfortunately, at the beginning of the 3rd millenium, we are stuck here between the proverbial rock and the proverbial hard place.

The Rock

The safest, most secure system is probably one with rigid, narrow, unquestioned beliefs that include a concrete depiction of the afterlife. This is the type of worldview that until the age of Darwin was prevalent in all cultures from the many small tribal ones to large ones such as ancient Egypt and Rome. And many millions, if not billions, of people, are still tucked securely into such belief systems. The need for such death-denying belief systems provides the only plausible explanation for how people smart enough to pull off the attacks on 9/11 could believe, firmly enough to sacrifice their lives, that their death would lead immediately to an encounter with 72 beautiful virgins! Unfortunately, although these types of worldviews may work for the believers in terms of psychological equanimity, as we have amply discussed, they often do so at great cost to those outside the culture.

The Hard Place

Conversely, those worldviews that are relativistic, less certain, more open, and tolerant of differences are better for those outside the culture but leave those within the culture open to pondering whether that on which they have based their whole sense of meaning and value is, in William James's (as quoted in Becker, 1962/1971, p. 112) words, "a mere mask, a tissue spun in happy hours." How secure, then, can we be? Well, without our martinis, marijuana, cocaine, Prozac, Zoloft, Paxil, and so on, it appears not very. If, as Marx said, religion is the opiate of the masses, then opiates and the other (legal and illegal) drugs du jour are the opiates for the rest of us, rich and poor.

A Middle Ground?

It seems as though most people and cultural worldviews can be characterized in one of these two ways, and the conflicts we have been examining can be characterized at least in part as involving a clash between them. But is there a middle ground for a mature humanity between the rock and the hard place? Is there a vision of reality substantial enough to serve our deep psychological needs for death-transcending meaning and value—but flexible enough to endure peaceably the existence of alternative worldviews? If we are unable to find this safer place, then perhaps the human race is doomed to ignominious self-extermination. On the other hand, humans have had a pretty good track record in the past in terms of making the seemingly impossible possible—after all, in a short span of time we have witnessed the end of the Cold War, the reunification of Germany, the end of apartheid in South Africa, and peace in Northern Ireland. Perhaps, then, we can continue to hope against hope that we will eventually come up with a way to live together in a world with ample physical resources and psychological security for all. And just maybe, as Becker (1975, p. 170) put it posthumously in his final written words, the tradition of existential psychodynamic thought that TMT and research carries forward can help "introduce just that minute measure of reason to balance destruction."

REFERENCES

Abdel-Khalek, A. M. (1998). The structure and measurement of death obsession. *Personality & Individual Differences, 24*(2), 159–165.

Abu-Nasr, D. (1995, January 30). Devout human bombs die in Allah's name. *Charleston Gazette*, p. 1A.

Adorno, T., Frenkel-Brunswick, E., Levinson, D., & Sanford, R. N. (1950). *The authoritarian personality*. New York: Harper.

Allen, G. (1897/2000). *The evolution of the idea of god*. Escondido, CA: The Book Tree.

Allen, J. (2001, October 1). Patriots at the mall. *U. S. News & World Report*, p. 18.

Allen, W. In Quoteworld. Retrieved from http://www.quoteworld.org.

Altemeyer, R. A. (1988). *Enemies of freedom: Understanding right-wing authoritarianism*. San Francisco, CA: Jossey-Bass.

American Psychiatric Association. (1994). *Diagnostic and statistical manual of mental disorders* (4th ed.). Washington, DC: Author.

Amnesty International Publications. (2001). *Racism and the administration of justice*. Introduction. AI Index: ACT 40/020/2001. Oxford, UK: The Alden Press. Retrieved from http://www.web.amnesty.org/aidoc/aidoc_pdf.nsf/index/ACT400202001ENGLISH/$File/ACT4002001.pdf

Anchors, S. (2001, September 16). Store owner killed in spree. *Arizona Republic*, p. A1.

Apple, R. W., Jr. (1990, August 16). Bush says Iraqi aggression threatens "our way of life." *New York Times*, p. A14.

Appleford, S., Bozza, A., Brackett, N., Dana, W., Delk, S., Diehl, M., et al. (2001, October 25). I heard the news today: A special report. *Rolling Stone Magazine, 880*, 21–41.

Arndt, J., Greenberg, J, & Cook, A. (in press). Mortality salience and the spreading activation of worldview-relevant constructs: Exploring the cognitive architecture of terror management. *Journal of Experimental Psychology: General*.

Arndt, J., Greenberg, J., Pyszczynski, T., & Solomon, S. (1997). Subliminal presentation of death reminders leads to increased defense of the cultural worldview. *Psychological Science, 8*, 379–385.

Arndt, J., Greenberg, J., Schimel, J., Pyszczynski, T., & Solomon, S. (in press). To belong or not to belong, that is the question: Terror management and identification with gender and ethnicity. *Journal of Personality and Social Psychology*.

Arndt, J., Greenberg, J., Solomon, S., Pyszczynski, T., & Simon, L. (1997). Suppression, accessibility of death-related thoughts, and cultural worldview defense: Exploring the psychodynamics of terror management. *Journal of Personality and Social Psychology, 73*, 5–18.

Arndt, J., & Solomon, S. (in press). The control of death and the death of control: The effects of mortality salience, neuroticism, and worldview threat on the desire for control. *Journal of Research in Personality*.

Bargh, J. (1996). Automaticity in social psychology. In E. T. Higgins & A. W. Kruglanski (Eds.), *Social psychology: Handbook of basic principles* (pp. 169–183). New York: Guilford Press.

Barr, C., & Peterson, S. (2001, September 15). Terror hunt. Text of fatwah urging jihad against Americans. Published in *Al-Quds al-'Arabi* on February 23, 1998. *Nationwide News Pty Limited. Courier Mail.* Retrieved April 22, 2002, from LexisNexis.

Bassili, J. N., & Smith, M. C. (1986). On the spontaneity of trait attribution: Converging evidence for the role of cognitive strategy. *Journal of Personality and Social Psychology, 50,* 239–245.

Beck, A. T. (1987). *Beck Depression Inventory (BDI).* San Antonio, TX: Psychological Corporation.

Becker, E. (1964). *The revolution in psychiatry.* New York: Free Press.

Becker, E. (1962/1971). *The birth and death of meaning.* New York: Free Press.

Becker, E. (1973). *The denial of death.* New York: Free Press.

Becker, E. (1975). *Escape from evil.* New York: Free Press.

Benner, P. E, & Wrubel, J. (1989). *The primacy of caring: Stress and coping in health and illness.* Reading, MA: Addison-Wesley/Addison Wesley Longman.

Bennett, D., & Holmes, D. (1975). Influence of denial (situation redefinition) and projection on anxiety associated with threat to self-esteem. *Journal of Personality and Social Psychology, 32,* 915–921.

Beyette, B. (2001, October 4). Boom in Bible, self-help book sales soothes the pain: Since September 11 there's been a run on titles dealing with loss and grief. *Los Angeles Times,* Section 5, p. 1.

bin Laden, O. (1998). Fatwa declaring jihad against America. Retrieved September, 2001, from http://www.fas.org

bin Laden, O. (1998, May). *Frontline* interview.

bin Laden, O. (2001, December 13). Transcript of Osama bin Laden videotape. Retrieved from http://www.cnn.com/2001/US/12/13/tape.transcript/

bin Laden, O. (2001, December 14). Tape seen as confession. *York News Times.* Retrieved from http://www.yorknewstimes.com/stories/121401/nat_1214010015.shtml

Bleich, A., Shalev, A., Shoham, S., & Solomon, Z. (1992). PTSD: Theoretical and practical considerations as reflected through Koach: An innovative treatment project. *Journal of Traumatic Stress, 5*(2), 265–271.

Bowlby, J. (1969). *Attachment.* New York: Basic Books.

Bowlby, J. (1973). *Separation: Anxiety and anger.* New York: Basic Books.

Bowlby, J. (1980). *Loss.* New York: Basic Books.

Brennan, K. A., Clark, C. L., & Shaver, P. R. (1998). Self-report measurement of adult attachment: An integrative overview. In J. A. Simpson & W. S. Rholes (Eds.), *Attachment theory and close relationships* (pp. 46–76). New York: Guilford Press.

Breslau, K. (2001, September 22). The final moments of United Flight 93. *Newsweek* Web exclusive. Retrieved June 20, 2002, from http://www.msnbc.com /news/632626.asp#BODY

Breslau, N., & Davis, G. C. (1992). Posttraumatic stress disorder in an urban population of young adults: Risk factors for chronicity. *American Journal of Psychiatry, 149(5),* 671–675.

British Columbia Schizophrenia Society. (January 2000). Retrieved from http://www.bcss.org/

Brockes, E. (2001, October 11). One month on: Ripple effect. *The Guardian* (London), p. 6.

Burger, J. M., & Cooper, H. M. (1979). The desirability of control. *Motivation & Emotion, 3(4),* 381–393.

Burns, G. L., Keortge, S. G., Formea, G. M., & Sternberger, L. G. (1996). Revision of the Padua Inventory of obsessive compulsive disorder symptoms: Distinctions between worry, obsessions, and compulsions. *Behaviour Research & Therapy, 34(2),* 163–173.

Burns, R. (1786/1885). *The complete works of Robert Burns.* New York: T. Y. Crowell.

Burros, M. (2001, December 5). In a stressed city, no room at the bar. *New York Times,* pp. F1, F5.

Carney, J., & Dickerson, J. F. (2001, October 22). A work in progress. *Time, 158,* 4.

Castano, E., Yzerbyt, V., Paladino, M., & Sacchi, S. (2002). I belong, therefore, I exist: Ingroup identification, ingroup entitativity, and ingroup bias. *Personality & Social Psychology Bulletin, 2,* 135–143.

Chaplin, S. (2000). *The psychology of time and death.* Ashland, OH: Sonnet Press.

Cicchetti, D., & Toth, S. (1997). *Developmental perspectives on trauma: Theory, research, and intervention.* Rochester, NY: University of Rochester Press.

Collins, L., & Lapierre, D. (1972). *O Jerusalem.* New York: Simon and Schuster.

Collins, N. L., & Feeney, B.C. (2000). A safe haven: An attachment theory perspective on support seeking and care-giving in intimate relationships. *Journal of Personality and Social Psychology, 78,* 1053–1073.

Costa, P. T., & McCrae, R. R. (1985). *The NEO Personality Inventory.* Odessa, FL: Psychological Assessment Resources.

Cross, M., & Ewen, D. (1969). *The Milton Cross new encyclopedia of the great composers and their music* (Vol. 2). Garden City, NY: Doubleday.

Crumbaugh, J. C. (1968). Cross-validation of Purpose-in-Life Test based on Frankl's concepts. *Journal of Individual Psychology, 24,* 78–81.

Crumbaugh, J. C., & Maholick, L. T. (1964). An experimental study in existentialism: The psychometric approach to Frankl's concept of noogenic neurosis. *Journal of Clinical Psychology, 20,* 200–207.

Curran, P. S., Bell, P., Murray, A., & Loughrey, G. (1990). Psychological consequences of the Enniskillen bombing. *British Journal of Psychiatry, 156,* 479–482.

Daniels, C. (2001). *Charlie Daniels Band: Lyrics.* Retrieved April 8, 2002, from http://www.charliedaniels.com/home_frame.html

Dawkins, R. (2001, September 15). Comment & analysis: Religion's misguided missiles. *The Guardian* (London), p. 20.

Dawson, M. E., Schell, A. M., & Filion, D. L. (1990). The electrodermal system. In J. T. Caioppo & L. G. Tassinary (Eds.), *Principles of psychophysiology: Physical, social, and inferential elements* (pp. 295–324). Cambridge, England: Cambridge University Press.

Dechesne, M., Greenberg, J., Arndt, J., & Schimel, J. (2000). Terror management and the vicissitudes of sports fan affiliation: The effects of mortality salience on optimism and fan identification. *European Journal of Social Psychology, 30,* 813–835.

Dechesne, M., Janssen, J., & van Knippenberg, A. (2000a). Derogation and distancing as terror management strategies: The moderating role of need for closure and permeability of group boundaries. *Journal of Personality & Social Psychology, 79,* 923–937.

Dechesne, M., Janssen, J., & van Knippenberg, A. (2000b). *Worldview allegiance vs. egotism in the face of existential threat: Need for closure as moderator of terror management strategies.* Unpublished manuscript, University of Nijmegen, Nijmegen, The Netherlands.

Dechesne, M., Pyszczynski, T., Ransom, S., Arndt, J., Sheldon, K., van Knippenberg, A., et al. (2002). *Literal and symbolic immortality: The effect of evidence of literal immortality on self-esteem striving and worldview defense in response to mortality salience.* Unpublished manuscript, University of Nijmegen, Nijmegen, The Netherlands.

Dempsey, J., Mackintosh, J., & Morris, H. (2002, April 11). Israel vows to continue "war of survival": Suicide bombing reinforces Sharon's resolve to defy US and press ahead with offensive. *The Financial Times* (London), Front page—first section, 1.

DeNeve, K. M., & Cooper, H. (1998). The happy personality: A meta-analysis of 137 personality traits and subjective well-being. *Psychological Bulletin, 124*(2), 197–229.

Dickens, C. (1843/1915). *A christmas carol.* Philadelphia: J. B. Lippincott.

Dickey, C. (With Ephron, D., Barry, J., Hosenball, M., & Isikoff, M.). (2002, April 15). Inside suicide, Inc. (see photo caption on p. 32). *Newsweek,* 26–32.

Dissanayake, E. (1992). *Homo aestheticus: Where art comes from and why.* New York: Free Press.

Drogin, B., & Mohan, G. (2002, February 22). The world; Reporter held captive is dead, videotape shows; Pakistan: Daniel Pearl was executed shortly after being kidnapped while pursuing terror links, officials say. Colleagues are in mourning. *Los Angeles Times* (Part A, Part 1, Foreign Desk), 1+.

Elliott, D. M., & Briere, J. (1995). Posttraumatic stress associated with delayed recall of sexual abuse: A general population study. *Journal of Traumatic Stress, 8*(4), 629–647.

Emmons, R. A. (1992). Abstract versus concrete goals: Personal striving level, physical illness, and psychological well-being. *Journal of Personality and Social Psychology, 62*, 292–300.

Epstein, S. (1983). The unconscious, the preconscious and the self-concept. In J. Suls & A. Greenwald (Eds.), *Psychological perspectives on the self,* (Vol. 2, pp. 219–247). Hillsdale, NJ: Erlbaum.

Epstein, S. (1994). Integration of the cognitive and the psychodynamic unconscious. *American Psychologist, 49*, 709–724.

Epstein, S., Lipson, A., Holstein, C., & Huh, E. (1992). Irrational reactions to negative outcomes: Evidence for two conceptual systems. *Journal of Personality and Social Psychology, 62*, 328–339.

Eysenck, H. J. (1952). *The scientific study of personality.* London, UK: Routledge & Kegan Paul.

Eysenck, H. J., & Eysenck, S. B. C. (1969). *Eysenck Personality Inventory (EPI).* San Diego, CA: EdITS/Educational and Industrial Testing Service.

Falwell, J. (2000, August 6). A national rebirth needed. Sermon delivered at Thomas Road Baptist Church. Retrieved June 20, 2002, from www.trbc.org/sermons/

Faulkner, W. (1936/1990). *Absalom, Absalom!* New York: Vintage International.

Fazio, R. H. (1990). Multiple processes by which attitudes guide behavior: The mode model as an integrative framework. In M. P. Zanna (Ed.), *Advances in experimental social psychology* (Vol. 23, pp. 91–159). San Diego, CA: Academic Press.

Filkins, D. (2002, April 6). A nation challenged: Afghanistan; U.S. warns of bounties posing threat to Westerners. *The New York Times* (Section A, Foreign Desk), 6.

First, M. B., Spitzer, R. L., Gibbon, M., & Williams, J. B. W. (1995). The structured clinical interview for DSM-III-R personality disorders (SCID-II): II. Multi-site test-retest reliability study. *Journal of Personality Disorders, 9*(2), 92–104.

Fiske, S. T., & Taylor, S. E. (1991). *Social cognition.* New York: McGraw-Hill.

Florian, V., & Kravitz, S. (1983). Fear of personal death: Attribution, structure, and relation to religious belief. *Journal of Personality and Social Psychology, 44*, 600–607.

Florian, V., & Mikulincer, M. (1997). Fear of death and the judgment of social transgressions: A multidimensional test of terror management theory. *Journal of Personality and Social Psychology, 73*, 369–380.

Florian, V., & Mikulincer, M. (1998). Symbolic immortality and the management of the terror of death: The moderating role of attachment style. *Journal of Personality & Social Psychology, 74*(3), 725–734.

Florian, V., & Mikulincer, M., & Hirschberger, G. (2002). The anxiety-buffering function of close relationships: Evidence that relationship commitment acts as a terror management mechanism. *Journal of Personality & Social Psychology, 82,* 527–542.

Freud, S. (1915/1959). *Thoughts for the time on war and death, 1915.* Collected papers, Vol. 4. New York: Basic Books.

Freud, S. (1933/1965). *New introductory lectures on psychoanalysis.* New York: Norton.

Fromm, E. (1941/1965). *Escape from freedom.* New York: Avon Books.

Fromm, E. (1973). *The anatomy of human destructiveness.* New York: Holt, Rinehart, and Winston.

Fukuyama, F. (2002, January). Issues 2002. *Newsweek.* Retrieved from http://www.msnbc.com/news/672440.asp

Gilbert, D. T., & Hixon, J. G. (1991). The trouble of thinking: Activation and application of stereotypic beliefs. *Journal of Personality and Social Psychology, 50,* 269–280.

Goisman, R. M. (1983). Therapeutic approaches to phobia: A comparison. *American Journal of Psychotherapy, 37(2),* 227–234,

Goldberg, J., True, W. R., Eisen, S. A., & Henderson, W. G. (1990). A twin study of the effects of the Vietnam War on posttraumatic stress disorder. *JAMA: Journal of the American Medical Association. 263(9),* 1227–1232.

Goldenberg, J. L., McCoy, S. K., Pyszczynski, T. Greenberg, J., & Solomon, S. (2000). The body as a source of self-esteem: The effects of mortality salience on identification with one's body, interest in sex, and appearance monitoring. *Journal of Personality and Social Psychology, 79,* 118–130.

Goldenberg, J. L., Pyszczynski, T., McCoy, S. K., Greenberg, J. & Solomon, S. (1999). Death, sex, love and neuroticism: Why is sex such a problem? *Journal of Personality and Social Psychology, 77,* 1173-1187.

Goldschmidt, W. (1990). *The human career: The self in the symbolic world.* Cambridge, MA: Basil Blackwell.

Gould, L. J. (1969). Manifest Alienation Measure. Conformity and marginality: Two faces of alienation. *Journal of Social Issues, 25,* 39–63.

Greenberg, J., Arndt, J., Simon, L., Pyszczynski, T., & Solomon, S. (2000). Proximal and distal defenses in response to reminders of one's mortality: Evidence of a temporal sequence. *Personality and Social Psychology Bulletin, 26,* 91-99.

Greenberg, J., Porteus, J., Simon, L., Pyszczynski, T., & Solomon, S. (1995). Evidence of a terror management function of cultural icons: The effects of mortality salience on the inappropriate use of cherished cultural symbols. *Personality and Social Psychology Bulletin, 21,* 1221–1228.

Greenberg, J., Pyszczynski, T., & Solomon, S. (1986). The causes and consequences of a need for self-esteem: A terror management theory. In R.F. Baumeister (Ed.), *Public self and private self* (pp. 189–212). New York: Springer-Verlag.

Greenberg, J., Pyszczynski, T., Solomon, S., Pinel, E., Simon, L., & Jordan, K. (1993). Effects of self-esteem on vulnerability-denying defensive distortions:

Further evidence of an anxiety-buffering function of self-esteem. *Journal of Experimental Social Psychology, 29*, 229–251.

Greenberg, J., Pyszczynski, T., Solomon, S., Rosenblatt, A., Veeder, M., Kirkland, S., et al. (1990). Evidence for terror management theory II: The effects of mortality salience on reactions to those who threaten or bolster the cultural worldview. *Journal of Personality and Social Psychology, 58*, 308–318.

Greenberg, J., Pyszczynski, T., Solomon, S., Simon, L., & Breus, M. (1994). Role of consciousness and accessibility of death-related thoughts in mortality salience effects. *Journal of Personality and Social Psychology, 67*, 627–637.

Greenberg, J., Schimel, J., Martens, A., Pyszczynski, T., & Solomon, S. (2001). Sympathy for the devil: Evidence that reminding whites of their mortality promotes more favorable reactions to white racists. *Motivation and Emotion, 25*, 113–133.

Greenberg, J., Simon, L., Harmon-Jones, E., Solomon, S., Pyszczynski, T., & Lyon, D. (1995). Testing alternative explanations for mortality salience effects: Terror management, value accessibility, or worrisome thoughts? *European Journal of Social Psychology, 25*, 417–433.

Greenberg, J., Simon, L., Porteus, J., Pyszczynski, T., & Solomon, S. (1995). Evidence of a terror management function of cultural icons: The effects of mortality salience on the inappropriate use of cherished cultural symbols. *Personality and Social Psychology Bulletin, 21*, 1221–1228.

Greenberg, J., Simon, L., Pyszczynski, T., Solomon, S., & Chatel, D. (1992). Terror management and tolerance: Does mortality salience always intensify negative reactions to others who threaten one's worldview? *Journal of Personality and Social Psychology, 63*, 212–220.

Greenberg, J., Solomon, S., & Pyszczynski, T. (1997). Terror management theory of self-esteem and cultural worldviews: Empirical assessments and conceptual refinements. In M. Zanna (Ed.), *Advances in experimental social psychology* (Vol. 29, pp. 61–139). Orlando, FL: Academic Press.

Greenberg, J., Solomon, S., Pyszczynski, T., Rosenblatt, A., Burling, J., Lyon, D., et al. (1992). Assessing the terror management analysis of self-esteem: Converging evidence of an anxiety-buffering function. *Journal of Personality and Social Psychology, 63*, 913–922.

Guardian Home Pages. (2001, September 22). In brief: Somalia offers backing to US. *The Guardian* (London), 10.

Harmon-Jones, E., Greenberg, J., Solomon, S., & Simon, L. (1995). The effects of mortality salience on intergroup bias between minimal groups. *European Journal of Social Psychology, 25*, 781.1–781.5.

Harmon-Jones, E., Simon, L., Greenberg, J., Pyszczynski, T., Solomon, S., & McGregor, H. (1997). Terror management theory and self-esteem: Evidence that increased self-esteem reduces mortality salience effects. *Journal of Personality and Social Psychology, 72*, 24–36.

Harris, J. F. (2001, September 14). God gave U.S. "What we deserve," Falwell says. *The Washington Post*, p. C03.

Heatherton, T. F., & Polivy, J. (1991). Development and validation of a scale for measuring state self-esteem. *Journal of Personality and Social Psychology, 60,* 895–910.

Heider, F. (1958). *The psychology of interpersonal relations.* New York: John Wiley.

Herdt, G. (1982). *Rituals of manhood.* Berkeley, CA: University of California Press.

Hjern, A., Angel, B., & Hoejer, B. (1991). Persecution and behavior: A report of refugee children from Chile. *Child Abuse & Neglect, 15*(3), 239–248.

Hoover, F. (2001, October 12). Many turn to God, but for how long. *The Columbus Dispatch,* p. F1.

Houston, B. K., & Holmes, D. (1974). Effectiveness of avoidant thinking and reappraisal in coping with threat involving temporary uncertainty. *Journal of Personality and Social Psychology, 30,* 382–388.

Hovland, C. I., Janis, I. L., & Kelley, H. H. (1953). *Communication and persuasion; psychological studies of opinion change.* New Haven, CT: Yale University Press.

Human Rights Watch. (1993). Rape in Bosnia-Hercegovina. Adapted from Helsinki Watch, *War crimes in Bosnia-Hercegovina.* (Vol. II). New York: Author. Retrieved June 20, 2002, from http://www.hrw.org/about/projects/womrep/General-25.htm

Huntington, Samuel P. (2002, January). The age of Muslim wars. Issues 2002. *Newsweek.* Retrieved June 20, 2002, from http://www.msnbc.com/news/672440.asp

Jacobs, A. (2001, September 30). A nation challenged: The haunted; for haunted survivors, the towers fall again and again. *The New York Times,* p. 1B.

Jacoby, J. (2001, September 23). Speaking out against terror. *The Boston Globe,* p. D7.

James, W. (1890/1918). *Principles of psychology.* Toronto, Ontario: General Publishing.

Janoff-Bulman, R. (1992). *Shattered assumptions: Towards a new psychology of trauma.* New York: The Free Press.

Jemmott, J. B., Ditto, P. H., & Croyle, R. T. (1986). Judging health status: Effects of perceived prevalence and personal relevance. *Journal of Personality and Social Psychology, 50,* 899–905.

Jonas, E., & Greenberg, J. (2002). *A terror management perspective on attitudes toward societal changes: The influence of mortality salience on Germans' reactions towards the German reunification and the euro.* Unpublished manuscript, Ludwig-Maximilians-Universitaet Muenchen, Munich, Germany.

Jonas, E., Schimel, J., Greenberg, J., & Pyszczynski, T. (in press). The Scrooge effect: Evidence that mortality salience increases prosocial attitudes and behavior. *Personality and Social Psychology Bulletin.*

Jones, K. (2001, December 29). India and Pakistan on threshold of war. World Socialist Web Site. WSWS: News & Analysis: Asia. Published by the International Committee of the Fourth International (ICFI). Retrieved from http://www.wsws.org/articles/2001/dec2001/ind-d29.shtml

Joyce, J. (1922/1960). *Ulysses.* New York: Penguin PBooks.

Judges, D. P. (1999). Scared to death: Capital punishment as authoritarian terror management. *U.C. Davis Law Review, 33,* 155–248.

Kaffman, M., & Elizur, E. (1984). Bereavement responses of kibbutz and non-kibbutz children following the death of the father. *Journal of Child Psychology & Psychiatry & Allied Disciplines, 24*(3), 435–442.

Kelman, H. (1987). The political psychology of the Israeli-Palestinian conflict: How can we overcome the obstacles to a negotiated solution? *Political Psychology, 8,* 347–363.

Kelman, H. (1997). Group processes in the resolution of international conflicts: Experiences from the Israeli-Palestinian case. *American Psychologist, 52,* 212–220.

Kelman, H. (1998). Building a sustainable peace: The limits of pragmatism in the Israeli-Palestinian negotiations. *Journal of Palestine Studies, 28*(1), 36–50.

Khadduri, M. (1999). Interpretations of Islam. *Journal of Palestine Studies, 28,* 98–100. Retrieved from ips.jps.org/jps/111/br_khadduri.html

Kienzle, R. (2001, December 23). Country goes to war since Pearl Harbor, patriotic anthems have rallied the nation. *Pittsburgh Post-Gazette,* p. G3.

Kihlstrom, J. F. (1987). The cognitive unconscious. *Science, 237,* 1445-1452.

Kingsolver, B. (2001, October 14). No glory in unjust war on the weak. *Los Angeles Times,* p. M1.

Kinzie, J. D., Sack, W. H., Angell, R. H., & Manson, S. M. (1986). The psychiatric effects of massive trauma on Cambodian children: I. The children. *Journal of the American Academy of Child Psychiatry, 25*(3), 370–376.

Kirkpatrick, L. A. & Epstein, A. (1992). Cognitive-experiential self theory and subjective probability: Further evidence for two conceptual systems. *Journal of Personality and Social Psychology, 63,* 534–544.

Koran (1909; Rev. J. M. Rodwell, trans.). New York: E. P. Dutton.

Kosterlitz, J. (2001). Troops and consequences. *National Journal, 33,* 3420–3425.

Kunda, Z. (1987). Motivated inference: Self-serving generation and evaluation of causal theories. *Journal of Personality and Social Psychology, 53,* 636–647.

Kunzendorf, R. G., & Maguire, D. (1995). *Depression: The reality of "no meaning" versus the delusion of negative meaning.* Unpublished manuscript, University of Massachusetts, Lowell, MA.

Kunzendorf, R. G., & McLaughlin, S. (1988). Depression: A failure to suppress the self-conscious "monitoring" of dismal cognitions. *Imagination, Cognition & Personality, 8*(1), 3–17.

Kunzendorf, R. G., Moran, C., & Gray, R. (1995). Personality traits and reality testing abilities, controlling for vividness of imagery. *Imagination, Cognition, and Personality, 105,* 113–132.

Kurosawa, A. (Director). (1952). *Ikiru.* [Motion picture]. Japan: Toho Films.

Lampman, J. (2001, November 29). Spiritual "resurgence" rises, falls in U.S; more in Europe identify as religious. *The Christian Science Monitor,* p. 14.

Landau, M. J., Pyszczynski, T., Greenberg, J., & Solomon, S. (2002). *Mortality salience and reminders of the terrorist attack on the World Trade Center in alienated and non-alienated college students.* Manuscript in preparation, University of Colorado at Colorado Springs, Colorado Springs, CO.

Laurance, J. (2001, September 29). War on terrorism: Psychology—Expression of feelings through art can be part of the healing process. *The Independent* (London), p. 3.

Lazarus, R. S. (1966). *Psychological stress and the coping process.* New York: McGraw-Hill.

Lazarus, R. S. (1995). Psychosocial factors play a role in health, but we have to tackle them with more sophisticated research and thought. *Advances, 11*(2), 14–18.

Lazarus, R. S., Opton, E. M., Nomikos, M. S., & Rankin, N. O. (1965). The principle of short-circuiting of threat: Further evidence. *Journal of Personality, 33,* 622–635.

LeDuff, C. (2001, December 5). A bleaker Santa's-eye view: Bell-ringer sees more anxiety and less giving. *New York Times,* p. D1.

Leeming, D. A., & Leeming, M. A. (1994). *Encyclopedia of creation myths.* Santa Barbara, CA: ABC-CLIO.

Lerner, M. J. (1980). *The belief in a just world: A fundamentalist decision.* New York: Plenum.

Lerner, M.J., & Miller, D.T. (1978). Just world research and the attribution process: Looking back and ahead. *Psychological Bulletin, 85,* 1030–1051.

Lessing, D. (1971/1981). *Briefing for a descent into hell.* New York: Vintage Books.

Lewis, B. (1990, September). The roots of Muslim rage. *The Atlantic Monthly, 226,* 47–60.

Lifton, R. J. (1968). *Revolutionary immortality: Mao Tse-Tung and the Chinese Cultural Revolution.* New York: Random House.

Lifton, R. J. (1979/1983). *The broken connection: On death and continuity of life.* New York: Simon and Schuster.

Linton, M. (2001, October 28). Feeling sad? You are not alone; Mental stress after Sept. 11 has many people depressed. *Toronto Sun,* p. 51.

Long, C. H. (1963). *Alpha: The myths of creation.* New York: George Braziller.

Macfarquhar, N. (2001, Oct. 19). A nation challenged: Education: Anti-Western and extremist views pervade Saudi schools. *New York Times,* Section p. B1.

Maclagan, D. (1977). *Creation myths: Man's introduction to the world.* New York: Thames and Hudson.

Maher, B., Geller, N., Grey, B., Brillstein, B., Gurvitz, M., Wilson, M., et al. (Executive Producers). (2001, September 9). *Politically incorrect with Bill Maher.* [Television broadcast]. New York and Washington, DC: American Broadcasting Corporation.

Mahoney, J. M., & Quick, B. G. (2000). Personality correlates of alienation in a university sample. *Psychological Reports, 87*(2), 1094–1100.

Maltby, J., & Day, L. (2000). The reliability and validity of the Death Obsession Scale among English university and adult samples. *Personality & Individual Differences, 28*(4), 695–700.

Marcuse, H. (1955). *Eros and civilization*. Boston, MA: Beacon Press.

Martin, L. L., & Tesser, A. (1993). *Thought processes following the attainment and non-attainment of goals*. Unpublished Manuscript, University of Georgia, Athens, Georgia.

Maslow, A. (1970). *Motivation and personality* (2nd ed.). New York: Harper & Row.

Mathews, R. C., & Kling, K. J. (1988). Self-transcendence, time perspective, and prosocial behavior. *Journal of Voluntary Action Research, 17*, 4–24.

McFarlane, A. C. (1992). Posttraumatic stress disorder among injured survivors of a terrorist attack: Predictive value of early intrusion and avoidance. In S. Mithen (Ed., 1996). *The prehistory of the mind: The cognitive origins of art, religion and science*. London, UK: Thames and Hudson.

McFarlane, A. C., & de Girolamo, G. (1996). The nature of traumatic stressors and the epidemiology of posttraumatic reactions. In B. A. van der Kolk, A. C., McFarlane, & L. Weisaeth (Eds.), *Traumatic stress: The effects of overwhelming experience on mind, body, and society* (pp. 129–154). New York: Guilford Press.

McGregor, H., Lieberman, J., Greenberg, J., Solomon, S., Arndt, J., Simon, L., et al. (1998). Terror management and aggression: Evidence that mortality salience promotes aggression toward worldview-threatening individuals. *Journal of Personality and Social Psychology, 74*, 590–605.

McNeill, W. H. (1999). *A world history* (4th ed.). New York: Oxford Press.

Meineke, S. (2001, December 13). Post-attack crowds thin at churches. *The Houston Chronicle*, p. 1.

Melville, H. (1851/1986). *Moby-Dick*. New York: Viking Penguin.

Mikulincer, M., & Florian, V. (1996). Coping and adaptation to trauma and loss. In M. Zeidner & N. S. Endler (Eds.), *Handbook of coping: Theory, research, applications* (pp. 554–572). New York: John Wiley & Sons.

Mikulincer, M., & Florian, V. (2000). Exploring individual differences in reactions to mortality salience—Does attachment style regulate terror management mechanisms? *Journal of Personality and Social Psychology, 79*, 260–273.

Mikulincer, M., Florian, V., Birnbaum, G., & Malishkevich, S. (2002). The death-anxiety buffering function of close relationships: Exploring the effects of separation reminders on death-thought accessibility. *Personality and Social Psychology Bulletin, 28*, 287–299.

Mikulincer, M., Florian, V., & Hirschberger, G. (in press). The existential function of close relationships: Introducing death into the science of love. *Personality and Social Psychology Review*.

Mikulincer, M., Florian, V., & Tolmacz, R. (1990). Attachment styles and fear of personal death: A case study of affect regulation. *Journal of Personality and Social Psychology, 58*, 273–280.

Milgram, S. (1967). The small-world problem. *Psychology Today, 1*, 60–67.

Miller, H. (1965). *Sexus*. New York: Grove Press.

Miller, S., Fleeman, M., Harrington, M., Laudadio, M., Wang, C., Warrick, P., et al. (2001). Finding a way to help. *People, 56*(15), 70–77.

Monmaney, T. (2001, September 29). Response to terror. *Los Angeles Times*, Part A, Part 1, p. 1.

Moomal, Z. (1999). The relationship between meaning in life and mental well-being. *South African Journal of Psychology, 29*(1), 36–41.

Morin, R., & Deane, C. (2001, October 8). Public support is overwhelming; poll finds 94% favor Bush's ordering strikes on Afghanistan. *The Washington Post*, p. A05.

Murder trial begins in toddler's death. (2000, May 16). *The St. Petersburg Times*, p. 3B.

Murphy, S. T., Monahan, J. L., & Zajonc, R. B. (1995). Additivity of nonconscious affect: combined effects of priming and exposure. *Journal of Personality and Social Psychology, 69*, 589–602.

Myers, D. G. (2002). *Social Psychology* (7th ed.). New York: McGraw-Hill.

Nagourney, A. (2001, December 13). Many rush to make wills. *New York Times*, pp. A1, D8.

A nation challenged: The president reports on progress; excerpts from the president's remarks on the war on terrorism. (2001, October 12). *New York Times*, p. B4.

Nelson, L. J., Moore, D. L., Olivetti, J., & Scott, T. (1997). General and personal mortality salience and nationalistic bias. *Personality and Social Psychology Bulletin, 23*, 884–892.

Nida'ul Islam. Mujahid Usama bin Laden talks exclusively to *Nida'ul Islam* about the new powder keg in the Middle East. Retrieved June 20, 2002, from www.islam.org.au/articles/15/LADIN.HTM

Nietzsche, F. (1886/2001). *Beyond good and evil: Prelude to a philosophy of the future*. Cambridge, UK: Cambridge University Press.

Nietzsche, F. (1887/1989). *On the genealogy of morals*. New York: Vintage Books.

Ochs, R. (2001, December 28). Post 9/11: Helping ourselves—but not to booze, drugs, food. *Newsday*, p. C4.

Ochsmann, R., & Mathy, M. (1994). *Depreciating of and distancing from foreigners: Effects of mortality salience*. Unpublished manuscript, Universitat Mainz, Mainz, Germany.

Officer's eggs allegedly spiked with hot sauce. (1995, April 6). *The Phoenix Gazette*, p. A2.

Panati, C. (1996). *Sacred origins of profound things: The stories behind the rites and rituals of the world's religions*. New York: Penguin Books USA.

Pauloutzian, R. F. (1981). Purpose in life and value changes following conversion. *Journal of Personality and Social Psychology, 41*, 1153–1160.

Pearson, P. R., & Sheffield, B. F. (1974). Purpose-in-Life and the Eysenck Personality Inventory. *Journal of Clinical Psychology, 30*(4), 562–564.

Pennebaker, J. W. (1989). Confession, inhibition, and disease. In L. Berkowitz, (Ed.), *Advances in experimental social psychology*, (Vol. 22, pp. 211–244). San Diego, CA: Academic Press.

Pressley, S. A. (1995, April 20). Bomb kills dozens in Oklahoma Federal Building. *Washington Post*, Section A, p. 1.

Pyszczynski, T., & Greenberg, J. (1987). Self-regulatory perseveration and the depressive self-focusing style: A self-awareness theory of the development and maintenance of reactive depression. *Psychological Bulletin, 102,* 122–138.

Pyszczynski, T., & Greenberg, J. (1992). *Hanging on and letting go: Understanding the onset, progression, and remission of depression.* New York: Springer-Verlag.

Pyszczynski, T., Greenberg, J., & Goldenberg, J. (in press). Fear versus freedom: On the defense, growth, and expansion of the self. In M. Leary & J. Tangney (Eds.), *Handbook of Self and Identity.* Thousand Oaks, CA: Sage Press.

Pyszczynski, T., Greenberg, J., & Solomon, S. (1999). A dual process model of defense against conscious and unconscious death-related thoughts. An extension of terror management theory. *Psychological Review, 106,* 835–845.

Pyszczynski, T., Greenberg, J., Solomon, S., & Hamilton, J. (1990). A terror management analysis of self-awareness and anxiety: The hierarchy of terror. *Anxiety Research, 2,* 177–195.

Pyszczynski, T., Wicklund, R., Floresku, S., Gauch, G., Koch, H., Solomon, S., et al. (1996). Whistling in the dark: Exaggerated consensus estimates in response to incidental reminders of mortality. *Psychological Science, 7,* 332–336.

Quattrone, G.A., & Tversky, A. (1984). Causal vs. diagnostic contingencies: On self-deception and on the voter's illusion. *Journal of Personality and Social Psychology, 46,* 237–248.

Rank, O. (1931/1961). *Psychology and the soul* (Perpetua Ed.). New York: A. S. Barnes.

Rank, O. (1932). *Art and artist: Creative urge and personality development.* New York: Alfred A. Knopf.

Rank, O. (1936/1945). *Will therapy.* New York: Alfred A. Knopf.

Rank, O. (1936/1978). *Truth and reality.* New York: Norton.

Rice, P. (2001, December 22). Religious books are rising to the occasion. *St. Louis Post-Dispatch,* Religion Section, p. 16.

Ritter, C., Benson, D. E, & Snyder, C. (1990). Belief in a just world and depression. *Sociological Perspectives, 33*(2), 235–252.

Robertson, P. (1986, August 18). Interview in *New York Magazine,* p. 24.

Robertson, P. (1990). *The new world order.* Dallas, TX: Word Publishing.

Robertson, P. (2001, September 13). *Transcript of Pat Robertson's interview with Jerry Falwell* on *The 700 Club* [Television broadcast]. Retrieved April 12, 2002, from the People for the American Way Web site: http://www.pfaw.org

Roheim, G. (1943). *The origin and function of culture.* (Nervous and Mental Disease Monograph No. 69). New York: Nervous and Mental Disease Monographs.

Rosenberg, M. (1965). *Society and the adolescent self-image.* Princeton, NJ: Princeton University Press.

Rosenblatt, A., Greenberg, J., Solomon, S., Pyszczynski, T., & Lyon, D. (1989). Evidence for terror management theory I: The effects of mortality salience on reactions to those who violate or uphold cultural values. *Journal of Personality and Social Psychology, 57*, 681–690.

Ross, L. (1977). The intuitive psychologist and his shortcomings: Distortions in the attribution process. *Advances in Experimental Social Psychology, 10*, 173–220.

Rushdie, S. (1989). *The satanic verses*. New York: Viking Press.

Sack, W. H., Angell, R. H., Kinzie, J. D., Rath, B. (1986). The psychiatric effects of massive trauma on Cambodian children: II. The family, the home, and the school. *Journal of the American Academy of Child Psychiatry, 25*(3), 377–383.

Sales, S. M. (1973). Threat as a factor in authoritarianism: An analysis of archival data. *Journal of Personality and Social Psychology, 28*, 44–57.

Sappington, A. A., Rice, J., Burleson, R., & Gordon, J. (1981). Emotionally based expectancies and willingness to use aversive therapy. *Basic and Applied Social Psychology, 2*, 227–234.

Sappington, A. A., Russell, J. C., Triplett, V., & Goodwin, J. (1980). Self-efficacy expectancies, response-outcome expectancies, emotionally based expectancies and their relationship to avoidance behavior. *Journal of Clinical Psychology, 37*, 737–744.

Schachter, S. (1959). *The psychology of affiliation: Experimental studies of the sources of gregariousness*. Stanford, CT: Stanford University Press.

Schimel, J., Simon, L., Greenberg, J., Pyszczynski, T., Solomon, S., Waxmonsky, J., et al. (1999). Stereotypes and terror management: Evident that mortality salience enhances stereotypic thinking and preferences. *Journal of Personality and Social Psychology, 77*, 905–926.

Segall, M. H., Campbell, D. T., & Herskovits, M. J. (1966). *The influence of culture on visual perception*. Indianapolis, IN: Bobbs-Merrill.

Shaver, P. R., & Hazan, C. (1993). Adult romantic attachment: Theory and evidence. In D. Perlman & W. Jones (Eds.), *Advances in personal relationships* (Vol. 4, pp. 29–70). London: Jessica Kingsley.

Simon, L., Arndt, J., Greenberg, J., Pyszczynski, T., & Solomon, S. (1998). Terror management and meaning: Evidence that the opportunity to defend the worldview in response to mortality salience increases the meaningfulness of life in the mildly depressed. *Journal of Personality, 66*(3), 359–382.

Simon, L., Greenberg, J., Arndt, J., Pyszczynski, T., Clement, R., & Solomon, S. (1997). Perceived consensus, uniqueness, and terror management: Compensatory responses to threats to inclusion and distinctiveness following mortality salience. *Personality and Social Psychology Bulletin, 23*, 1055–1065.

Simon, L., Greenberg, J., Clement, R., Pyszczynski, T., Arndt., J., & Solomon, S. (1997). Fitting in and standing out: The effects of mortality salience on optimal distinctiveness striving. *Personality and Social Psychology Bulletin, 23*, 1055–1065.

Simon, L., Greenberg, J., Harmon-Jones, E., Solomon, S., & Pyszczynski, T. (1996). Mild depression, mortality salience, and defense of the worldview: Evidence of intensified terror management in the mildly depressed. *Personality & Social Psychology Bulletin*, 22(1), 81–90.

Simon, L., Greenberg, J., Harmon-Jones, E., Solomon, S., Pyszczynski, T., Arndt, J., et al. (1997). Terror management and cognitive-experiential self-theory: Evidence that terror management occurs in the experiential system. *Journal of Personality and Social Psychology*, 72, 1132–1146.

Sloan, J., & Peterson, L. (2002, February 7). I will make you pay! *The Tampa Tribune*, p. 1.

Smith, A. (1857/1934). *Dreamthorp: A book of essays written in the country*. Garden City, New York: Doubleday, Doiran.

Snyder, C. R. (2000). The hope mandala: Coping with the loss of a loved one. In J. E. Gillham. (Ed.), *The science of optimism and hope: Research essays in honor of Martin E. P. Seligman. Laws of life symposia series* (pp. 129–142). Philadelphia: Templeton Foundation Press.

Snyder, C. R, & Ingram, R. E. (2000). Psychotherapy: Questions for an evolving field. In C. R. Snyder & R. E. Ingram (Eds.), *Handbook of psychological change: Psychotherapy processes & practices for the 21st century* (pp. 707–726). New York: John Wiley & Sons.

Solomon, S., Greenberg, J., & Pyszczynski, T. (1991a). A terror management theory of social behavior: The psychological functions of self-esteem and cultural worldviews. In M. Zanna (Ed.), *Advances in experimental social psychology* (Vol. 24, pp. 91–159). Orlando, FL: Academic Press.

Solomon, S., Greenberg, J., & Pyszczynski, T. (1991b). Terror management theory. In C. R. Snyder & D. Forsyth (Eds.), *Handbook of clinical and social psychology: The health perspective*. New York: Pergamon.

Solomon, S., Greenberg, J., & Pyszczynski, T. (in press). Fear of death and social behavior: The anatomy of human destructiveness. In N. Dess & R. Bloom (Eds.), *Evolutionary psychology and violence: A primer for policymakers and public policy*. Westport, CT: Praeger.

Solomon, Z., Laor, N., & McFarlane, A. C. (1996). Acute posttraumatic reactions in soldiers and civilians. In B. A. van der Kolk, A. C. McFarlane, & A. C. L. Weisaeth (Eds.), *Traumatic stress: The effects of overwhelming experience on mind, body, and society* (pp. 102–114). New York: Guilford Press.

Spiegel, D., Bloom, J. R., & Yalom, I. (1981). Group support for patients with metastatic cancer: A randomized prospective outcome study. *Archives of General Psychiatry*, 38(5), 527–533.

Spielberger, C. D., Gorsuch, R. L., & Lushene, R. E. (1970). *Trait Anxiety Inventory (self-evaluation questionnaire)*. Palo Alto, CA: Consulting Psychologists Press.

Srull, T. K., & Wyer, R. S., Jr. (1980). Category accessibility and social perception: Some implications for the study of person memory and interpersonal judgments. *Journal of Personality and Social Psychology*, 38, 841–856.

Strachan, E., Pyszczynski, T., Greenberg, J., & Solomon, S. (2001). Coping with the inevitability of death: Terror management and mismanagement. In C. R. Snyder (Ed.), *Coping with stress: Effective people and processes* (pp. 144–136). New York: Oxford University Press.

Stone, W. F. (1980). The myth of left-wing authoritarianism. *Political Psychology, 2,* 3–20.

Substance abuse up since 9/11. (2001, December 7). *Newsday,* p. A13.

Suppression of dissent echoes McCarthyism. Wellington Newspapers Limited. (2001, November 1). *The Evening Post,* p. 6.

Swift, J. (1726/2001). *Gulliver's travels.* Indianapolis, IN: Bobbs-Merrill.

Tajfel, H., Billig, M. G., Bundy, R. P., & Flament, C. (1971). Social categorization and intergroup behavior. *European Journal of Social Psychology, 1,* 149–178.

Tattersall, I. (2000). Once we were not alone. *Scientific American, 282,* 56–62.

Taubman Ben-Ari, O., Florian, V., & Mikulincer, M. (1999). The impact of mortality salience on reckless driving: A test of terror management mechanisms. *Journal of Personality and Social Psychology, 76,* 35–45.

Taubman Ben-Ari, O., Florian, V., & Mikulincer, M. (in press). The effects of mortality salience on relationship strivings and beliefs—the moderating role of attachment style. *British Journal of Social Psychology.*

Taylor, S. E, & Brown, J. D. (1988). Illusion and well-being: A social psychological perspective on mental health. *Psychological Bulletin, 103*(2), 193–210.

Text of Fatwah urging Jihad against Americans. (1998, February 23). *Al-Quds al-'Arabi.* Retrieved from http://www.ict.org.il/articles/fatwah.htm

Tillich, P. (1959/1964). Theology of culture. R. Kimball, (Ed.). New York: Oxford University Press.

Toner, R., & Elder, J. (2001, December 12). Public is wary but supportive on rights curbs. *New York Times,* p. 1.

Transcript of the comments by Bush on air strikes against the Iraqis. (1991, January 17). As recorded by the *New York Times,* p. A14.

Tversky, A., & Kahneman, D. (1973). *Judgment under uncertainty: Heuristics and biases.* Eugene, Oregon: Oregon Research Institute.

Tversky, A., & Kahneman, D. (1974). Judgment under uncertainty: Heuristics and biases. *Science, 125,* 1124–1131.

Two care providers plead not guilty in child-abuse case. (1989, January 24). *Los Angeles Times.* Metro Part 2, p.1.

Tyrangiel, J. (2001, December 9). The Taliban next door. *Time.* Retrieved June 20, 2002, from http://www.time.com/time/nation/printout/0,8816,187564,00.html

Ullman, C. (1982). Cognitive and emotional antecedents of religious concern. *Journal of Personality and Social Psychology, 43,* 183–192.

van der Kolk, B. A., McFarlane, A. C., & Weisaeth, L. (Eds.). (1996). *Traumatic stress: The effects of overwhelming experience on mind, body, and society.* New York: The Guilford Press.

Vaughn, K. & Klack, N. (1999, April 24). Note blames the victims. *Rocky Mountain News*. Retrieved June 20, 2002, from http://www.rockymoutainnews.com

Viorst, M. (1998). The shadow of the prophet: The struggle for the soul of Islam. New York: Anchor Books.

Watson, D., & Clark, L. A. (1984). Negative affectivity: The disposition to experience aversive emotional states. *Psychological Bulletin, 96*, 465–490.

Watson, D., Clark, L. A., & Tellegen, A. (1988). Development and validation of brief measures of positive and negative affect: The PANAS scales. *Journal of Personality and Social Psychology, 53*, 1063–1070.

Watson, P. (2002, March 16). The world; Temple supporters march in India; Religion: Police keep the peace and bar the Hindu procession in Ayodhya from reaching the disputed site where a mosque once stood. *Los Angeles Times* (Part A; Part 1; Foreign Desk), 3.

Weeks, L. (2001, December 15). "Let's roll": A 9-11 call to arms. Booker T. and Neil Young salute Flight 93's heroes. *The Washington Post*, p. C01.

Wegner, D. M. (1994). Ironic processes of mental control. *Psychological Review, 101*, 34–52.

Wegner, D. M., & Erber, R. (1992). The hyperaccessibility of suppressed thoughts. *Journal of Personality and Social Psychology, 63*, 903–912.

Weisaeth, L. (1993). Disasters: Psychological and psychiatric aspects. In L. Goldberger & S. Breznitz (Eds.), *Handbook of stress: Theoretical and clinical aspects*, 2nd ed. (pp. 591–616). New York: The Free Press.

Wenzlaff, R. M., Wegner, D. M., & Roper, D. W. (1988). Depression and mental control: The resurgence of unwanted negative thoughts. *Journal of Personality & Social Psychology, 55*(6), 882–892.

We shall overcome. (2001, September 24). *Newsweek*, 18–25.

Williams, C. J. (2002, April 4). The world; The Middle East; Europe sees a tinderbox in its streets; Conflict: Spate of anti-Semitic attacks has officials worried about roxy fighting between Jewish and Arab groups. *Los Angeles Times* (Part A; Part 1, Foreign Desk), 1+.

Woodruff, C. (2001, December 16). More seek help in handguns. *Albany Times Union*, pp. A1, A9.

Woolf, V. (1929/1981). *A room of one's own*. New York: Harcourt Brace Jovanovich.

Wortman, C. B, & Silver, R. C. (1992). Reconsidering assumptions about coping with loss: An overview of current research. In L. Montada, & F. Sigrun-Heide (Eds.), *Life crises and experiences of loss in adulthood* (pp. 341–365). Hillsdale, NJ: Lawrence Erlbaum Associates.

Yacoub, S. N. (2002, April 16). Saddam Hussein calls Palestinian suicide bombings "legitimate." Compiled by The Associated Press (International News section).

Yalom, I. D. (1980). *Existential psychotherapy*. New York: Basic Books.

Zakaria, F. (2001, October 15). Why do they hate us? *Newsweek, 138* (16), 22–28.

Zillmann, D. (1971). Excitation transfer in communication-mediated aggressive behavior. *Journal of Experimental Social Psychology, 7*, 419–434.

AUTHOR INDEX

SUBJECT INDEX

worldview and living with concept of, 16–18

Death-related thoughts,
  accessibility of, 58–59
  defensive processes activated by, 70
  and mortality salience
    accessibility and suppression of, 60–62
    accessibility of worldview constructs in, 68
    after separation reminders, 67–68
    after worldview defense, 66–67

Depression, 123–124

Derogation, of alternative worldviews, 30–31

Dewey, John, 13

Dickens, Charles, 87

Dissent suppression, 102–104

Distal defense(s), 56, 59–60, 191
  after 9/11 terrorist attacks, 100–106

Distractive pursuits, 56–59, 96–97

Emery, Gary, 140

Ethnopolitical violence, ideology and, 153–154

Excitation transfer, 48

Falwell, Jerry, 106, 160, 176

Foda, Farag, 177

Frankl, Victor, 117

Freud, Sigmund, 11, 119, 147

Fromm, Erich, 11, 99

Fukuyama, Francis, 158, 159, 160, 180

Fundamental attribution error, 144

Fundamentalist ideology, 161–163
  Islamic and Christian, 158–161

Goffman, Erving, 11

Graham, Inez, 128

Greenberg, Jeff, 17

Greenwood, Lee, 8, 101

Group identifications, in terror management, 89–91

Guadagno, Rich, 109

Harris, Eric, 196

Heider, Fritz, 137–138

Hero appreciation, 109, 141

Hitler, Adolf, 12, 33–34

Human behavior, assumptions regarding, 12–13

Hussein, Saddam, 170, 194

Hutchinson, Kay Bailey, 145

Ideology,
  atheistic, 148
  and ethnopolitical violence, 153–154
  fundamentalist, 161–163
    Islamic and Christian, 158–161
  proselytizing, 150–152
  and sacrifice of life, 147–148
  terror management and, 148–150
  Western secular, 158–161

Igarashi, Hitoshi, 177

Ikira, 141

Immortality,
  cultural concepts of, 19–22
  symbolic, and mortality salience, 83–84

Intergroup conflict,
  aggression in, 74–77
  and confirmation of worldview, 78–81
  in minimal groups, 77
  prejudice in, 72–74

Islam, and secular democracy, 183–184

Islamic fundamentalism, 21, 158–161

Islamic terrorism, 154–157
  elimination of, as tool of social change, 185–187
  Islamic fundamentalism and, 158–161
  political agenda of, 168–170
  reasons for targeting United States, 157–161

Israel, state of, 164–166. *See also* Palestinian statehood, establishment of

James, William, 12, 197

Jefferson, Lisa, 109

Kaslow, Florence, 129

Kelman, Herb, 185

Kierkegaard, Søren, 11, 15, 117

Kissinger, Henry, 168

Law enforcement, changes in, 99–100

Lewis, Bernard, 146

Lifton, Robert Jay, 20, 83, 117, 147

Limbaugh, Rush, 7

Lyles, CeeCee, 109

Madonna, 7, 102

Mafouz, Naguib, 177

Maher, Bill, 103

Marcuse, Herbert, 146

May, Rollo, 117

Meaning, and value, 100–101, 135–140

Mental illness. *See* Psychopathology

Middle East,
    democratic and theocratic government
      in, 179–183
    diversion from political and economic
      problems, 157–161
    education and employment in, 177–179
    fundamentalist teachings in, support
      for, 156–157
    Islamic and secular government in,
      183–184
    needs of people living in, 173–174
    Palestinian statehood in, 184–185
    political repression in, 179–181
    terror as tool of social change in,
      185–187
    U. S. policies in, 163–168
    worldviews and achieving peace in,
      174–177
Midler, Bette, 109
Miller, Henry, 122
Morris, Walter, 75
Mortality, development of sense of, 26–27
Mortality salience, 45
    and anxiety-provoking events, 48–49
    and consciousness, 62–64
    and death-related thoughts
      accessibility and suppression, 60–62
      and accessibility of worldview con-
        structs, 68
      after separation reminders, 67–68
      after worldview defense, 66–67
    and delay and distraction, 56–59
    and dual defense model, 54–56
    and excitation transfer, 48
    and moral transgression, 45–50
    and proximal and distal defenses, 56,
      59–60
    and psychodynamics of terror manage-
      ment, 68–70
    and secure attachment, 84–85
    and self-esteem, 89–92
    and social connections, 89–91
    and symbolic immortality, 83–84
    and worldview defense, 49, 50–52,
      81–86
Mundine, Anthony, 104

Nesin, Aziz, 177
Neuroticism, 121–123
9/11 terrorist attacks,
    provisions for coping with, 134

      building self-esteem, 141
      social support, 134–135
      understanding/meaning, 135–140
    proximal defenses in, 96–100
    psychological impact of, 93–95
      altruistic actions, 108–109
      in children, 129–133
      dissent suppression, 102–104
      distractive pursuits, 96–97
      fear of future attacks, 112–113
      hero appreciation, 109–110
      individual, 110–112
      meaning and value seeking, 100–101
      negation or disbelief, 96
      patriotic sentiment, 101–102
      prejudice and bigotry, 104–108
      protective measures, 98–100
      renewal of religious beliefs, 100–101
      terror mismanagement and, 128–129
Nygaard, William, 177

Obsessive–compulsive behavior, 119–121

Palestinian statehood, 184–185
    conflict over, 193–195
    establishment of, 165
Panati, Charles, 21
Patriotism, and nationalism, 101–102,
    146–154
Peaceful coexistence, 12
    accommodation and, 32
    annihilation and, 32–34, 149–150
    assimilation and, 31–32
    conversion and, 30
    derogation and, 30–31
    difficulty of, 29–30
Pearl, Daniel, 193
Peirce, Charles, 13
Penner, Louis, 108
Pentagon, 94
Phobias, 119–121
Posttraumatic stress disorder, 124–125
    as reaction to terrorist attacks, 125–126
    from terror mismanagement perspec-
      tive, 126–127
Powell, Colin, 7
Prejudice,
    after 9/11 attacks, 104–108
    and terror management, 72–74
Priming, 110
Protective measures, 98–100
Proximal defense(s), 56, 59–60, 191

and worldview confirmation, 78–81. *See also* Worldview(s)
Self-perception, changes in, 88–89
Self-preservation,
  biological disposition to, 13–14
  consciousness of, 14–15
    fear and, 15
Separation reminders, 67–68
September 11 terrorist attacks. *See* 9/11 terrorist attacks.
Shamni, Abdulla, 21
Shawa, Ali Abu, 145
Shelby, Richard, 145
Social support, in disasters, 101–102, 134–135
Sodhi, Balbir Singh, 6, 105
Solomon, Sheldon, 139
Swift, Jonathan, 77–78
Symbolic immortality, and mortality salience, 83–84

Taliban government,
  as repressive theocracy, 180–181
  and support for al Qaeda, 155
  U. S. attacks on Afghanistan and, 102–103
Terror. *See also* Mortality salience
  potential for, 27–28
Terrorist attacks,
  attributing causes to, 143–145
  finding meaning in aftermath of, 135
    appreciation of life, 139–140
    causes of human behavior, 137–138
    information gathering, 135–137
    personal growth, 138–139
  motivation behind, 154–156
    ethnopolitical, 146–154
  in United States, 4
    September 11, 2002, (9/11), 3–7, 93–113. *See also* 9/11 terrorist attacks
  terror management theory and, 7–9
Terror management. *See also* Terror management theory; Worldview(s)
  in children, 129–133
  daily, 195–196
  disruption of, 9
  and ideology, 148–154
  and Islamic terrorism, 154–157
  in minimal groups, 77
  and peace efforts, 171–173. *See also* Middle East
  prejudice and intergroup conflict in, 72–81

psychodynamics of, 54–56, 68–70
  consciousness, 62–64
  death-related thought accessibility, 60–62, 66–68
  delay and distraction, 56–59
  mortality salience, 54–56
  proximal and distal defenses, 56, 59–60
  separation reminders, 67–68
  worldview defense, 66–67
  and psychopathology, 115–123. *See also* Psychopathology
  and social connections, 89–92
  studies on. *See* Research, terror management
  worldview in, 146–154
    mitigating factors, 81–85
Terror management theory, 7–8, 27–28, 190–191
  core proposition of, 16–18
  development of, 11–12
  and 9/11 attack, 189–190, 191–193
  validity of, 34–35. *See also* Research, terror management
Threat-focused defenses, 59–60
Tillich, Paul, 161–162

Wahhabi sect, 156–157
World Trade Center towers, 94
Worldview(s), 16–18
  changes in, 172–173
  confirmation of, and terror management, 78–81
  cultural, 18–23, 85–86
  designated inferiors in, 78–81
  and protection against anxiety, 149
  reducing threat of alternative, 174–177
  tolerant, 82–83
Worldview defense, 66–67
  and concern about mortality, 58
  and death-related thought accessibility, 66–68
  delayed, 60–62
  ethnopolitical motivation of, 146–154
  mortality salience and, 50–52, 81–86
  studies of, 50–52

Yalom, Irvin, 17–18, 116, 117, 129–130, 139
Young, Neil, 109

Zakaria, Fareed, 179–180, 181

ABOUT THE AUTHORS

Tom Pyszczynski, Sheldon Solomon, and **Jeff Greenberg** began doing research together as graduate students at the University of Kansas, where they each received a PhD in psychology in the early 1980s.

Inspired by the work of the Pulitzer Prize–winning cultural anthropologist Ernest Becker, they developed Terror Management Theory as a conceptual framework to illuminate the interrelatedness of various forms of human behavior and motivation. The theory integrates ideas from existential psychology, psychoanalysis, and evolutionary theory into a framework that is amenable to rigorous scientific testing. In so doing, their work lays the groundwork for an experimental existential psychology, a new perspective on the human condition influencing current thinking on a wide range of issues within psychology. Their work has yielded a wealth of new insights into diverse aspects of the human condition, including self-esteem striving, prejudice, intergroup conflict, human sexuality, unconscious motives, conformity, aggression, creativity, altruism, and love.

Currently, the three authors are professors of psychology—Dr. Pyszczynski at the University of Colorado at Colorado Springs, Dr. Solomon at Skidmore College, and Dr. Greenberg at the University of Arizona.